HELLBOY ™

THE TROLL
WITCH
and OTHERS

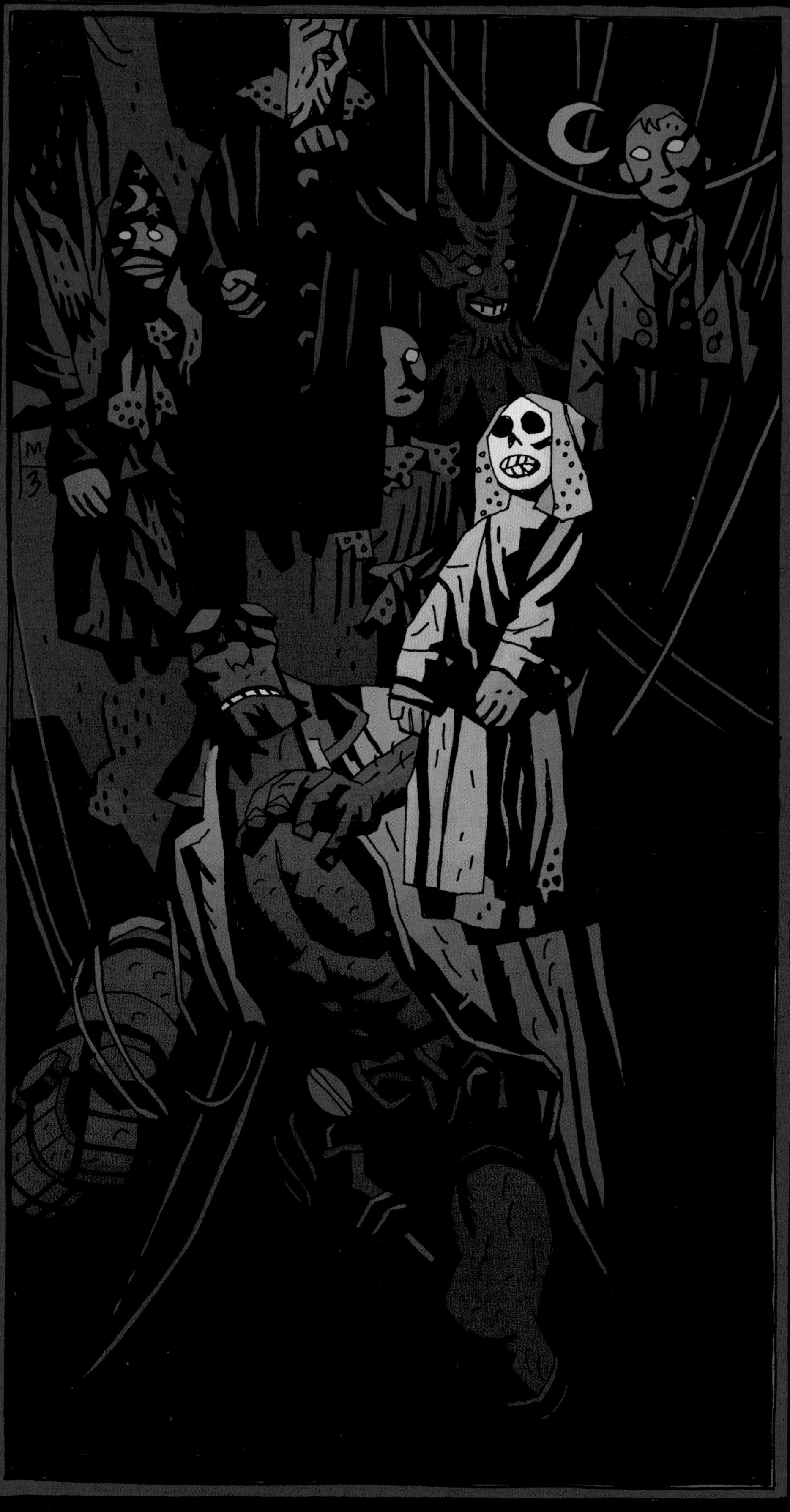

HELLBOY™

THE TROLL WITCH and OTHERS

by
MIKE MIGNOLA
RICHARD CORBEN
P. CRAIG RUSSELL

DAVE STEWART • CLEM ROBINS
LOVERN KINDZIERSKI • GALEN SHOWMAN

✠

Introduction by
WALTER SIMONSON

Edited by
SCOTT ALLIE

Hellboy logo designed by
KEVIN NOWLAN

Collection designed by
MIKE MIGNOLA & CARY GRAZZINI

Publisher
MIKE RICHARDSON

DARK HORSE BOOKS®

All stories written by MIKE MIGNOLA.

"The Penanggalan," "The Hydra and the Lion," "The Troll Witch,"
"Dr. Carp's Experiment," and "The Ghoul" drawn by MIKE MIGNOLA,
colored by DAVE STEWART, lettered by CLEM ROBINS.

"The Vampire of Prague" drawn by P. CRAIG RUSSELL,
colored by LOVERN KINDZIERSKI, lettered by GALEN SHOWMAN.

"Makoma" drawn by RICHARD CORBEN,
colored by DAVE STEWART, lettered by CLEM ROBINS.

NEIL HANKERSON ✠ Executive Vice President

TOM WEDDLE ✠ Chief Financial Officer

RANDY STRADLEY ✠ Vice President of Publishing

MICHAEL MARTENS ✠ Vice President of Business Development

ANITA NELSON ✠ Vice President of Marketing, Sales, and Licensing

DAVID SCROGGY ✠ Vice President of Product Development

DALE LaFOUNTAIN ✠ Vice President of Information Technology

DARLENE VOGEL ✠ Director of Purchasing

KEN LIZZI ✠ General Counsel

DAVEY ESTRADA ✠ Editorial Director

SCOTT ALLIE ✠ Senior Managing Editor

CHRIS WARNER ✠ Senior Books Editor, Dark Horse Books

ROB SIMPSON ✠ Senior Books Editor, M Press/Dark Horse Books

DIANA SCHUTZ ✠ Executive Editor

CARY GRAZZINI ✠ Director of Design and Production

LIA RIBACCHI ✠ Art Director

CARA NIECE ✠ Director of Scheduling

Published by
Dark Horse Books
A division of Dark Horse Comics, Inc.
10956 SE Main St.
Milwaukie, OR 97222

First Edition
November 2007
ISBN-10: 1-59307-860-9
ISBN-13: 978-1-59307-860-7

This volume collects stories from the Dark Horse comic-book series *Hellboy: Makoma*; from the books *The Dark
Horse Book of Hauntings*, *The Dark Horse Book of Witchcraft*, *The Dark Horse Book of the Dead*, and *The Dark Horse Book
of Monsters*; from the comic book *Hellboy Premiere Edition*; and the original story "The Vampire of Prague."

1 3 5 7 9 10 8 6 4 2

PRINTED IN CHINA

INTRODUCTION
by WALTER SIMONSON

Mike Mignola once told me that when he was fairly new in the business, he visited my wife, Louise, and me in our old apartment back in New York City. And there, during a hotly contested video game of Pong, I referred to him as a "spaz"! Frankly, given my own reflexes or lack thereof, I can't imagine that I was any better at that damn game.

However, it was clear from the beginning—and has only become more apparent with time—that creatively, Mike is anything *but* a "spaz." He is cranky, low-key, extremely funny, cranky, wonderfully inventive, generous, cranky, and, artistically, inspired.

Did I mention that Mike is cranky?

And with the world of Hellboy, he has produced a body of work creating a "Secondary World," as Tolkien would have called it, in which others have taken delight not only reading, but enlarging.

The book you hold in your hands is the proof of that.

Almost blisteringly prosaic in the face of miracles, Hellboy is a proud member of that pulp tradition in which the hero solves problems with a fight that serves up both entertainment and catharsis. Except of course, in a case like that of "The Troll Witch," in which he doesn't. Hellboy's actions and attitude would be recognizable to anyone familiar with the heroes of the pulp tradition— the tall, laconic, unflappable, immensely courageous protagonist of its honorable tradition. But Hellboy exists in and walks through a dream world of nightmare. His is a syncretic world fashioned of bits of obscure lore and strange untapped corners of mythology and legend. There is the occasional whiff, however faint, that is reminiscent of Baudelaire and fever dreams.

In Hellboy's world, he walks down these mean streets, not as the last honest man in the politically corrupt world of men, but as the last best hope of mankind against a sea of unseen but very real dangers. Mignola's masterly abstraction of form enables him to insinuate a world of dark possibilities without being explicit. His draftsmanship suggests a concretely real world and at the same time, his abstraction suggests a world unseen, a world of more dangers than we can imagine lurking just out of sight. That world waits with immense patience for us to stand too close to the border. Criss-crossing our familiar planet from Malaysia to Alaska to Long Island, it is Hellboy's lot to enter into that terra incognito to face its attendant dangers.

Mike's storytelling is interestingly conservative, with its rectilinear layouts and measured pacing. No mad bleeds, inset panels, or radical page layouts here. But the visual sense of order belies the underlying sense of chaos. His transitions from the mundane to the supernatural, as in "Dr. Carp's Experiment," are almost hallucinogenic in their simplicity. The known falls away from us as we cross a simple panel border and we find ourselves captured by the nightmare. With his use of the occasional small panels presented as panes of atmospheric pattern scattered throughout his stories, Mignola evokes a sense of almost religious iconography, traces of that hidden world in which meaning is too powerful or overwhelming to be completely understood.

And his dialogue throughout the stories is sparse to the point of demanding that the reader bring their own interpretations to the material, an approach that both obscures the meaning of the word and at the same time enlarges it. "There are more things in heaven and earth, Horatio, Than are dreamt of in your philosophy." And where else but in Hellboy's world would we observe a fragment of a puppet production of Shakespeare's *Hamlet*?

Essentially—and I do not say this lightly—this is work I would like to have done myself.

It really *is* too cool for school!

I would also like to add a few words about the other artists who are a part of this collection.

Okay. Here's all you have to know about Rich Corben, a gentleman I've never met, darn it. There's nobody like him in comics. And probably not anywhere else, for that matter. From the first work of Rich's I ever saw, back in the late sixties or early seventies, Corben's voice was utterly individualistic. I don't know where he came from, who his influences were, or why he chose to do comics. But he did them like nobody else, with an intensity that made the realization of his work at world building completely convincing. And he was the whole package—brilliant, gripping draftsmanship; fascinating stories both on his own and in collaboration with others; and a grasp of explosive black-and-white and color that was the hallmark of a mature artist right from the beginning. I'm delighted he's here in this package of Hellboy. And given the nature of Rich's own fantasy work, it's a perfect fit.

Ever since I've known him, Craig Russell has been a creator with an abiding passion for opera. I haven't asked Craig if he likes all opera or is simply particularly passionate about Wagner, clearly one of his great delights. But the echoes of that passion ring throughout his work, even in that work not directly derived from operatic theater. He has always brought to his craft an arresting quality of thoroughly considered stagecraft. His drawings reveal a care in the staging of his dramas as well as in his designs for the settings within which these dramas are enacted. Craig's protagonists are clothed in richly conceived costumes, revealing carefully considered designs of imagination. There is a formalism in his visualizations that cloak his stories with an aura of inevitability. In the end, Craig's work seems to me to give the reader a glimpse as through a proscenium arch into another world, where characters enact their dramas to preordained ends that have something to do with the workings of an implacable fate.

The Penanggalan

I FIRST DISCOVERED this beautifully odd thing about a zillion years ago, in Bernhardt J. Hurwood's *Passport to the Supernatural*, the first great book I ever read about supernatural creatures from all over the world. The Penanggalan kicking her own head off, the swollen intestines and the vinegar, all that is taken from Malaysian folklore—because you just can't make up stuff like that.

"The Penanggalan" was originally published in 2004, as part of a special comic through *Wizard* magazine. For this collection I've redrawn two panels. I usually don't do things like that, but those two panels were *really* bugging me.

✠

The Hydra and the Lion

MY DAUGHTER KATIE AND I COBBLED this one together one night at an Italian restaurant somewhere in New York City. Back then she was still telling people (anyone who would listen) that she was half lion, and she had perfected a sort of lion roar to prove it. Her favorite creature back then was the Hydra (thanks to Disney's *Hercules*), and she explained to me that the lion girl would probably be pulling the Hydra's teeth out with pliers. Okay. The whole thing never made much sense, but I told the story to my long-suffering editor (the very patient Scott Allie) and then forgot all about it. A few years later, Scott put together *The Dark Horse Book of Monsters* and asked for the Hydra story. Damn. At the last minute, I added that bit about the Thespian and Nemean lions, so now, at least, we could have a couple guys *trying* to make sense of the story.

I've always said that in supernatural stories you need bits that are beyond human comprehension—this one is pretty much made of those bits.

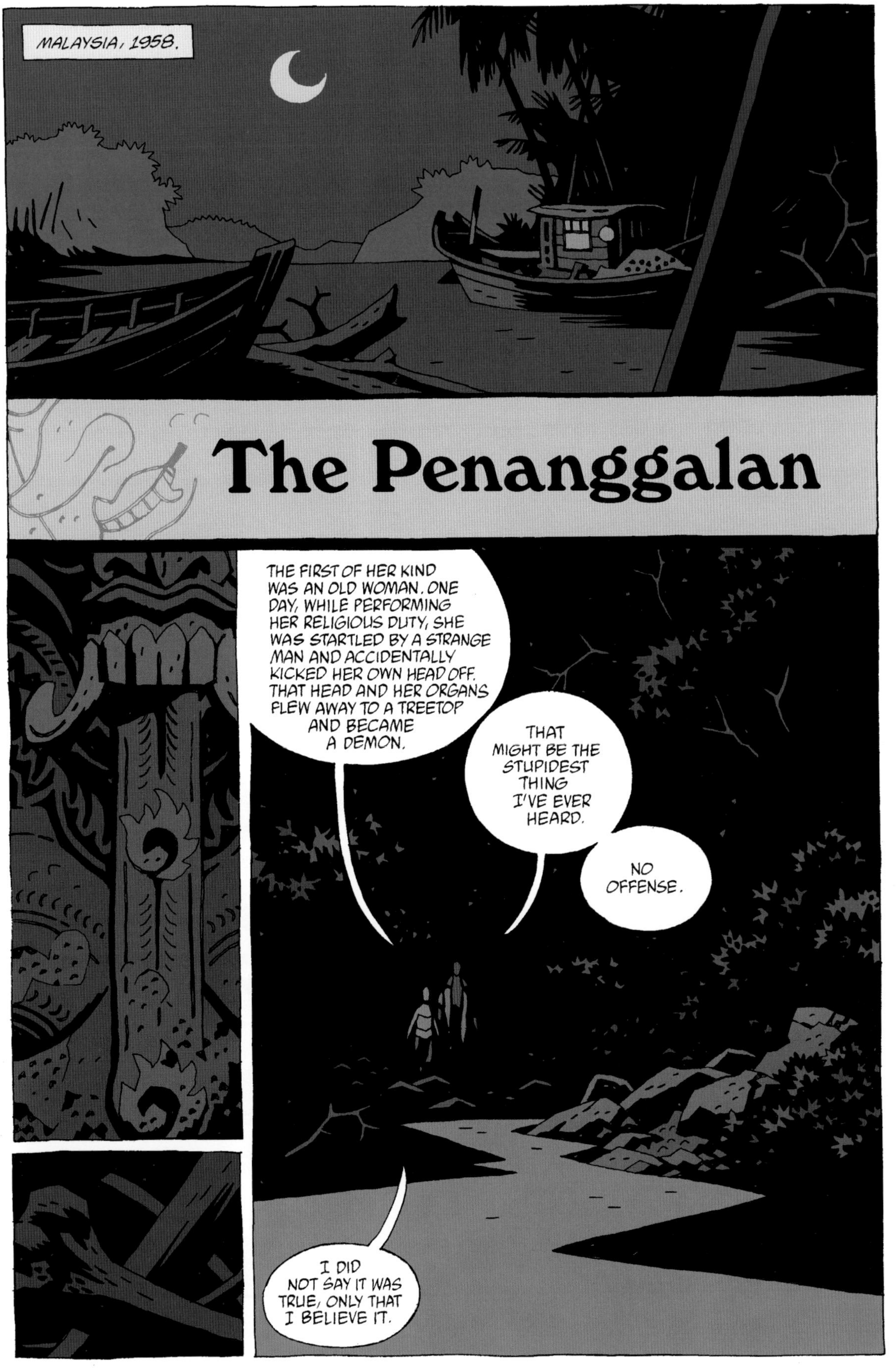
MALAYSIA, 1958.
The Penanggalan
THE FIRST OF HER KIND WAS AN OLD WOMAN. ONE DAY, WHILE PERFORMING HER RELIGIOUS DUTY, SHE WAS STARTLED BY A STRANGE MAN AND ACCIDENTALLY KICKED HER OWN HEAD OFF. THAT HEAD AND HER ORGANS FLEW AWAY TO A TREETOP AND BECAME A DEMON.
THAT MIGHT BE THE STUPIDEST THING I'VE EVER HEARD.
NO OFFENSE.
I DID NOT SAY IT WAS TRUE, ONLY THAT I BELIEVE IT.

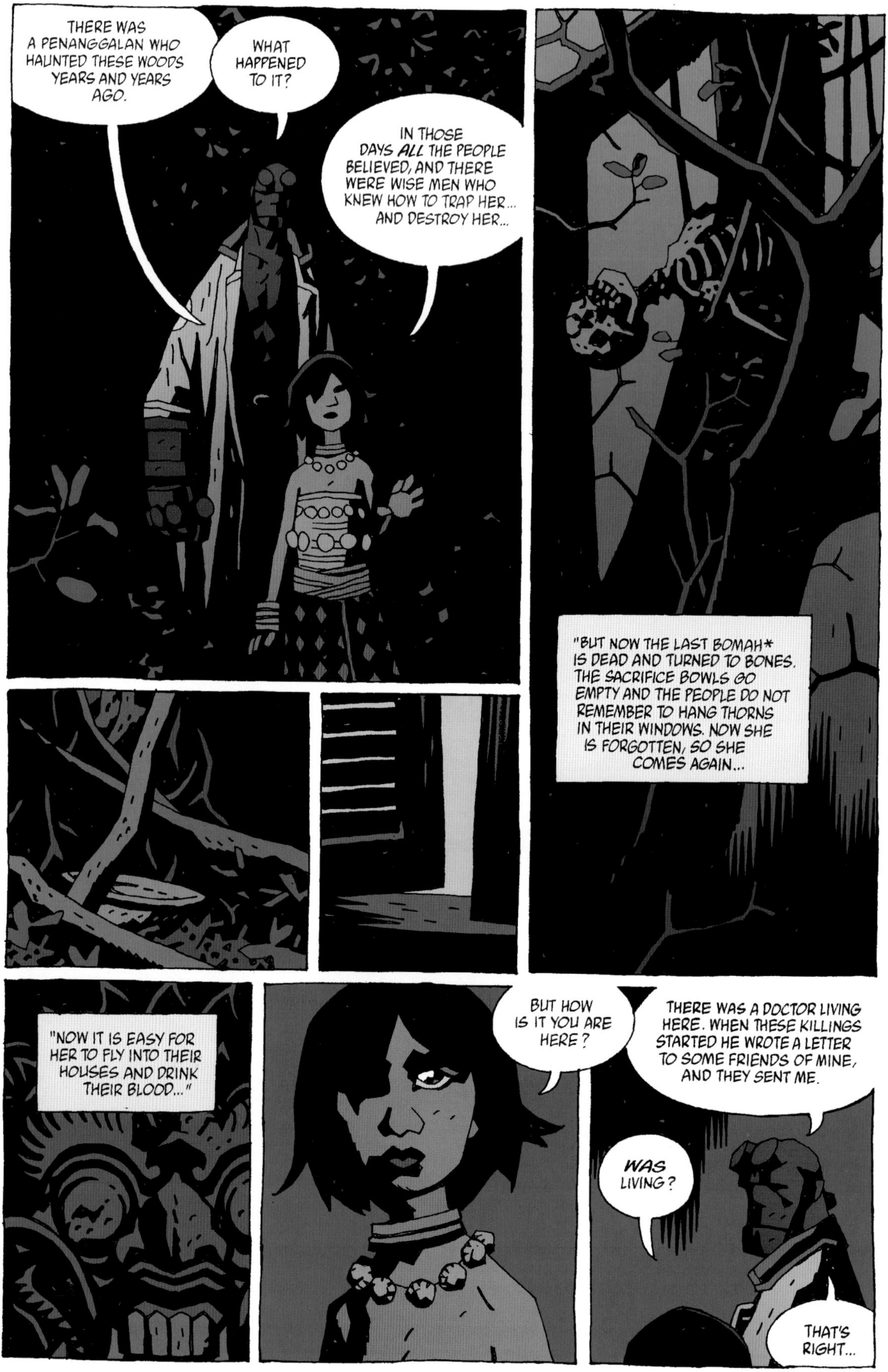

THERE WAS A PENANGGALAN WHO HAUNTED THESE WOODS YEARS AND YEARS AGO.
WHAT HAPPENED TO IT?
IN THOSE DAYS ALL THE PEOPLE BELIEVED, AND THERE WERE WISE MEN WHO KNEW HOW TO TRAP HER... AND DESTROY HER...
"BUT NOW THE LAST BOMAH* IS DEAD AND TURNED TO BONES. THE SACRIFICE BOWLS GO EMPTY AND THE PEOPLE DO NOT REMEMBER TO HANG THORNS IN THEIR WINDOWS. NOW SHE IS FORGOTTEN, SO SHE COMES AGAIN...
"NOW IT IS EASY FOR HER TO FLY INTO THEIR HOUSES AND DRINK THEIR BLOOD..."
BUT HOW IS IT YOU ARE HERE?
THERE WAS A DOCTOR LIVING HERE. WHEN THESE KILLINGS STARTED HE WROTE A LETTER TO SOME FRIENDS OF MINE, AND THEY SENT ME.
WAS LIVING?
THAT'S RIGHT...

*A MALAYSIAN SHAMAN

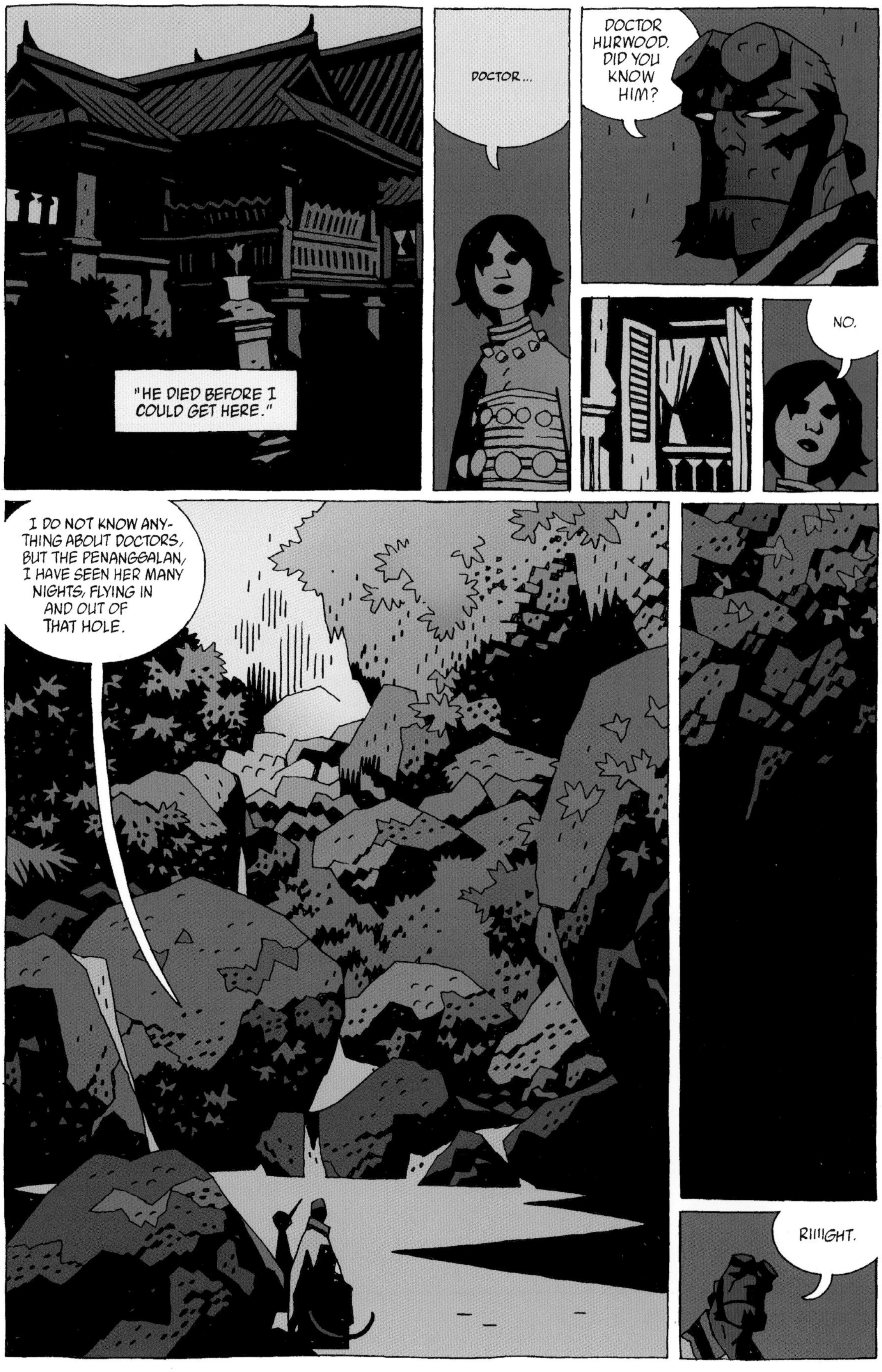
"HE DIED BEFORE I COULD GET HERE."
DOCTOR...
DOCTOR HURWOOD. DID YOU KNOW HIM?
NO.
I DO NOT KNOW ANYTHING ABOUT DOCTORS, BUT THE PENANGGALAN, I HAVE SEEN HER MANY NIGHTS, FLYING IN AND OUT OF THAT HOLE.
RIIIGHT.

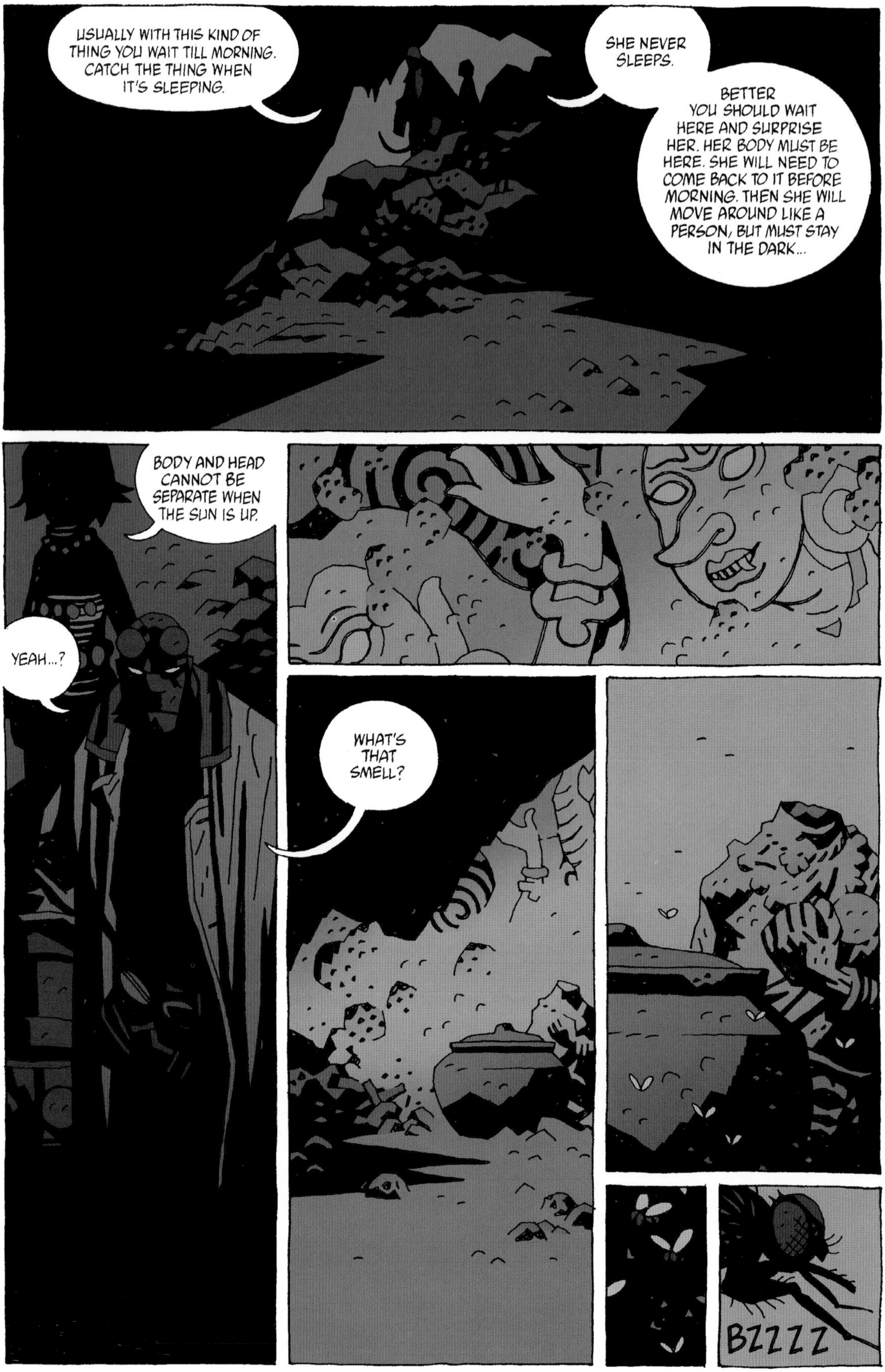
USUALLY WITH THIS KIND OF THING YOU WAIT TILL MORNING. CATCH THE THING WHEN IT'S SLEEPING.
SHE NEVER SLEEPS.
BETTER YOU SHOULD WAIT HERE AND SURPRISE HER. HER BODY MUST BE HERE. SHE WILL NEED TO COME BACK TO IT BEFORE MORNING. THEN SHE WILL MOVE AROUND LIKE A PERSON, BUT MUST STAY IN THE DARK...
BODY AND HEAD CANNOT BE SEPARATE WHEN THE SUN IS UP.
YEAH...?
WHAT'S THAT SMELL?
BZZZZ

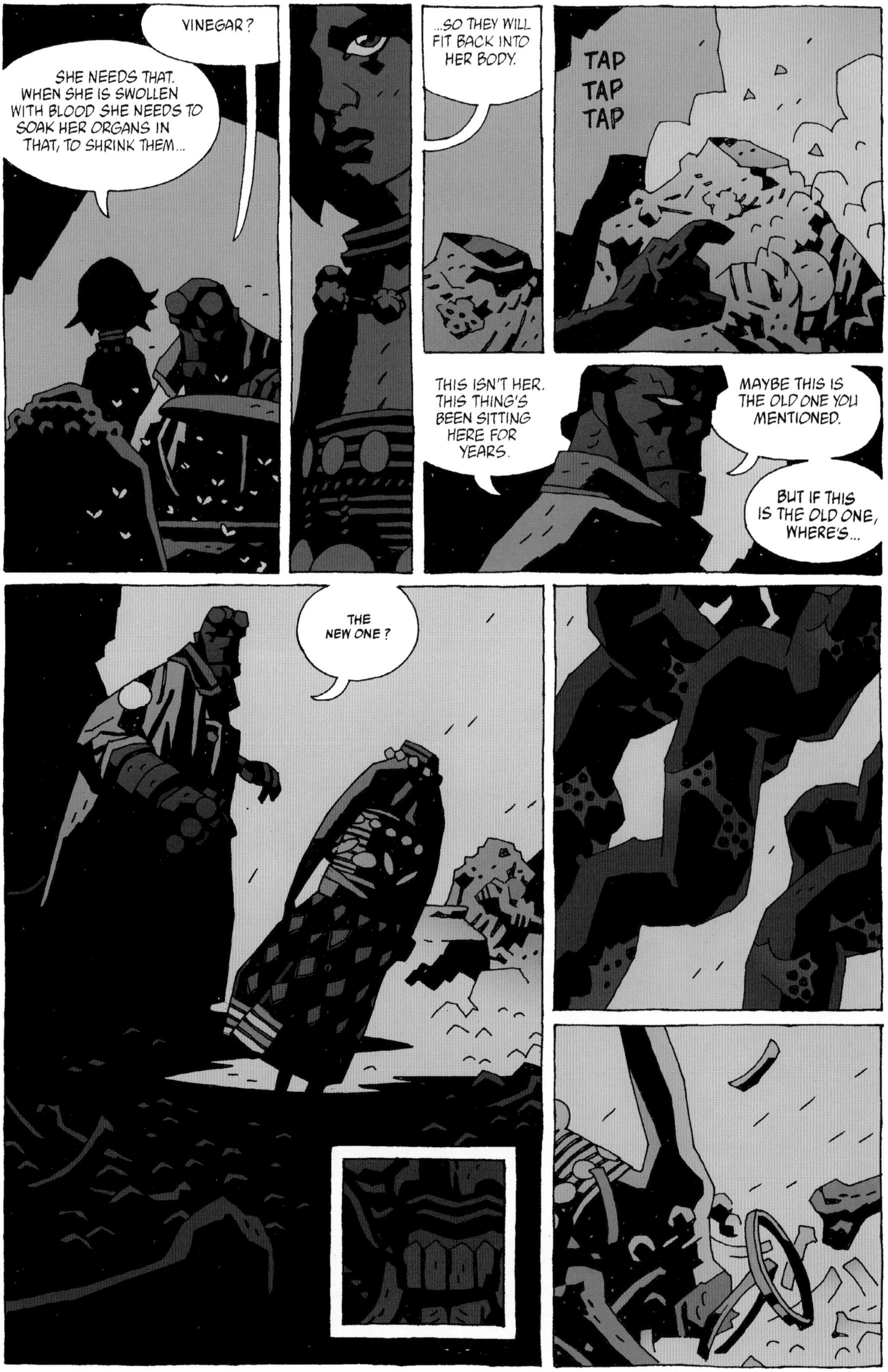

VINEGAR?
SHE NEEDS THAT. WHEN SHE IS SWOLLEN WITH BLOOD SHE NEEDS TO SOAK HER ORGANS IN THAT, TO SHRINK THEM...
...SO THEY WILL FIT BACK INTO HER BODY.
TAP TAP TAP
THIS ISN'T HER. THIS THING'S BEEN SITTING HERE FOR YEARS.
MAYBE THIS IS THE OLD ONE YOU MENTIONED.
BUT IF THIS IS THE OLD ONE, WHERE'S...
THE NEW ONE?

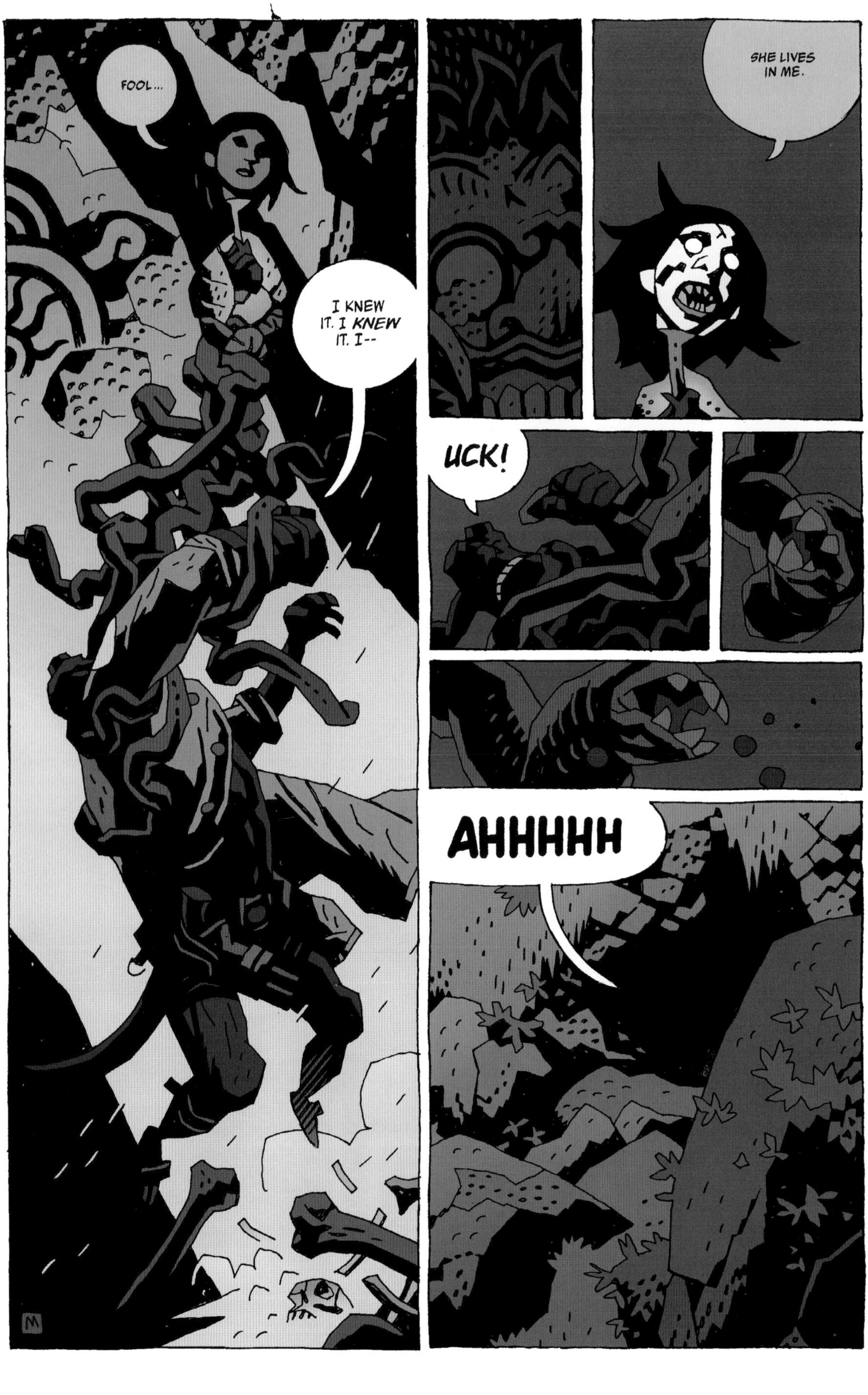
FOOL...
I KNEW IT. I KNEW IT. I--
SHE LIVES IN ME.
UCK!
AHHHHH

AHHHHHHHHHHH

SON OF A--

FWOOOOOOSH

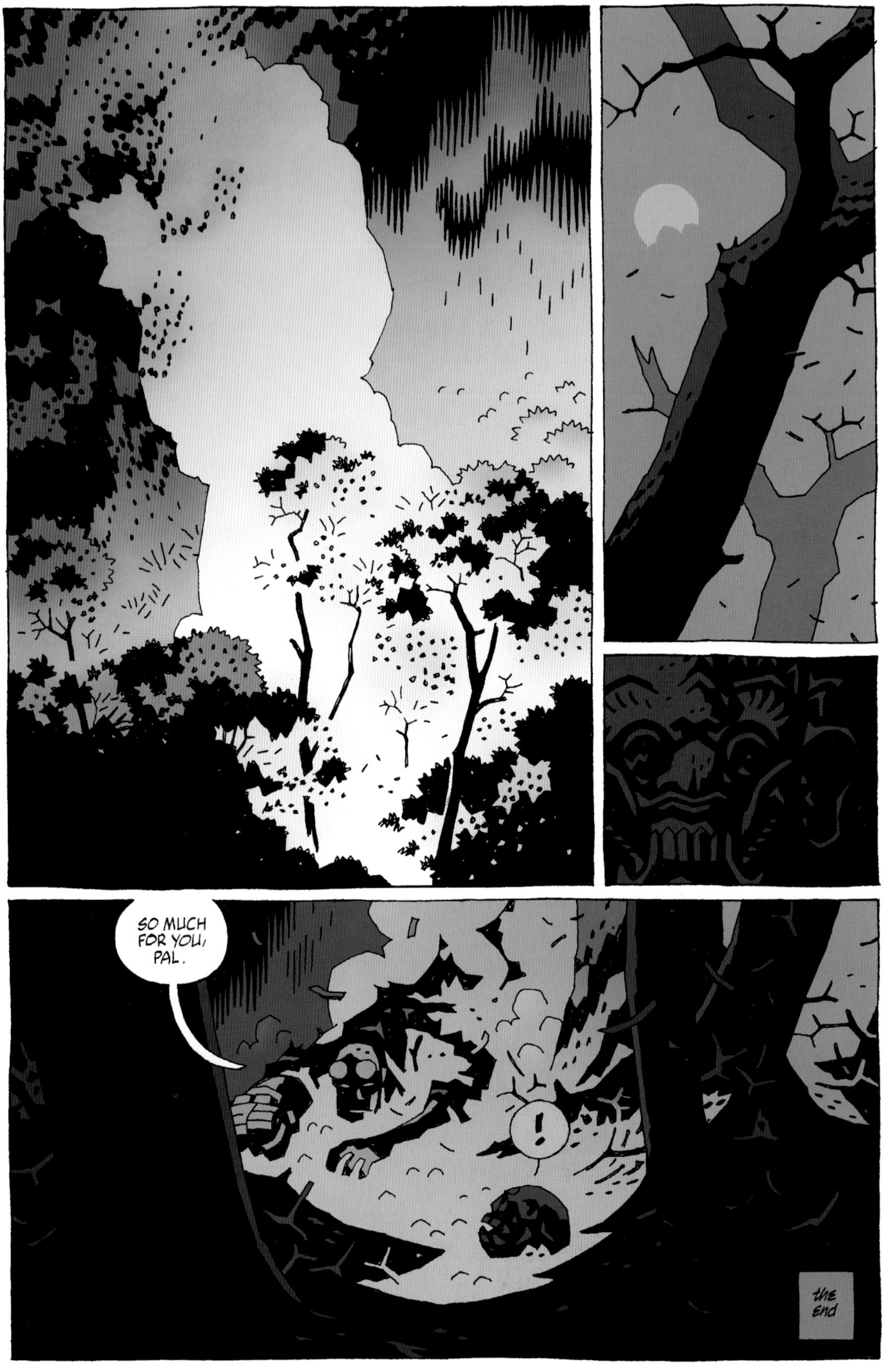
SO MUCH FOR YOU, PAL.
!
the End

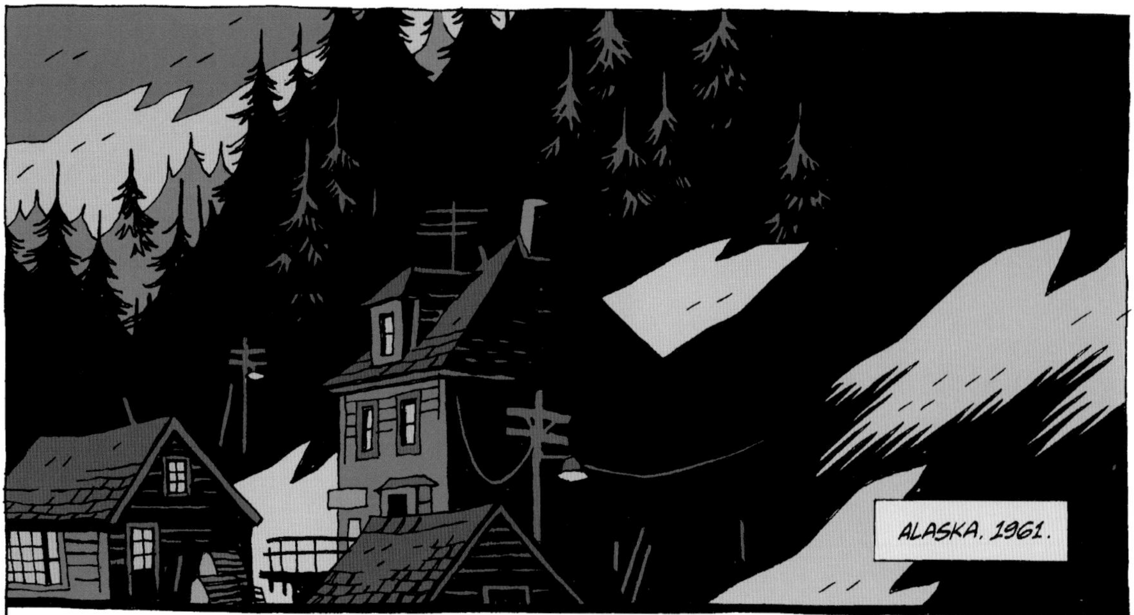
ALASKA. 1961.

The Hydra and the Lion

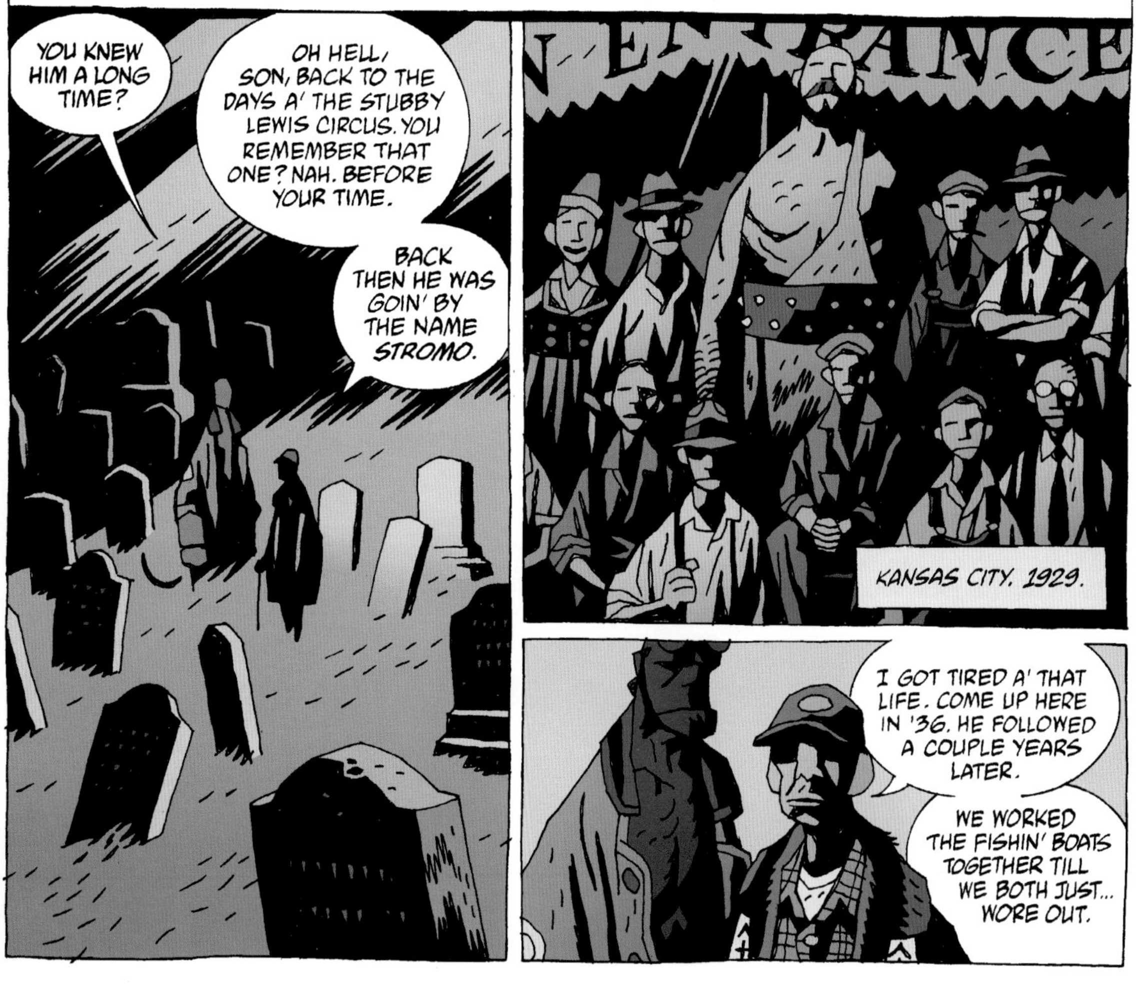
YOU KNEW HIM A LONG TIME?
OH HELL, SON, BACK TO THE DAYS A' THE STUBBY LEWIS CIRCUS. YOU REMEMBER THAT ONE? NAH. BEFORE YOUR TIME.
BACK THEN HE WAS GOIN' BY THE NAME STROMO.
KANSAS CITY. 1929.
I GOT TIRED A' THAT LIFE. COME UP HERE IN '36. HE FOLLOWED A COUPLE YEARS LATER.
WE WORKED THE FISHIN' BOATS TOGETHER TILL WE BOTH JUST... WORE OUT.

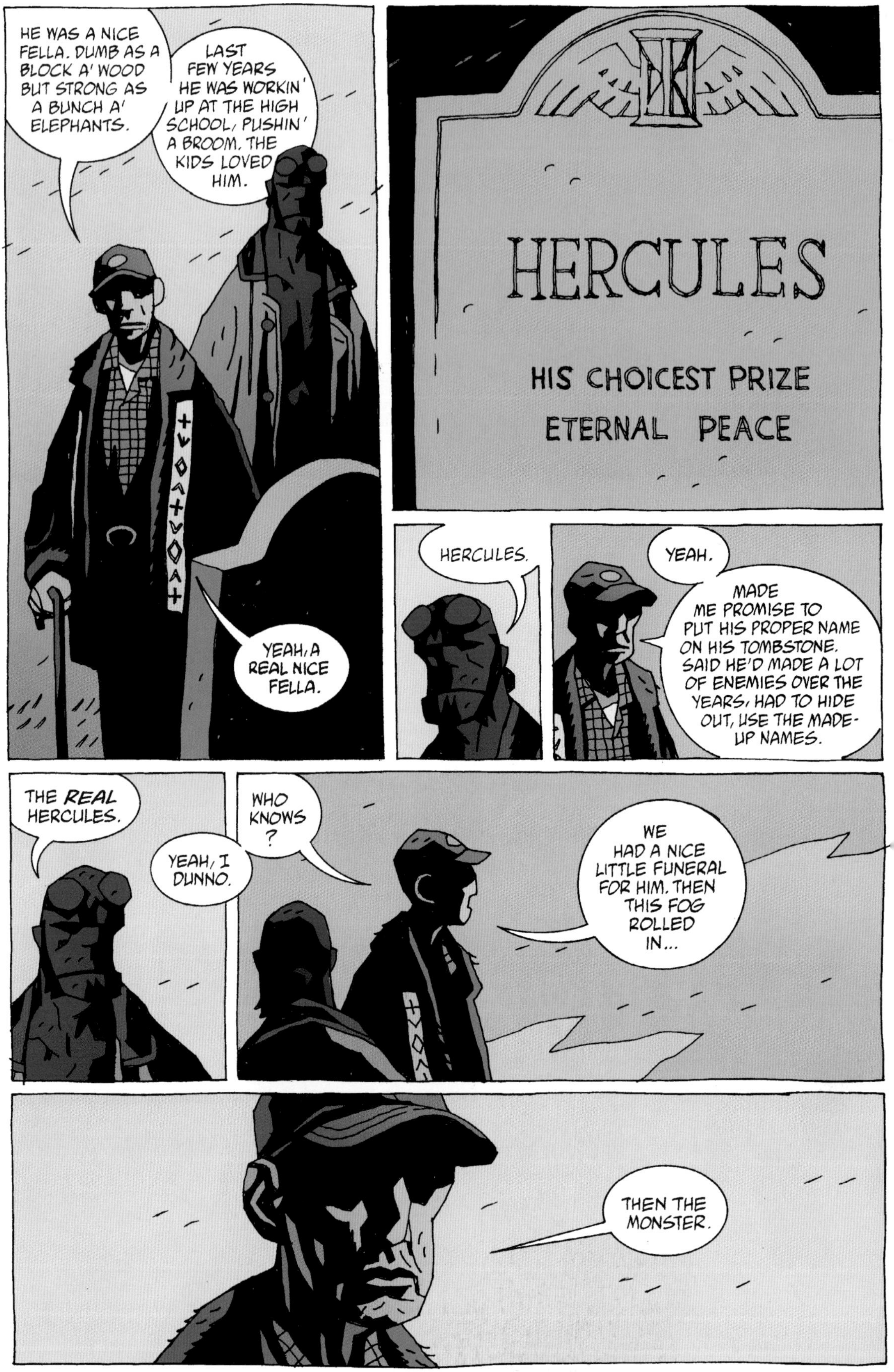
HE WAS A NICE FELLA. DUMB AS A BLOCK A' WOOD BUT STRONG AS A BUNCH A' ELEPHANTS.
LAST FEW YEARS HE WAS WORKIN' UP AT THE HIGH SCHOOL, PUSHIN' A BROOM. THE KIDS LOVED HIM.
YEAH, A REAL NICE FELLA.
HERCULES
HIS CHOICEST PRIZE
ETERNAL PEACE
HERCULES.
YEAH.
MADE ME PROMISE TO PUT HIS PROPER NAME ON HIS TOMBSTONE. SAID HE'D MADE A LOT OF ENEMIES OVER THE YEARS, HAD TO HIDE OUT, USE THE MADE-UP NAMES.
THE *REAL* HERCULES.
YEAH, I DUNNO.
WHO KNOWS?
WE HAD A NICE LITTLE FUNERAL FOR HIM. THEN THIS FOG ROLLED IN...
THEN THE MONSTER.

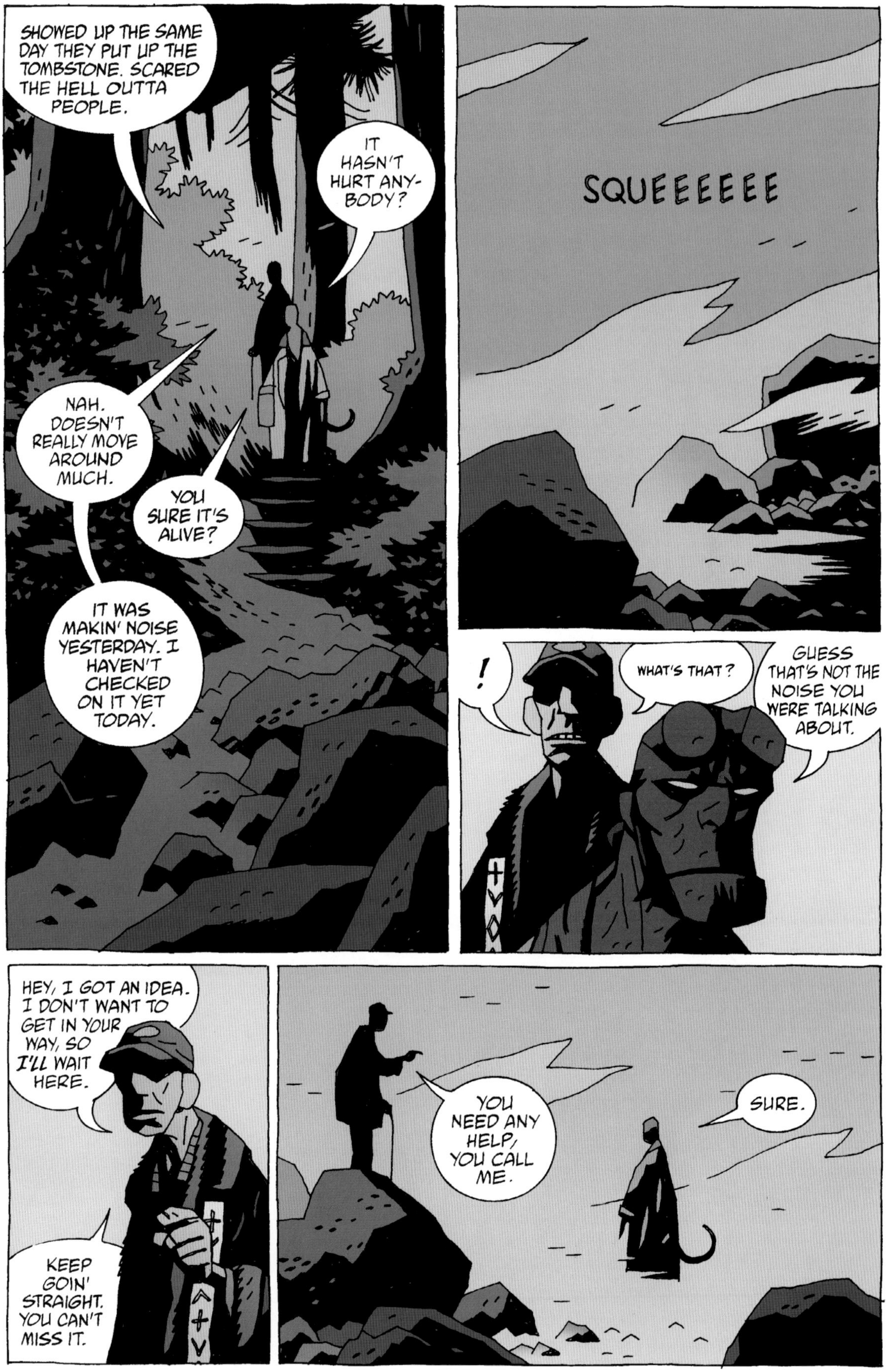
SHOWED UP THE SAME DAY THEY PUT UP THE TOMBSTONE. SCARED THE HELL OUTTA PEOPLE.
IT HASN'T HURT ANY-BODY?
NAH. DOESN'T REALLY MOVE AROUND MUCH.
YOU SURE IT'S ALIVE?
IT WAS MAKIN' NOISE YESTERDAY. I HAVEN'T CHECKED ON IT YET TODAY.
SQUEEEEEEE
!
WHAT'S THAT?
GUESS THAT'S NOT THE NOISE YOU WERE TALKING ABOUT.
HEY, I GOT AN IDEA. I DON'T WANT TO GET IN YOUR WAY, SO I'LL WAIT HERE.
KEEP GOIN' STRAIGHT. YOU CAN'T MISS IT.
YOU NEED ANY HELP, YOU CALL ME.
SURE.

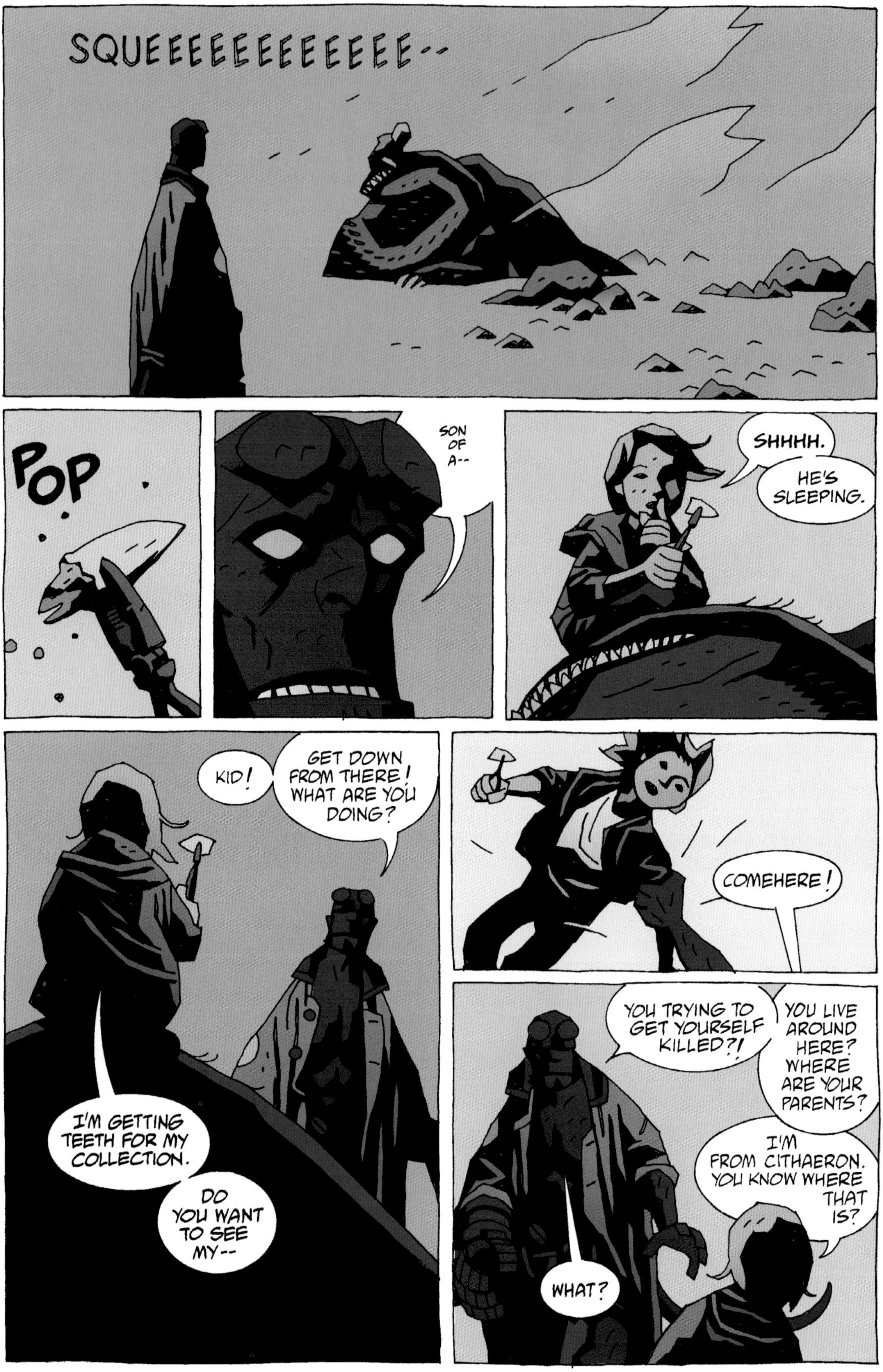
SQUEEEEEEEEEEEE--
POP
SON OF A--
SHHHH.
HE'S SLEEPING.
KID!
GET DOWN FROM THERE! WHAT ARE YOU DOING?
I'M GETTING TEETH FOR MY COLLECTION.
DO YOU WANT TO SEE MY--
COMEHERE!
YOU TRYING TO GET YOURSELF KILLED?!
YOU LIVE AROUND HERE? WHERE ARE YOUR PARENTS?
I'M FROM CITHAERON. YOU KNOW WHERE THAT IS?
WHAT?

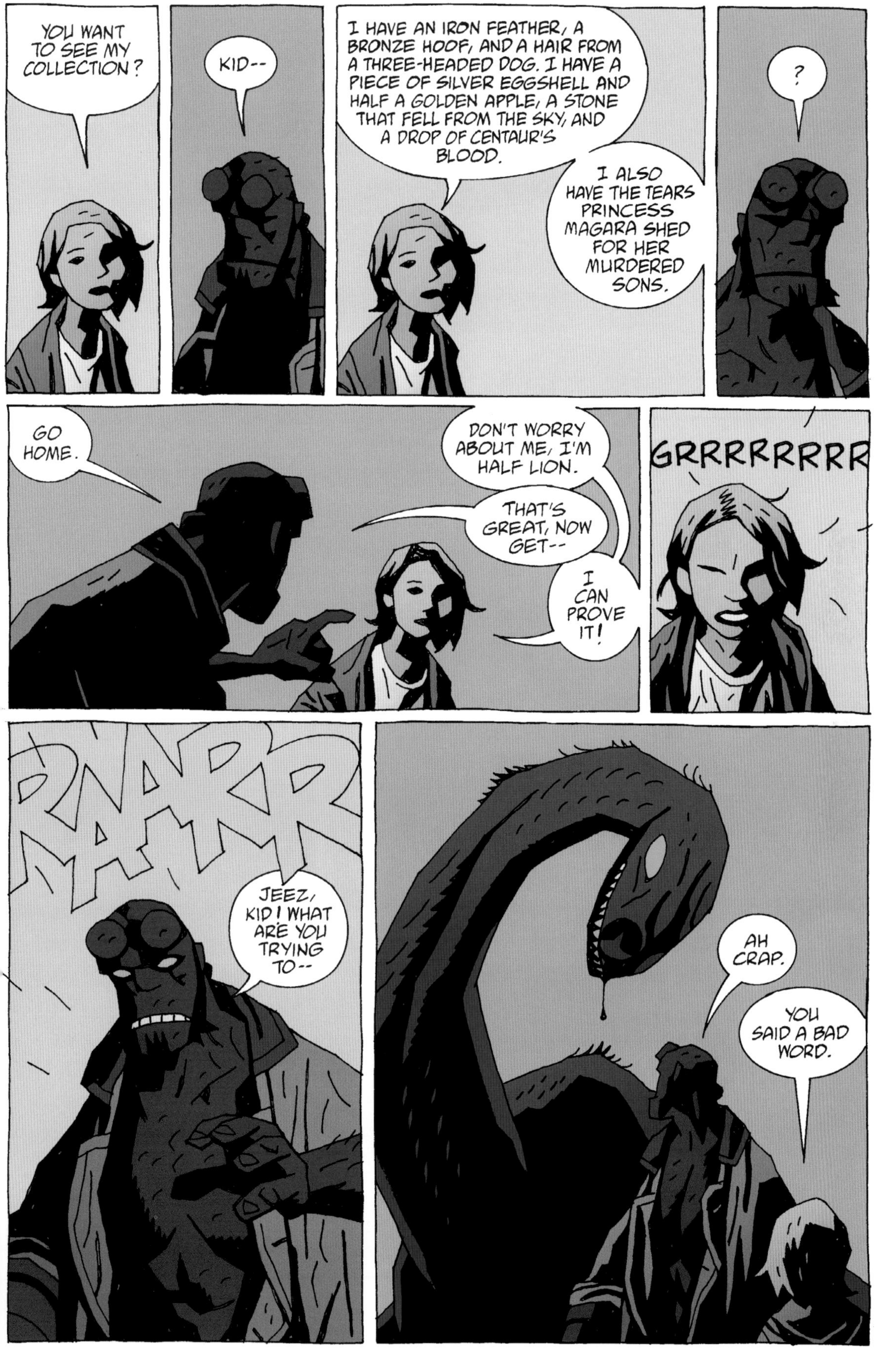
YOU WANT TO SEE MY COLLECTION?
KID--
I HAVE AN IRON FEATHER, A BRONZE HOOF, AND A HAIR FROM A THREE-HEADED DOG. I HAVE A PIECE OF SILVER EGGSHELL AND HALF A GOLDEN APPLE, A STONE THAT FELL FROM THE SKY, AND A DROP OF CENTAUR'S BLOOD.
I ALSO HAVE THE TEARS PRINCESS MAGARA SHED FOR HER MURDERED SONS.
?
GO HOME.
DON'T WORRY ABOUT ME, I'M HALF LION.
THAT'S GREAT, NOW GET--
I CAN PROVE IT!
GRRRRRRRR
RAAARRR
JEEZ, KID! WHAT ARE YOU TRYING TO--
AH CRAP.
YOU SAID A BAD WORD.

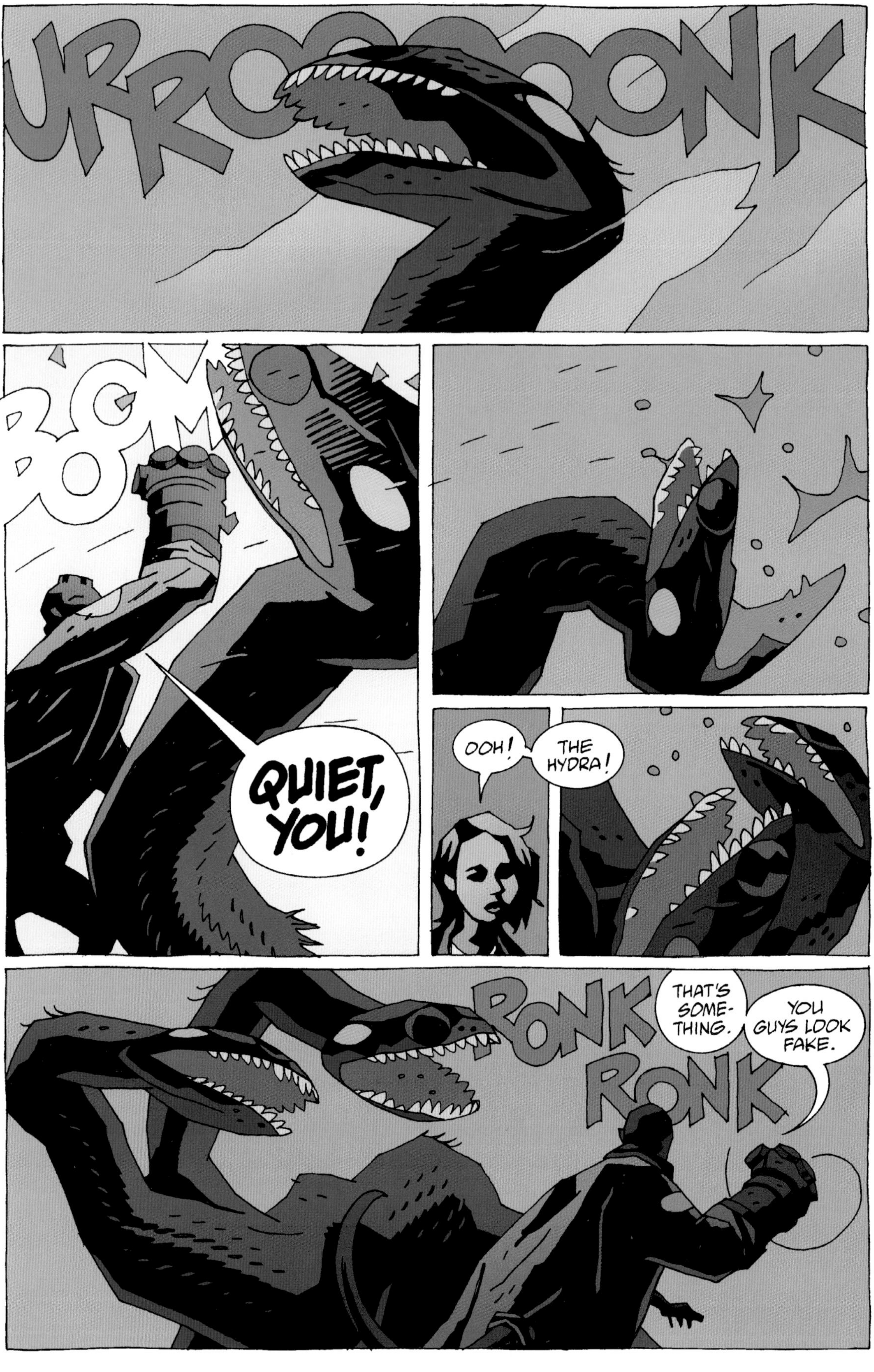
URROOOOOONK
BOOM
QUIET, YOU!
OOH!
THE HYDRA!
RONK RONK
THAT'S SOME-THING.
YOU GUYS LOOK FAKE.

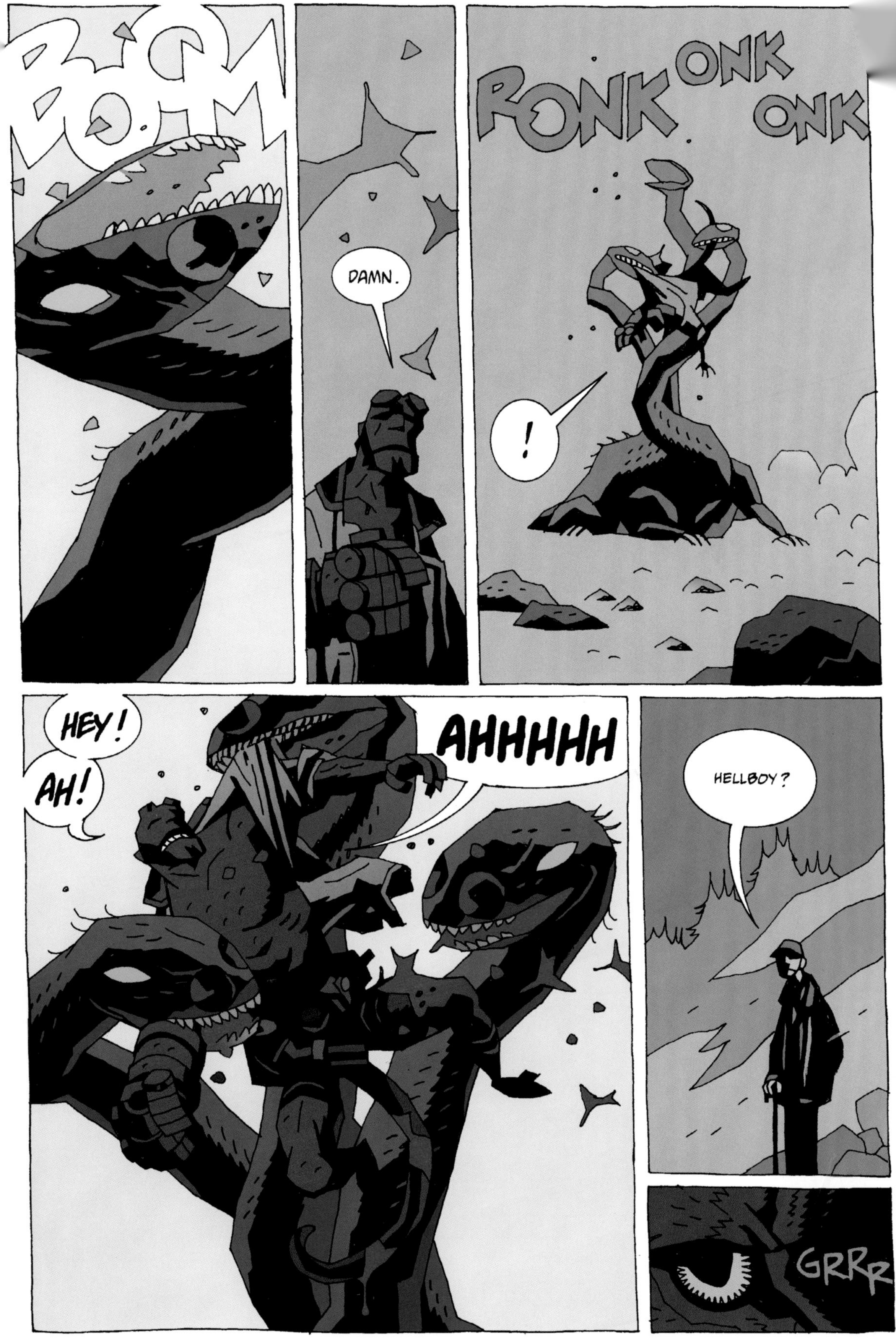
BOOM
DAMN.
RONK ONK ONK
!
HEY!
AH!
AHHHHH
HELLBOY?
GRRR

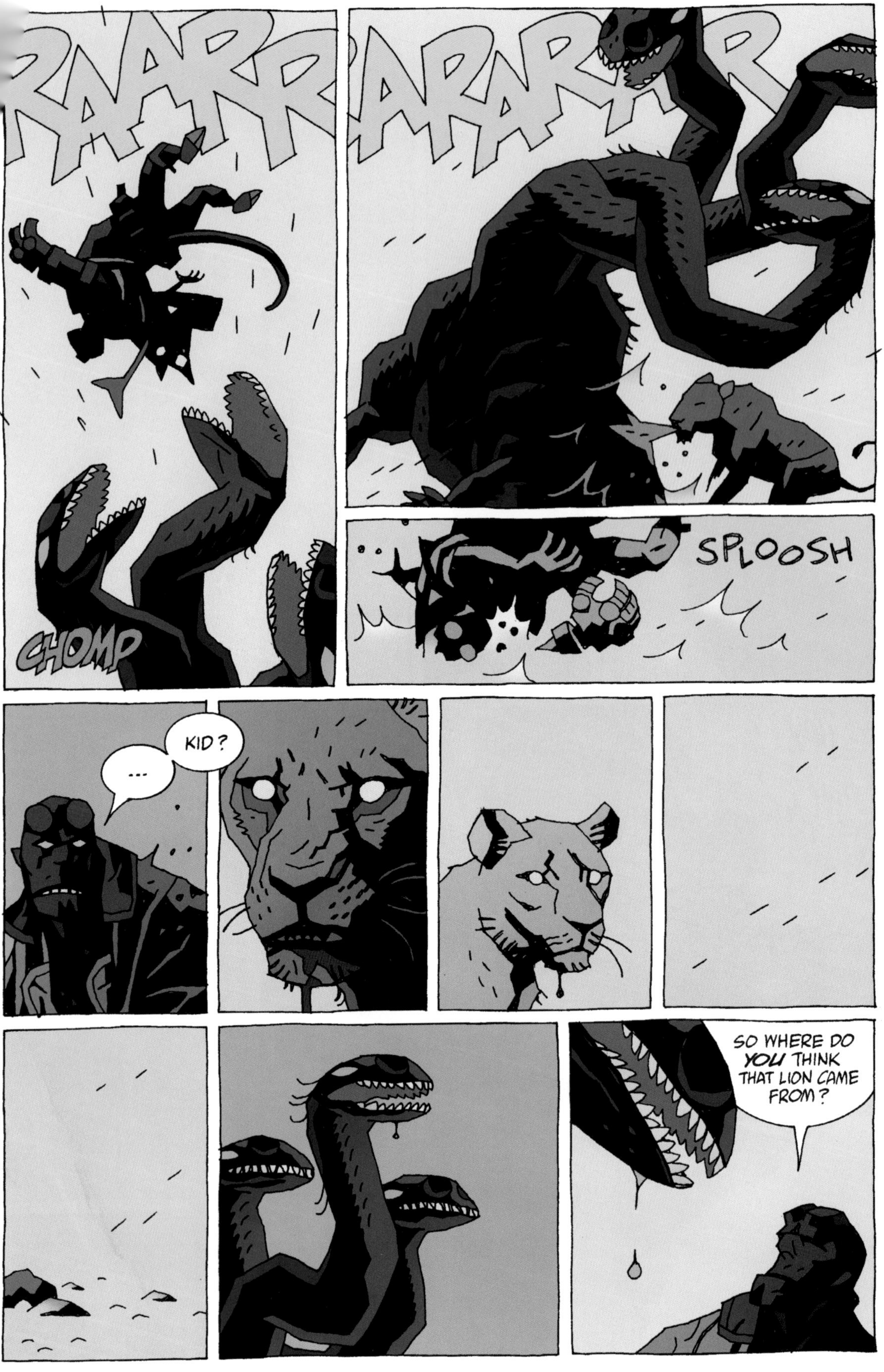
RAARR
RARARR
CHOMP
SPLOOSH
KID?
...
SO WHERE DO *YOU* THINK THAT LION CAME FROM?

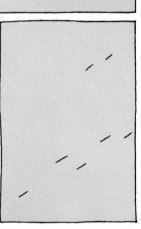

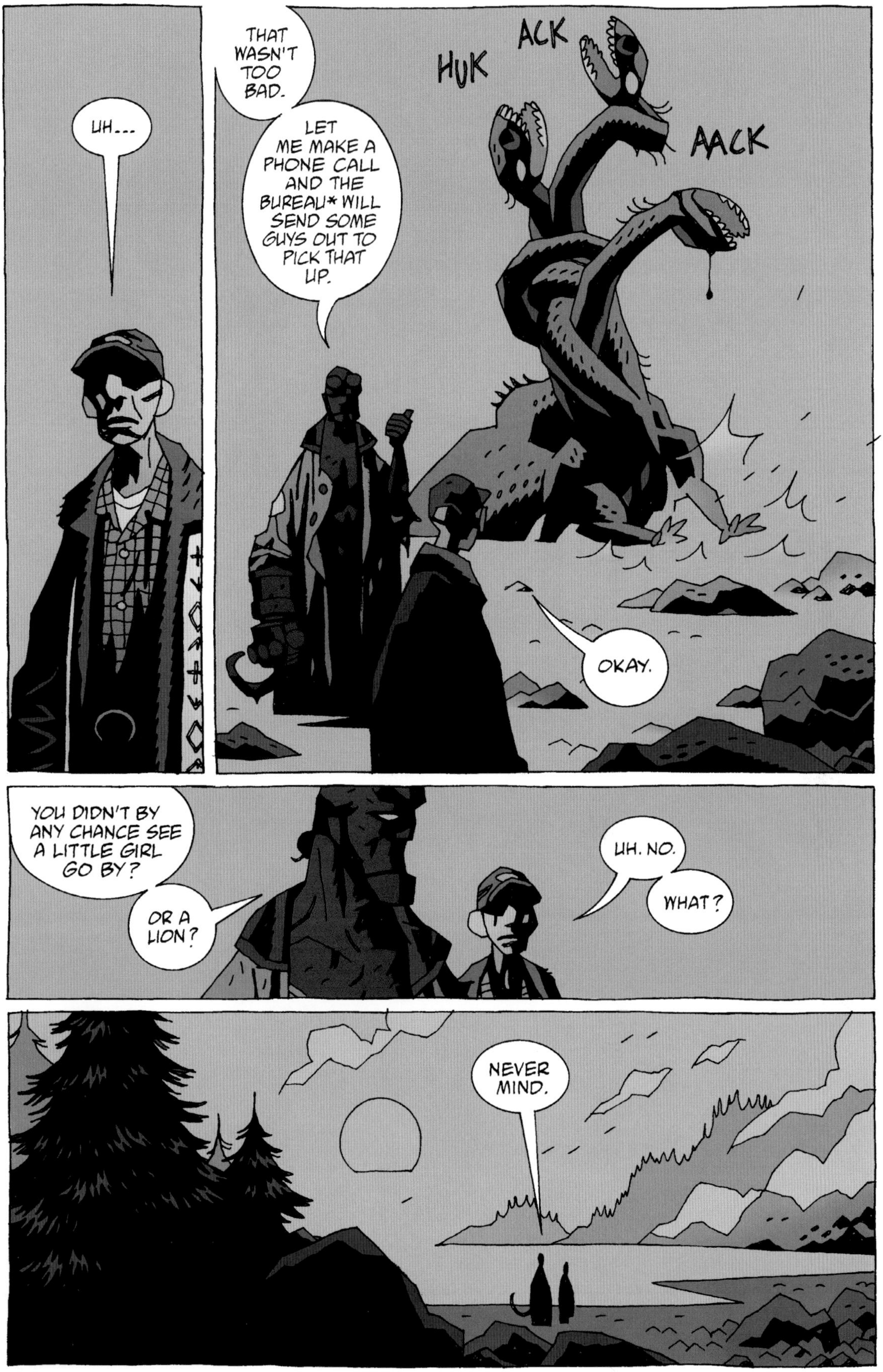
UH...
THAT WASN'T TOO BAD.
LET ME MAKE A PHONE CALL AND THE BUREAU* WILL SEND SOME GUYS OUT TO PICK THAT UP.
HUK
ACK
AACK
OKAY.
YOU DIDN'T BY ANY CHANCE SEE A LITTLE GIRL GO BY?
OR A LION?
UH. NO.
WHAT?
NEVER MIND.

*BUREAU FOR PARANORMAL RESEARCH AND DEFENSE

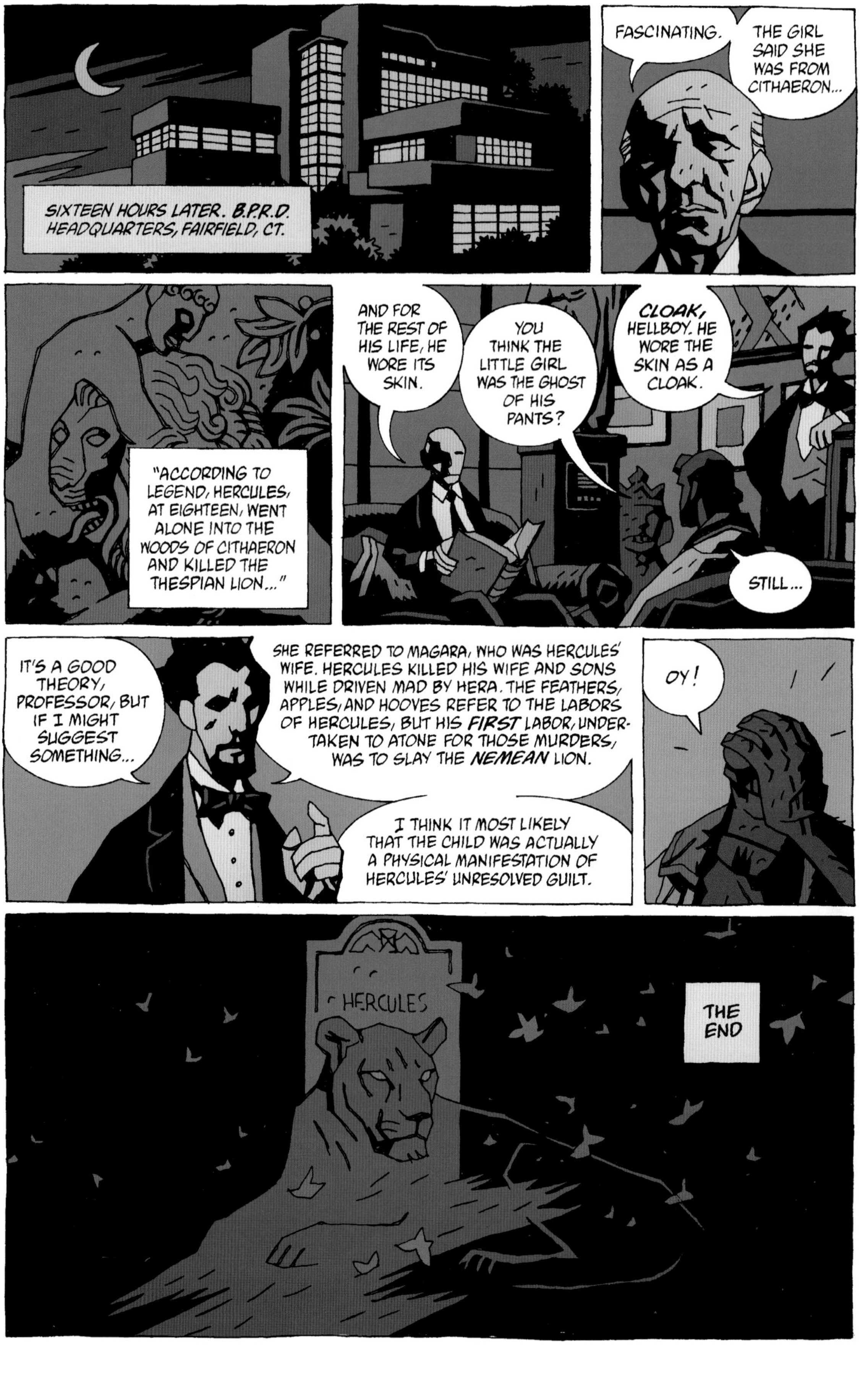
SIXTEEN HOURS LATER. B.P.R.D. HEADQUARTERS, FAIRFIELD, CT.
FASCINATING.
THE GIRL SAID SHE WAS FROM CITHAERON...
"ACCORDING TO LEGEND, HERCULES, AT EIGHTEEN, WENT ALONE INTO THE WOODS OF CITHAERON AND KILLED THE THESPIAN LION..."
AND FOR THE REST OF HIS LIFE, HE WORE ITS SKIN.
YOU THINK THE LITTLE GIRL WAS THE GHOST OF HIS PANTS?
CLOAK, HELLBOY. HE WORE THE SKIN AS A CLOAK.
STILL...
IT'S A GOOD THEORY, PROFESSOR, BUT IF I MIGHT SUGGEST SOMETHING...
SHE REFERRED TO MAGARA, WHO WAS HERCULES' WIFE. HERCULES KILLED HIS WIFE AND SONS WHILE DRIVEN MAD BY HERA. THE FEATHERS, APPLES, AND HOOVES REFER TO THE LABORS OF HERCULES, BUT HIS FIRST LABOR, UNDERTAKEN TO ATONE FOR THOSE MURDERS, WAS TO SLAY THE NEMEAN LION.
I THINK IT MOST LIKELY THAT THE CHILD WAS ACTUALLY A PHYSICAL MANIFESTATION OF HERCULES' UNRESOLVED GUILT.
OY!
HERCULES
THE END

The Troll-witch

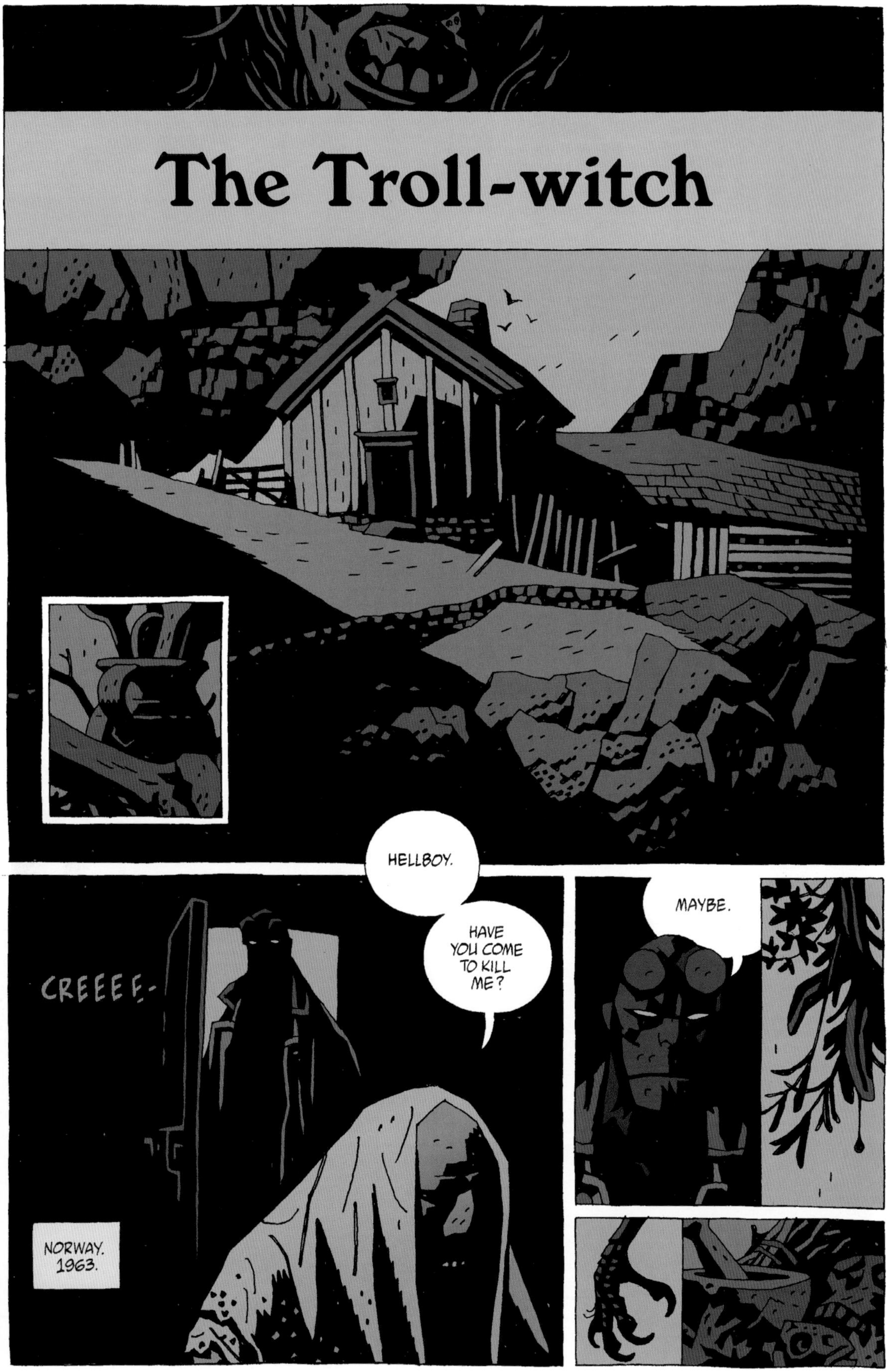

CREEEE-
HELLBOY.
HAVE YOU COME TO KILL ME?
NORWAY. 1963.
MAYBE.

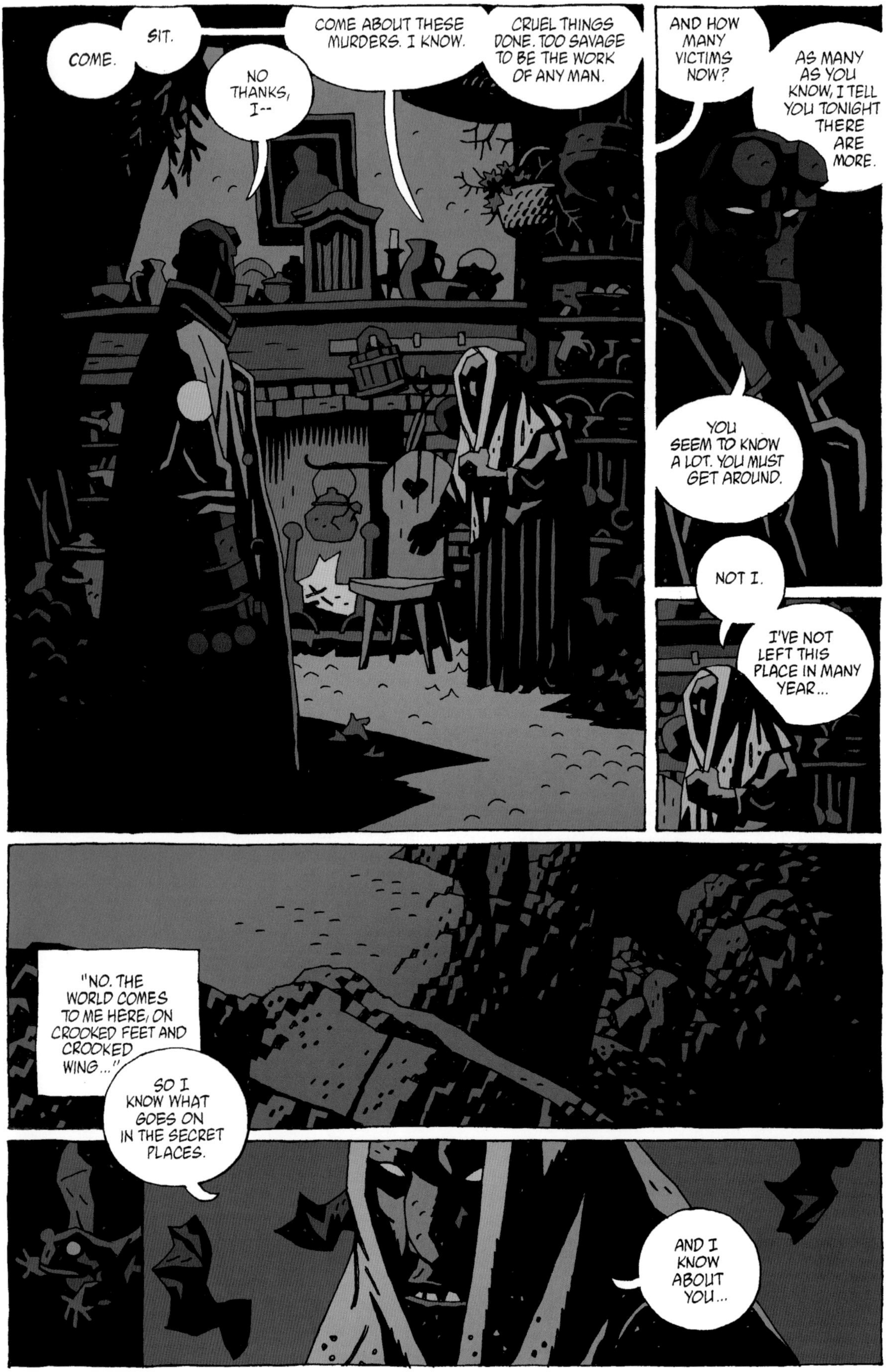
COME.
SIT.
NO THANKS, I--
COME ABOUT THESE MURDERS. I KNOW.
CRUEL THINGS DONE. TOO SAVAGE TO BE THE WORK OF ANY MAN.
AND HOW MANY VICTIMS NOW?
AS MANY AS YOU KNOW, I TELL YOU TONIGHT THERE ARE MORE.
YOU SEEM TO KNOW A LOT. YOU MUST GET AROUND.
NOT I.
I'VE NOT LEFT THIS PLACE IN MANY YEAR...
"NO. THE WORLD COMES TO ME HERE, ON CROOKED FEET AND CROOKED WING..."
SO I KNOW WHAT GOES ON IN THE SECRET PLACES.
AND I KNOW ABOUT YOU...

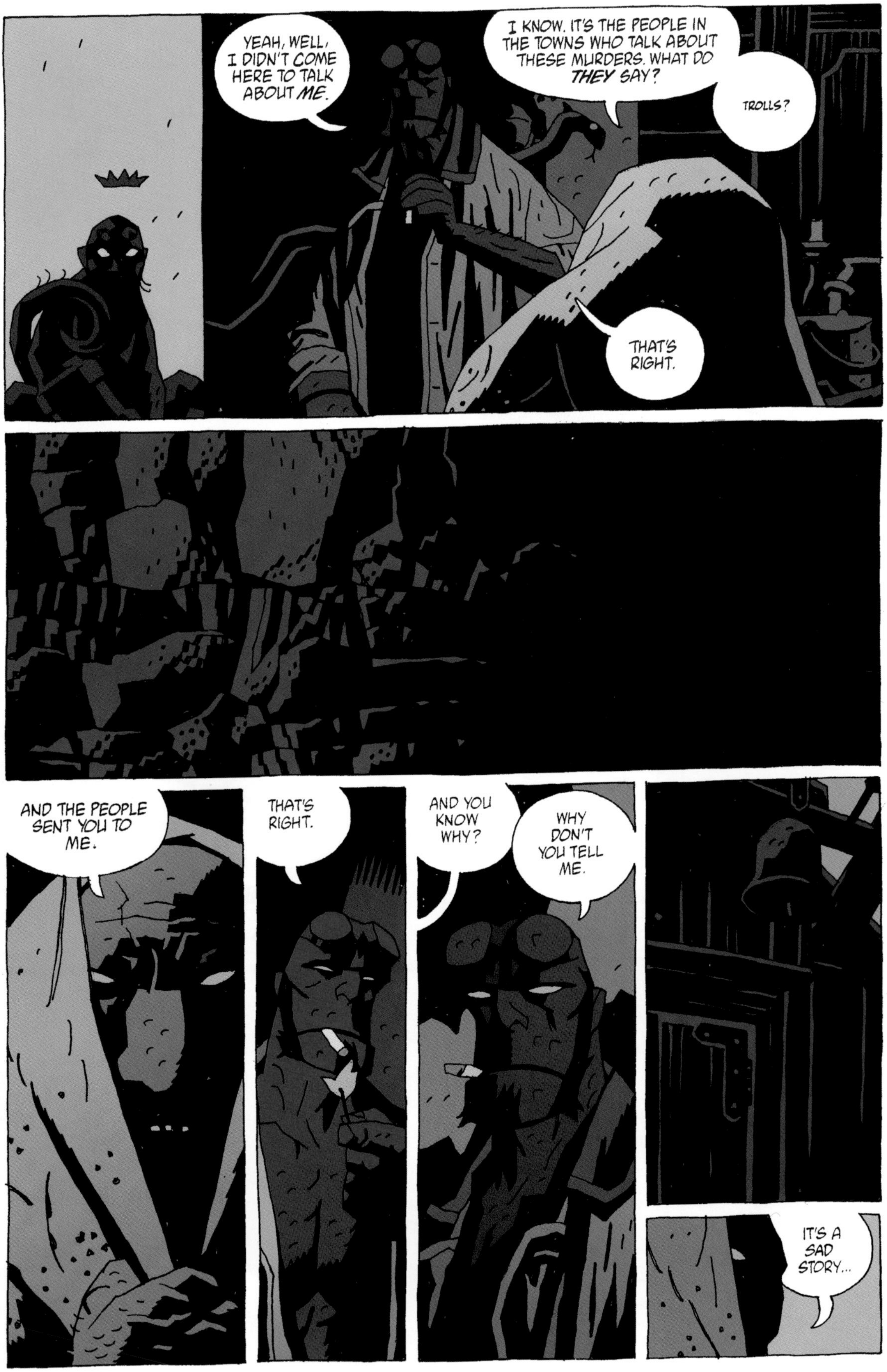

YEAH, WELL, I DIDN'T COME HERE TO TALK ABOUT *ME*.
I KNOW. IT'S THE PEOPLE IN THE TOWNS WHO TALK ABOUT THESE MURDERS. WHAT DO *THEY* SAY?
TROLLS?
THAT'S RIGHT.
AND THE PEOPLE SENT YOU TO ME.
THAT'S RIGHT.
AND YOU KNOW WHY?
WHY DON'T YOU TELL ME.
IT'S A SAD STORY...

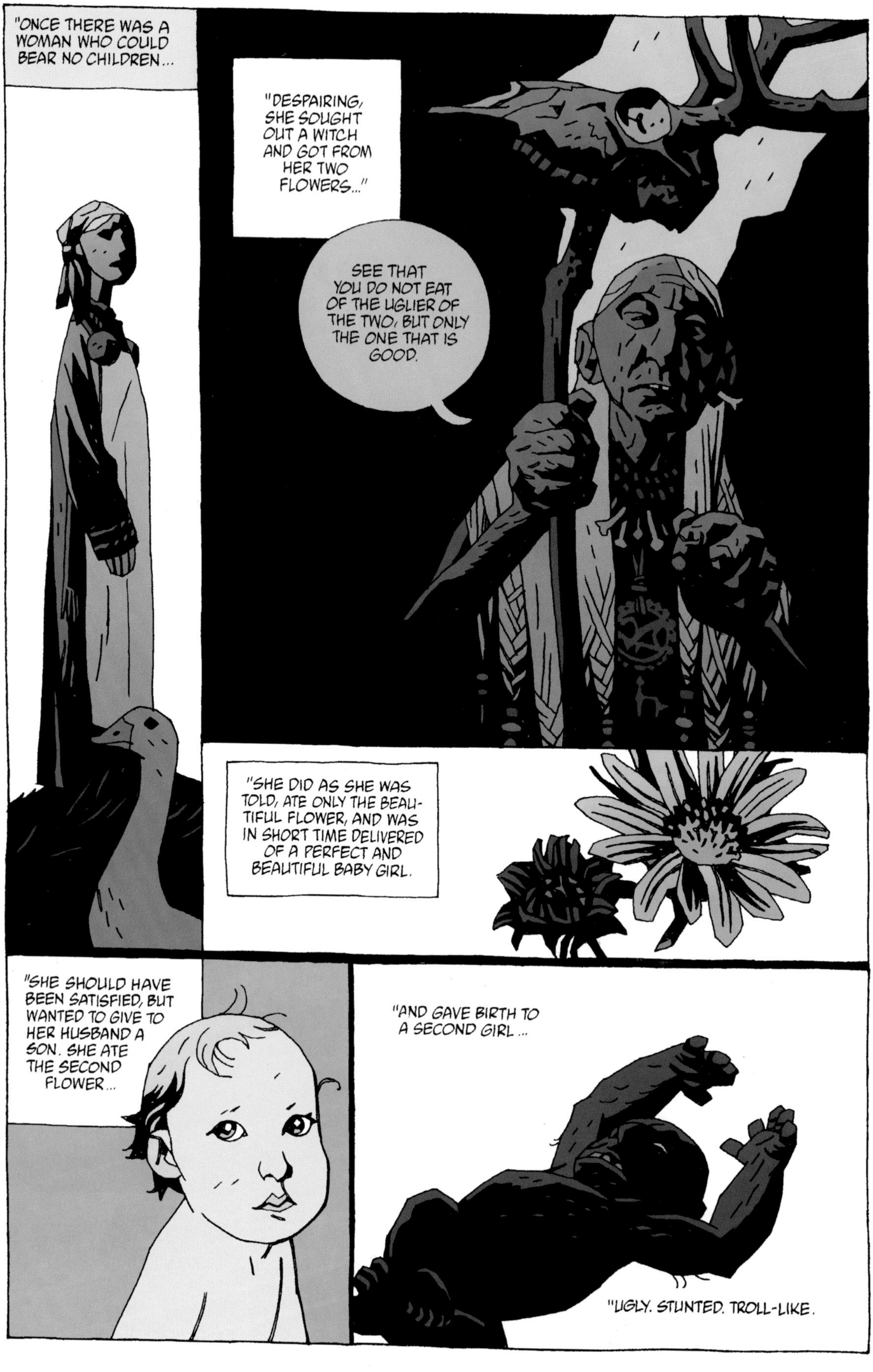
"ONCE THERE WAS A WOMAN WHO COULD BEAR NO CHILDREN...
"DESPAIRING, SHE SOUGHT OUT A WITCH AND GOT FROM HER TWO FLOWERS..."
SEE THAT YOU DO NOT EAT OF THE UGLIER OF THE TWO, BUT ONLY THE ONE THAT IS GOOD.
"SHE DID AS SHE WAS TOLD, ATE ONLY THE BEAU-TIFUL FLOWER, AND WAS IN SHORT TIME DELIVERED OF A PERFECT AND BEAUTIFUL BABY GIRL.
"SHE SHOULD HAVE BEEN SATISFIED, BUT WANTED TO GIVE TO HER HUSBAND A SON. SHE ATE THE SECOND FLOWER...
"AND GAVE BIRTH TO A SECOND GIRL...
"UGLY. STUNTED. TROLL-LIKE.

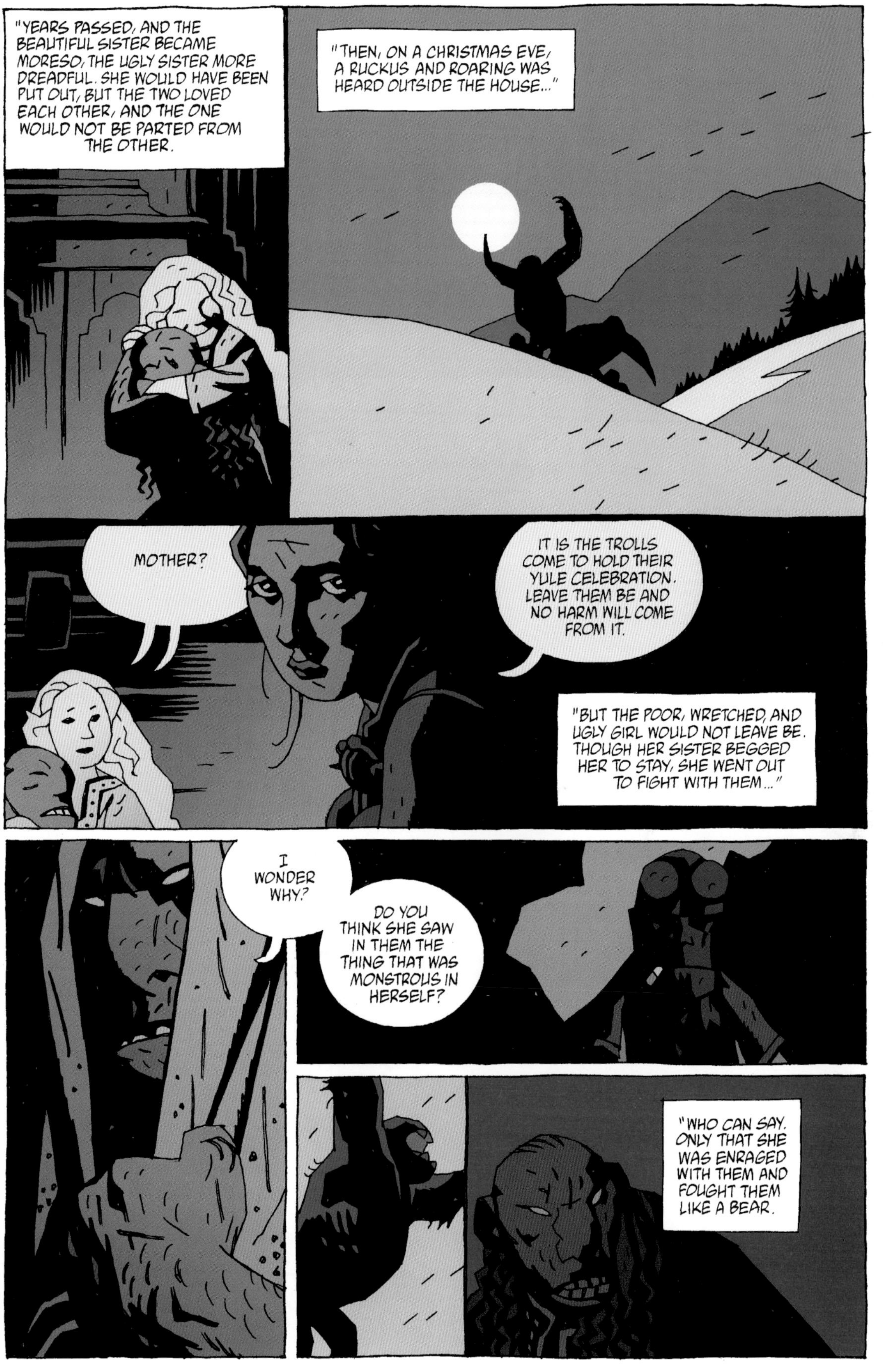
"YEARS PASSED, AND THE BEAUTIFUL SISTER BECAME MORESO, THE UGLY SISTER MORE DREADFUL. SHE WOULD HAVE BEEN PUT OUT, BUT THE TWO LOVED EACH OTHER, AND THE ONE WOULD NOT BE PARTED FROM THE OTHER.
"THEN, ON A CHRISTMAS EVE, A RUCKUS AND ROARING WAS HEARD OUTSIDE THE HOUSE..."
MOTHER?
IT IS THE TROLLS COME TO HOLD THEIR YULE CELEBRATION. LEAVE THEM BE AND NO HARM WILL COME FROM IT.
"BUT THE POOR, WRETCHED, AND UGLY GIRL WOULD NOT LEAVE BE. THOUGH HER SISTER BEGGED HER TO STAY, SHE WENT OUT TO FIGHT WITH THEM..."
I WONDER WHY?
DO YOU THINK SHE SAW IN THEM THE THING THAT WAS MONSTROUS IN HERSELF?
"WHO CAN SAY. ONLY THAT SHE WAS ENRAGED WITH THEM AND FOUGHT THEM LIKE A BEAR.

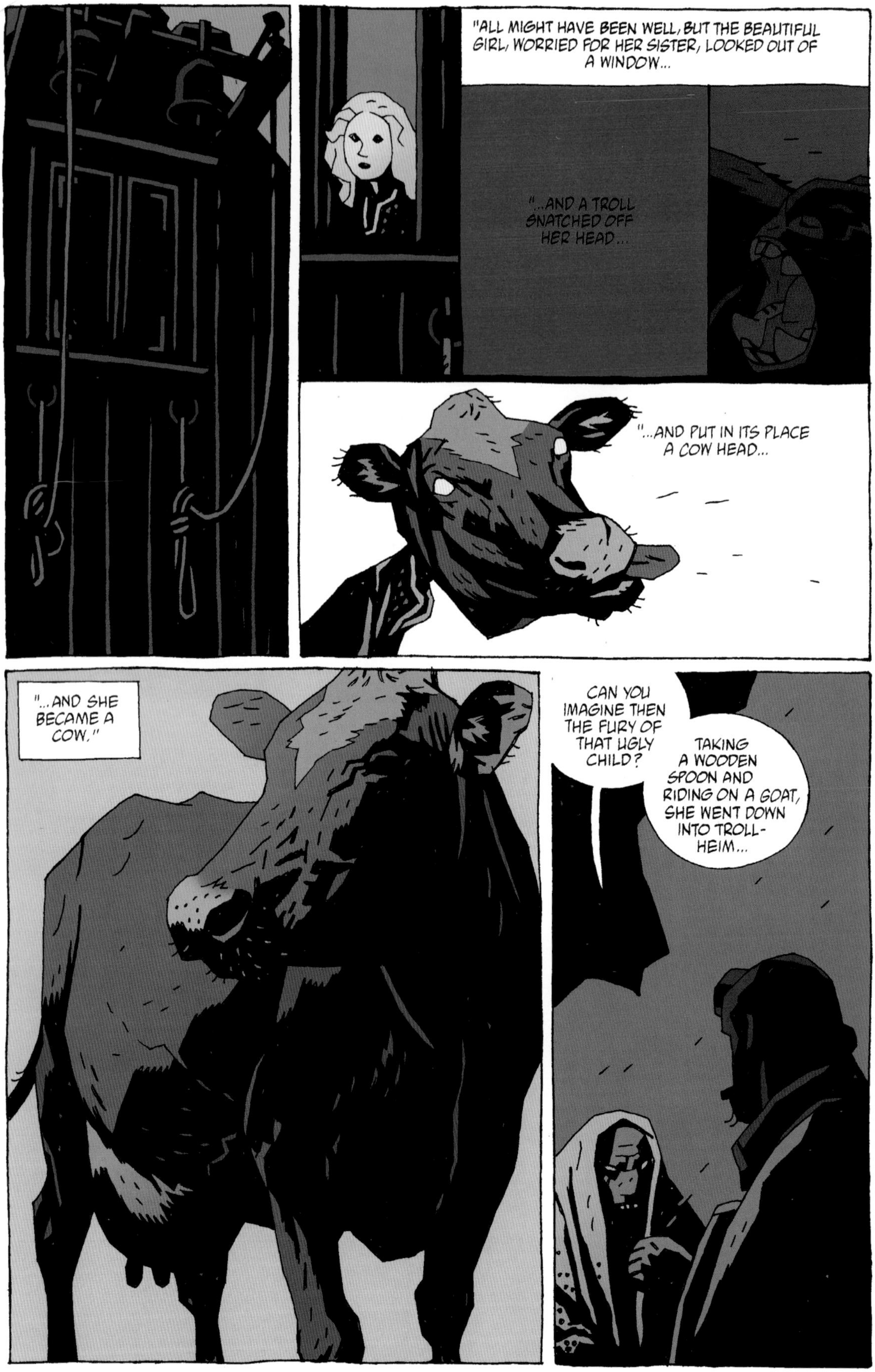
"ALL MIGHT HAVE BEEN WELL, BUT THE BEAUTIFUL GIRL, WORRIED FOR HER SISTER, LOOKED OUT OF A WINDOW...
"...AND A TROLL SNATCHED OFF HER HEAD...
"...AND PUT IN ITS PLACE A COW HEAD...
"...AND SHE BECAME A COW."
CAN YOU IMAGINE THEN THE FURY OF THAT UGLY CHILD?
TAKING A WOODEN SPOON AND RIDING ON A GOAT, SHE WENT DOWN INTO TROLL-HEIM...

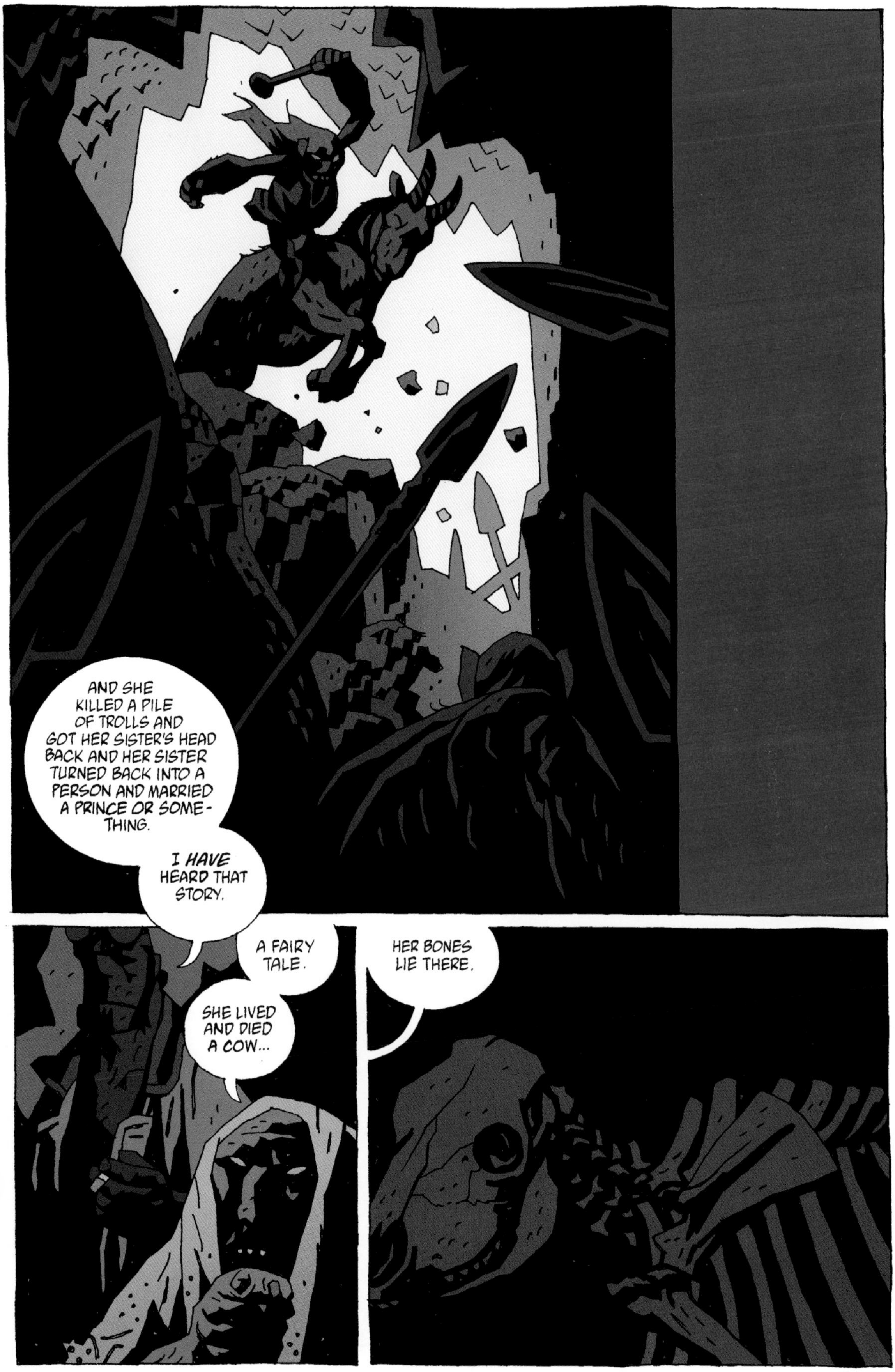
AND SHE KILLED A PILE OF TROLLS AND GOT HER SISTER'S HEAD BACK AND HER SISTER TURNED BACK INTO A PERSON AND MARRIED A PRINCE OR SOME-THING.
I *HAVE* HEARD THAT STORY.
A FAIRY TALE.
SHE LIVED AND DIED A COW...
HER BONES LIE THERE.

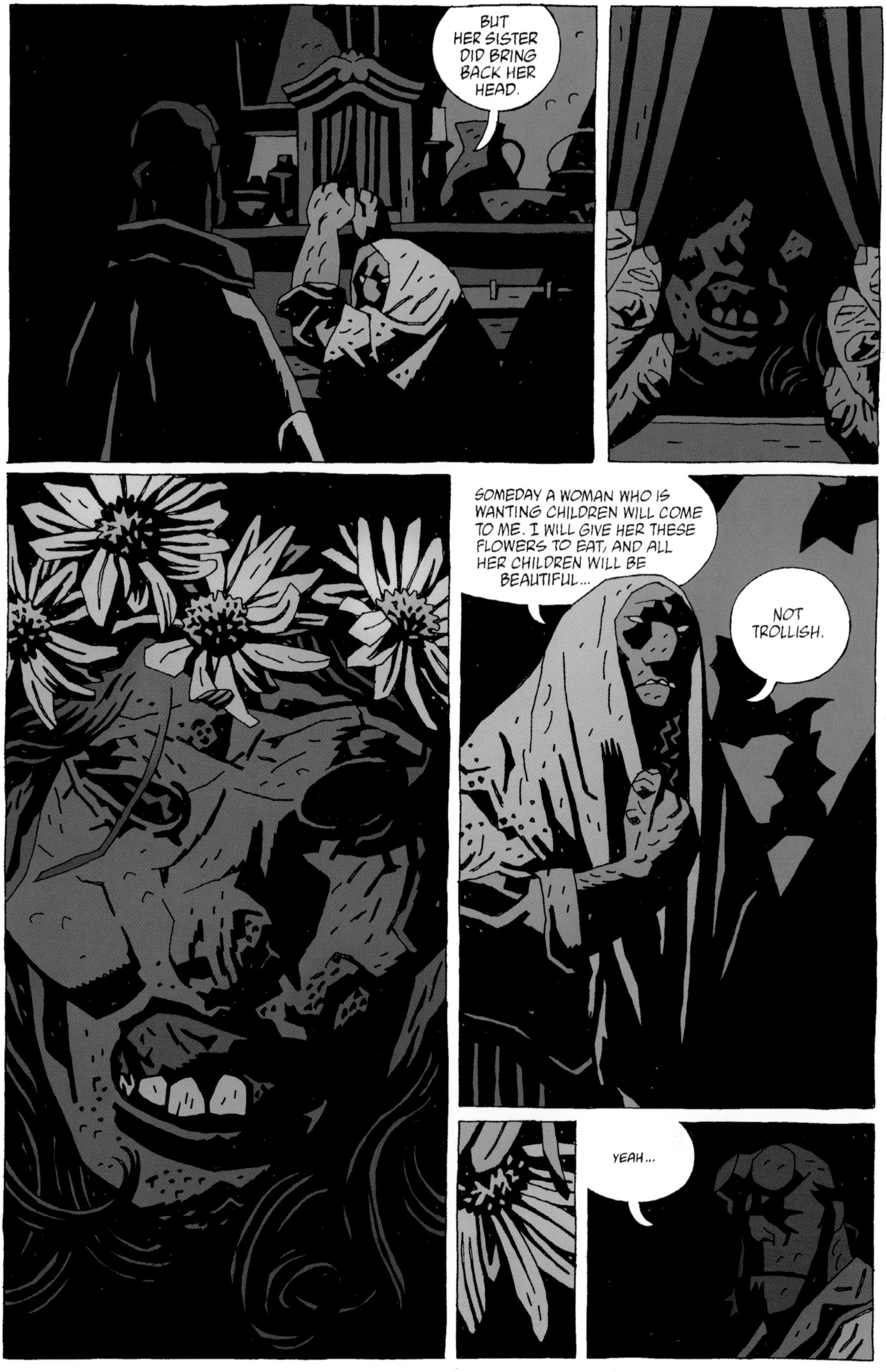
BUT HER SISTER DID BRING BACK HER HEAD.
SOMEDAY A WOMAN WHO IS WANTING CHILDREN WILL COME TO ME. I WILL GIVE HER THESE FLOWERS TO EAT, AND ALL HER CHILDREN WILL BE BEAUTIFUL...
NOT TROLLISH.
YEAH...

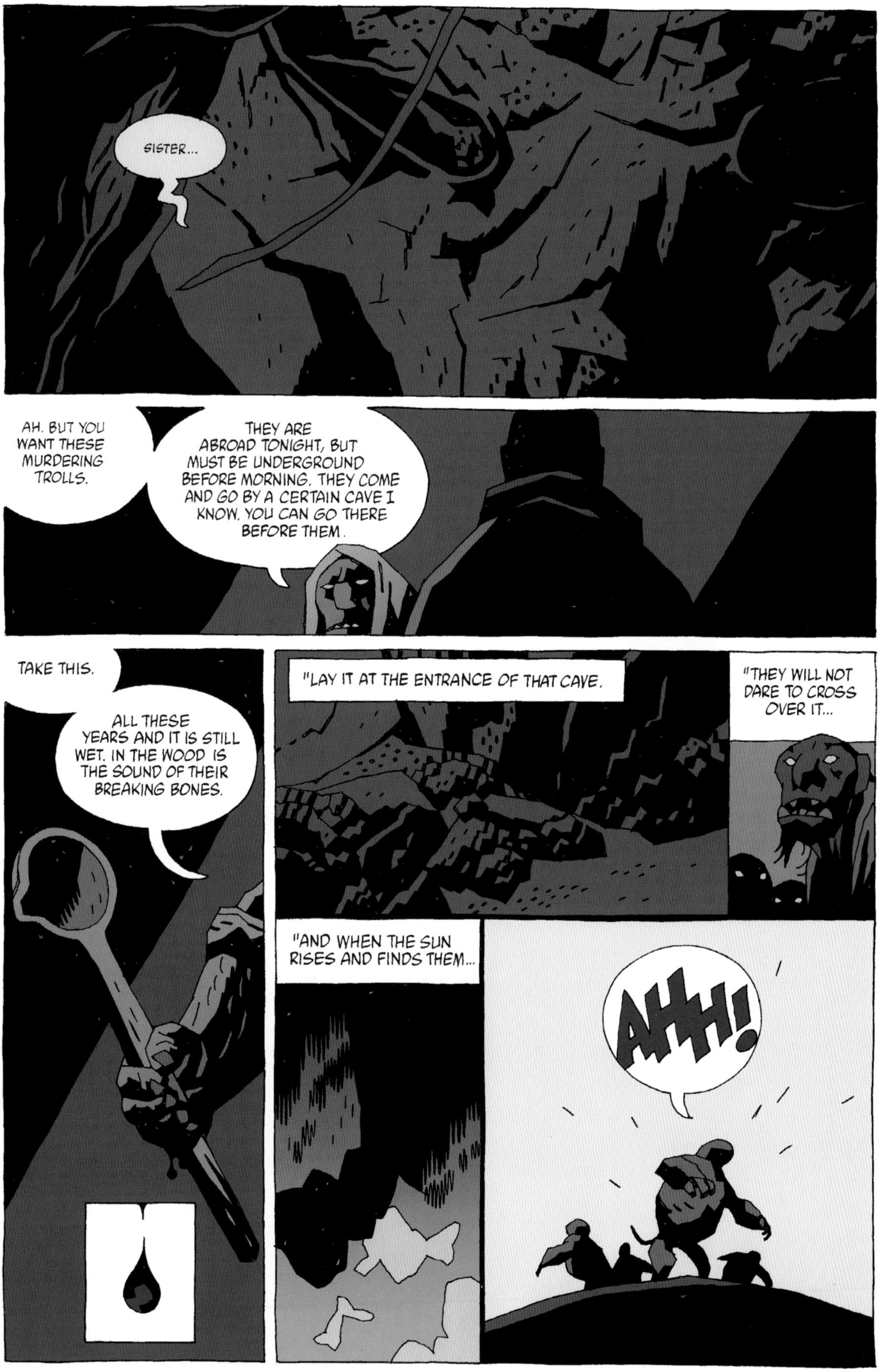
SISTER...
AH. BUT YOU WANT THESE MURDERING TROLLS.
THEY ARE ABROAD TONIGHT, BUT MUST BE UNDERGROUND BEFORE MORNING. THEY COME AND GO BY A CERTAIN CAVE I KNOW. YOU CAN GO THERE BEFORE THEM.
TAKE THIS.
ALL THESE YEARS AND IT IS STILL WET. IN THE WOOD IS THE SOUND OF THEIR BREAKING BONES.
"LAY IT AT THE ENTRANCE OF THAT CAVE.
"THEY WILL NOT DARE TO CROSS OVER IT...
"AND WHEN THE SUN RISES AND FINDS THEM...
AHH!

"THEY WILL TURN TO STONE.

"NO BLOW STRUCK...

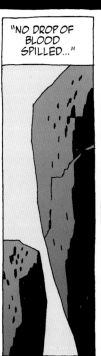

"NO DROP OF BLOOD SPILLED..."

AND I WONDER... HOW WILL YOU FEEL ABOUT THAT?

THE END

The Troll Witch

THIS IS ONE OF MY FAVORITES. The story of the two sisters is based on a Norwegian folktale. In the original story, the one sister *does* rescue the other's head and she does turn back into a person and she marries a prince, etc. I liked her better as a cow. The reveal of the sister's head was probably unconsciously inspired by the end of John Huston's *The Man Who Would Be King*, my all-time favorite "boy movie."

"The Troll Witch" was published in 2004, in *The Dark Horse Book of Witchcraft*.

✠

The Vampire of Prague

MY FIRST TRIP TO PRAGUE was with director Guillermo del Toro, back in 2000, to scout locations for his film *Blade II* and to look for Kafka puppets. We had better luck with the locations. Guillermo *did* finally find a Kafka puppet (but it had no coat or hat and I think a proper Kafka puppet needs both), but the puppet we both fell in love with was a horrible, pop-eyed, green-faced thing with little playing cards tucked into its sleeve. Pinned to its coat was a little book telling the legend of the gambler ghost of Prague. For this story I've stayed faithful to the gambler legend but have taken the liberty of turning him into a vampire. There are supposedly a few vampires who haunt Prague, but they tend to be pathetic characters—one waits for people to hurt themselves so he can lick their blood off the ground. Another lives in a pond and eats fish. Sad.

Most of the little puppet shops in Prague are gone now, but there are still a few good ones on the castle side of the Charles Bridge. The best of these was the inspiration for the last part of this story.

I originally planned to draw this one myself, but when it became clear that was never going to happen, the only artist I could think of for it was P. Craig Russell. I've been a fan of Craig's work for a very long time—everything from *Killraven* and *Elric* to his super-epic *Ring of the Nibelung*. We've worked together several times over the years, but always with Craig inking my pencil drawings. This was my first time writing for him, and to say I was intimidated, well, that doesn't even begin to cover it. I gave Craig a script with all the dialogue (I usually write the dialogue after it's drawn) and then a very loose description of the action. I didn't try to tell Craig how to do anything. I didn't break the plot down by pages. I didn't even say how many pages the story had to be. I just turned it over to Craig (with some pictures of that gambler-ghost puppet) and got the hell out of his way.

"The Vampire of Prague" was done specifically for this collection, with Craig's regular colorist, Lovern Kindzierski, and letterer, Galen Showman.

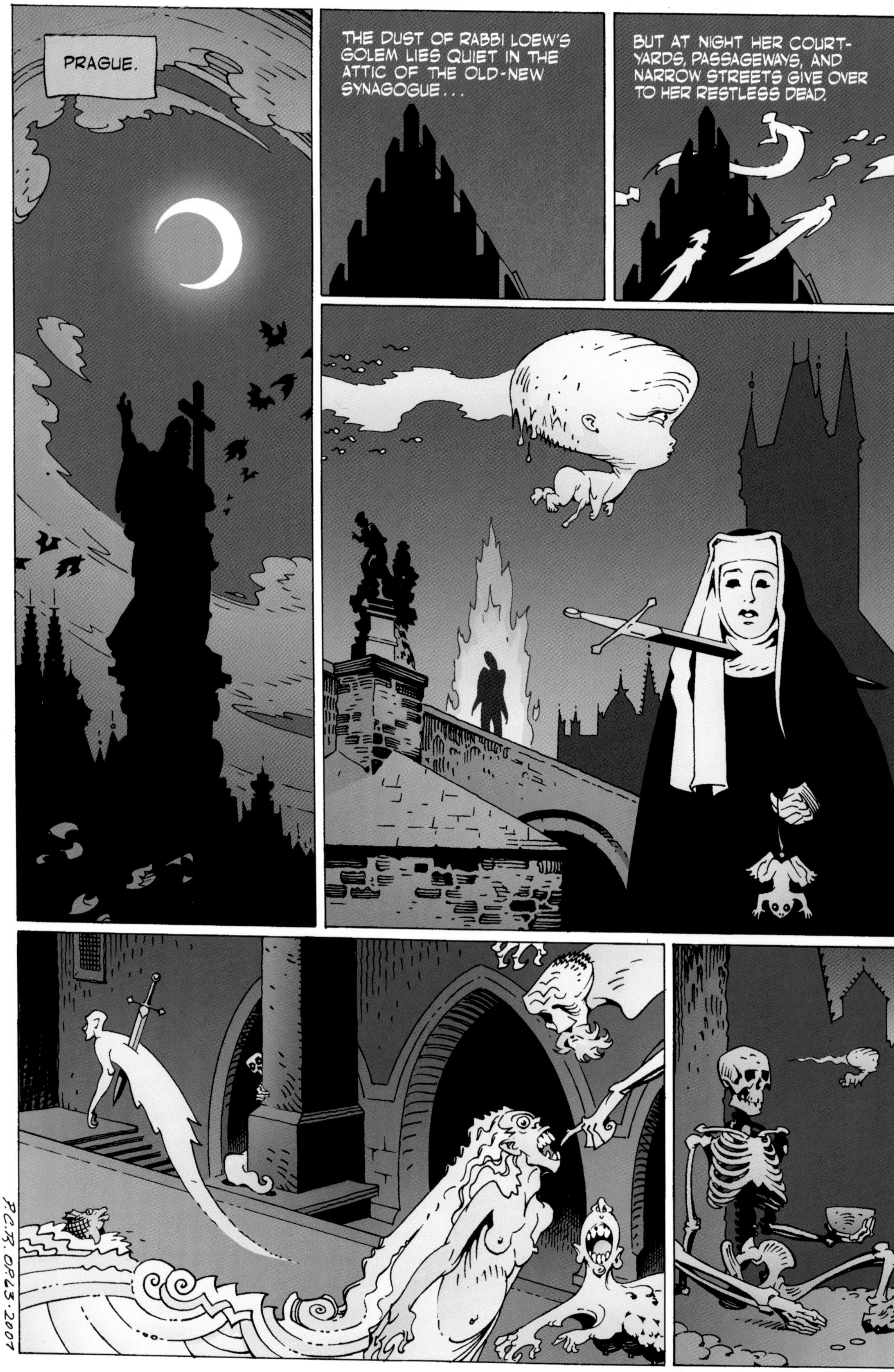
PRAGUE.
THE DUST OF RABBI LOEW'S GOLEM LIES QUIET IN THE ATTIC OF THE OLD-NEW SYNAGOGUE . . .
BUT AT NIGHT HER COURT-YARDS, PASSAGEWAYS, AND NARROW STREETS GIVE OVER TO HER RESTLESS DEAD.

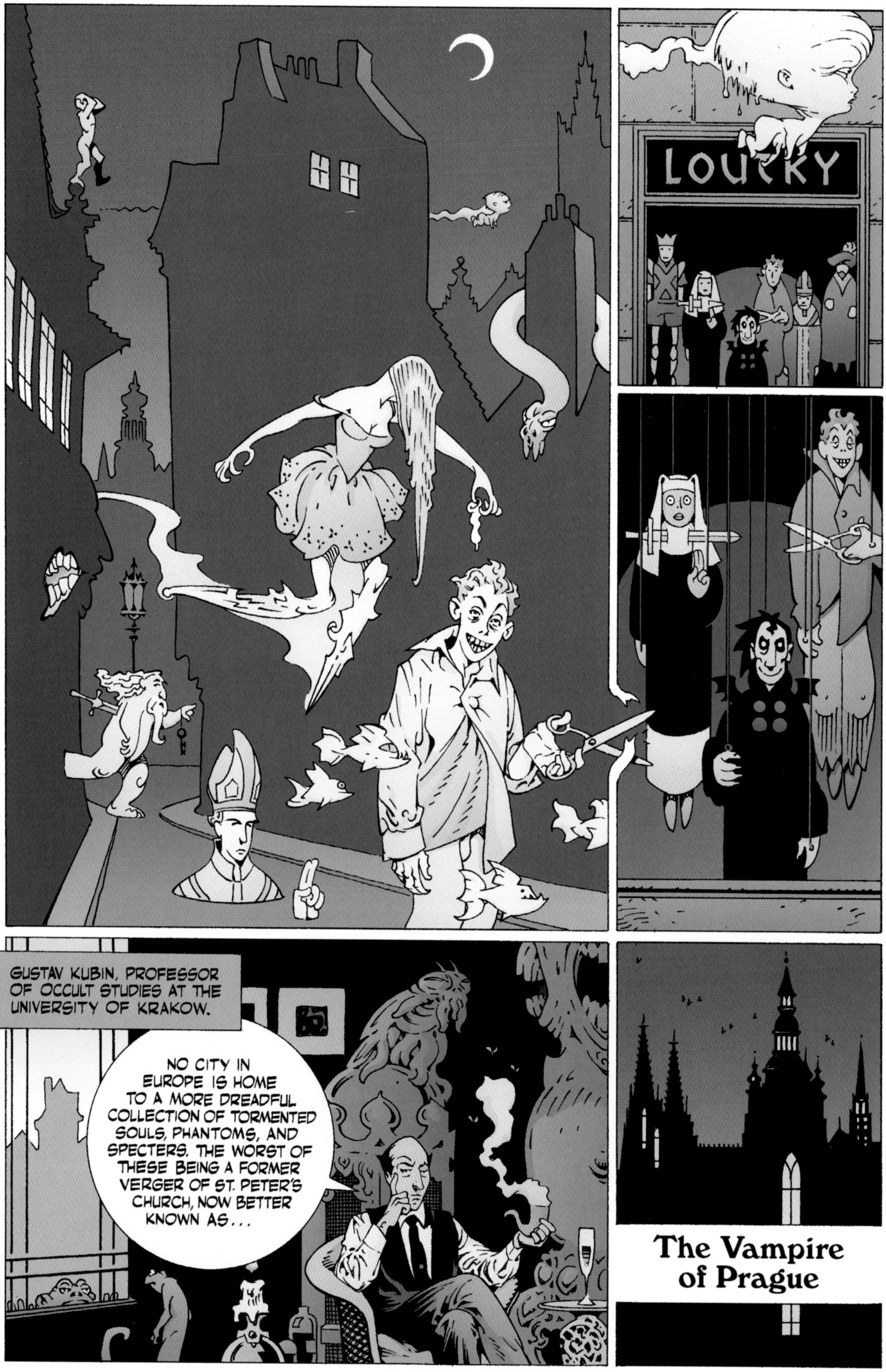
LOUČKY
GUSTAV KUBIN, PROFESSOR OF OCCULT STUDIES AT THE UNIVERSITY OF KRAKOW.
NO CITY IN EUROPE IS HOME TO A MORE DREADFUL COLLECTION OF TORMENTED SOULS, PHANTOMS, AND SPECTERS. THE WORST OF THESE BEING A FORMER VERGER OF ST. PETER'S CHURCH, NOW BETTER KNOWN AS...
The Vampire of Prague

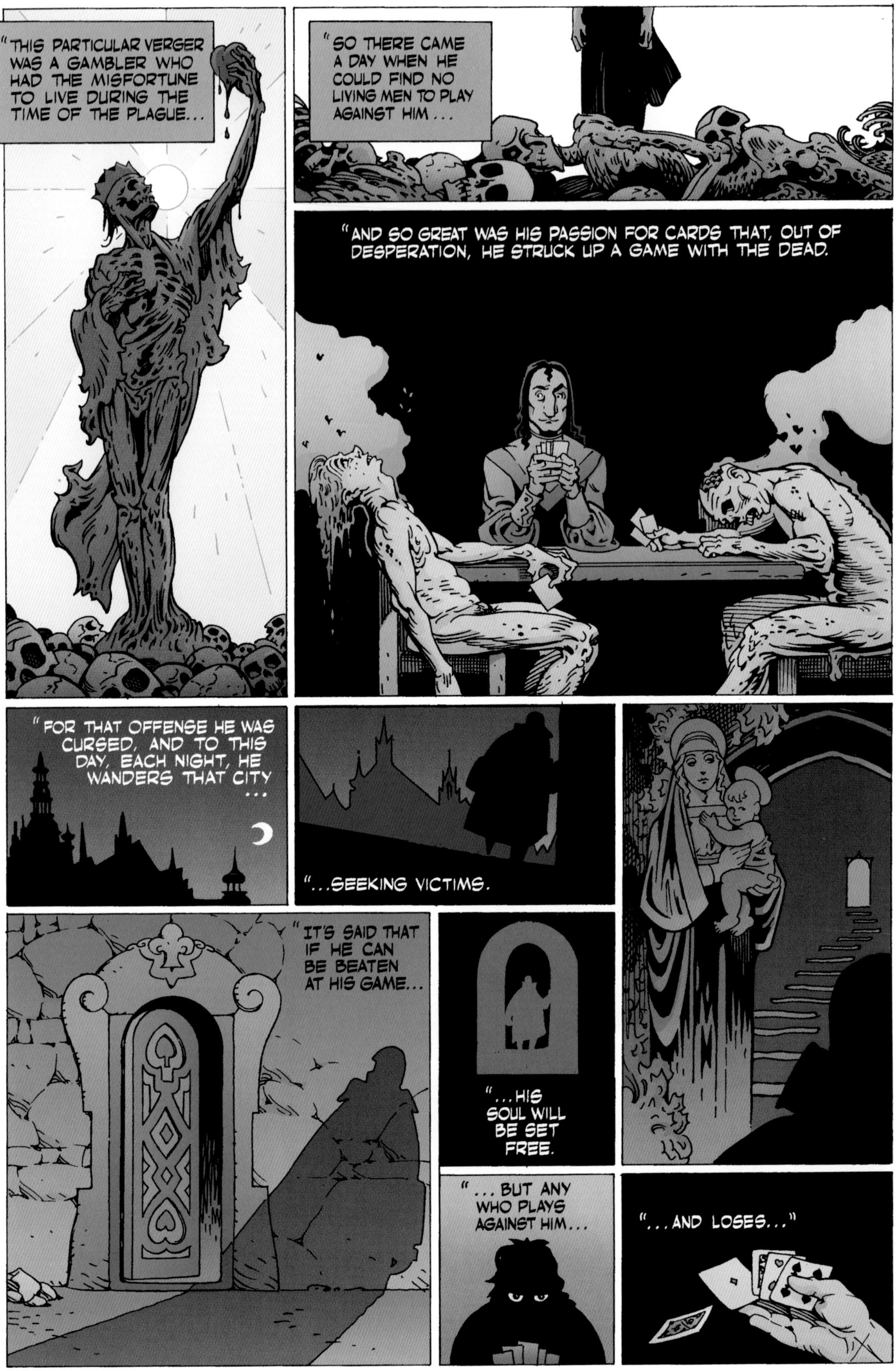
"THIS PARTICULAR VERGER WAS A GAMBLER WHO HAD THE MISFORTUNE TO LIVE DURING THE TIME OF THE PLAGUE...
"SO THERE CAME A DAY WHEN HE COULD FIND NO LIVING MEN TO PLAY AGAINST HIM...
"AND SO GREAT WAS HIS PASSION FOR CARDS THAT, OUT OF DESPERATION, HE STRUCK UP A GAME WITH THE DEAD.
"FOR THAT OFFENSE HE WAS CURSED, AND TO THIS DAY, EACH NIGHT, HE WANDERS THAT CITY...
"...SEEKING VICTIMS.
"IT'S SAID THAT IF HE CAN BE BEATEN AT HIS GAME...
"...HIS SOUL WILL BE SET FREE.
"...BUT ANY WHO PLAYS AGAINST HIM...
"...AND LOSES..."

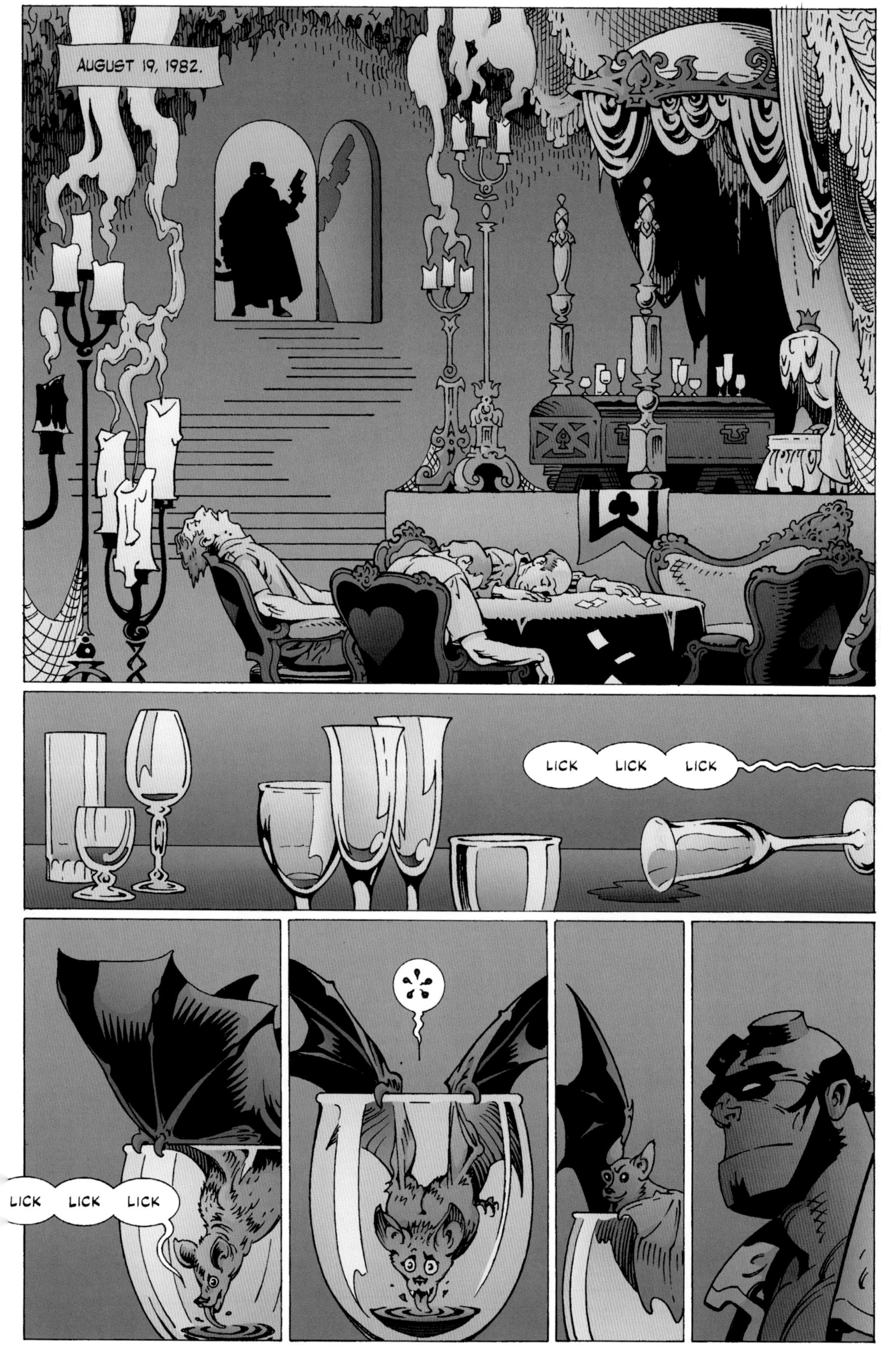
AUGUST 19, 1982.
LICK LICK LICK
LICK LICK LICK

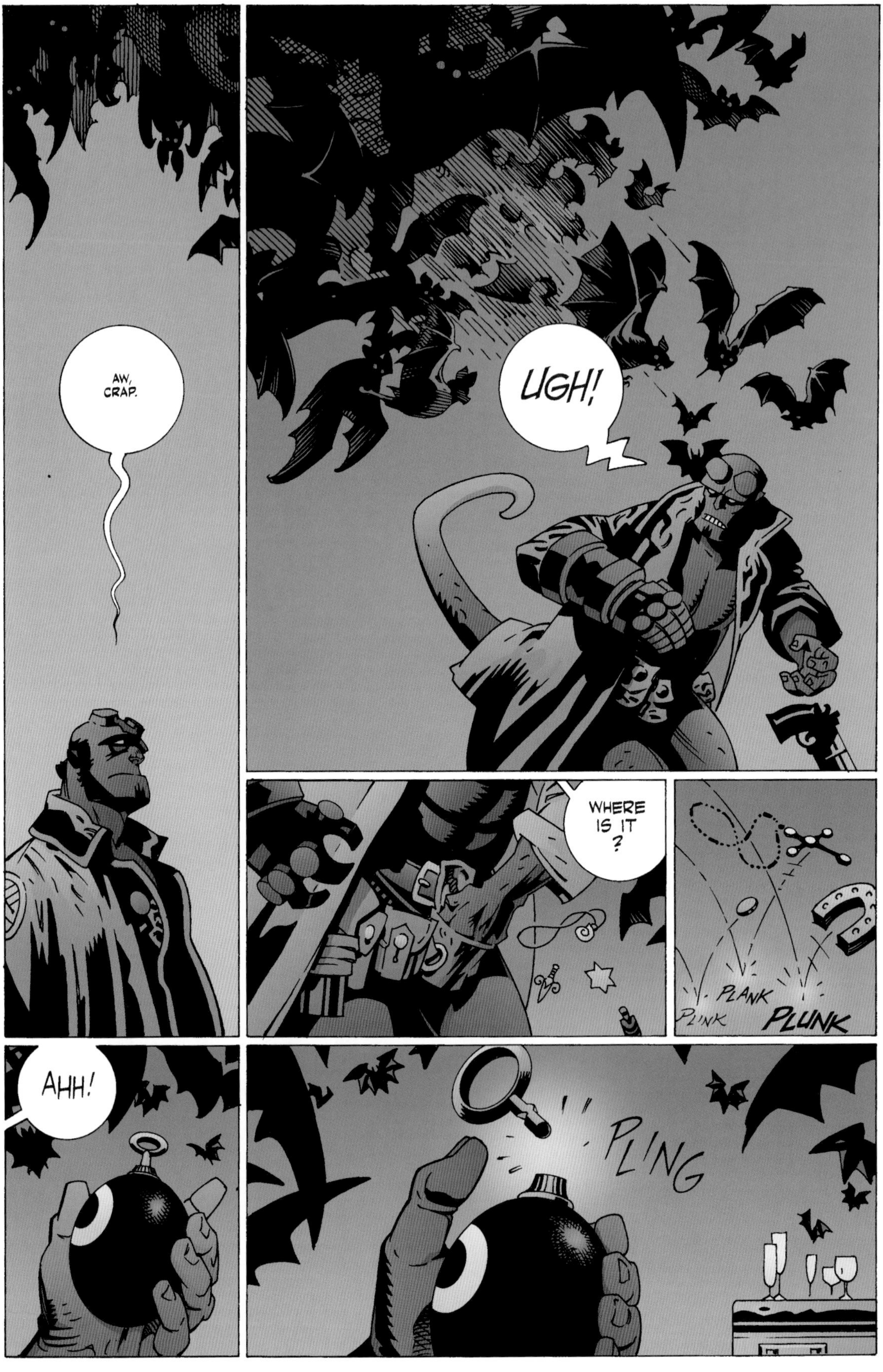
AW, CRAP.
UGH!
WHERE IS IT ?
PLANK
PLINK
PLUNK
AHH!
PLING

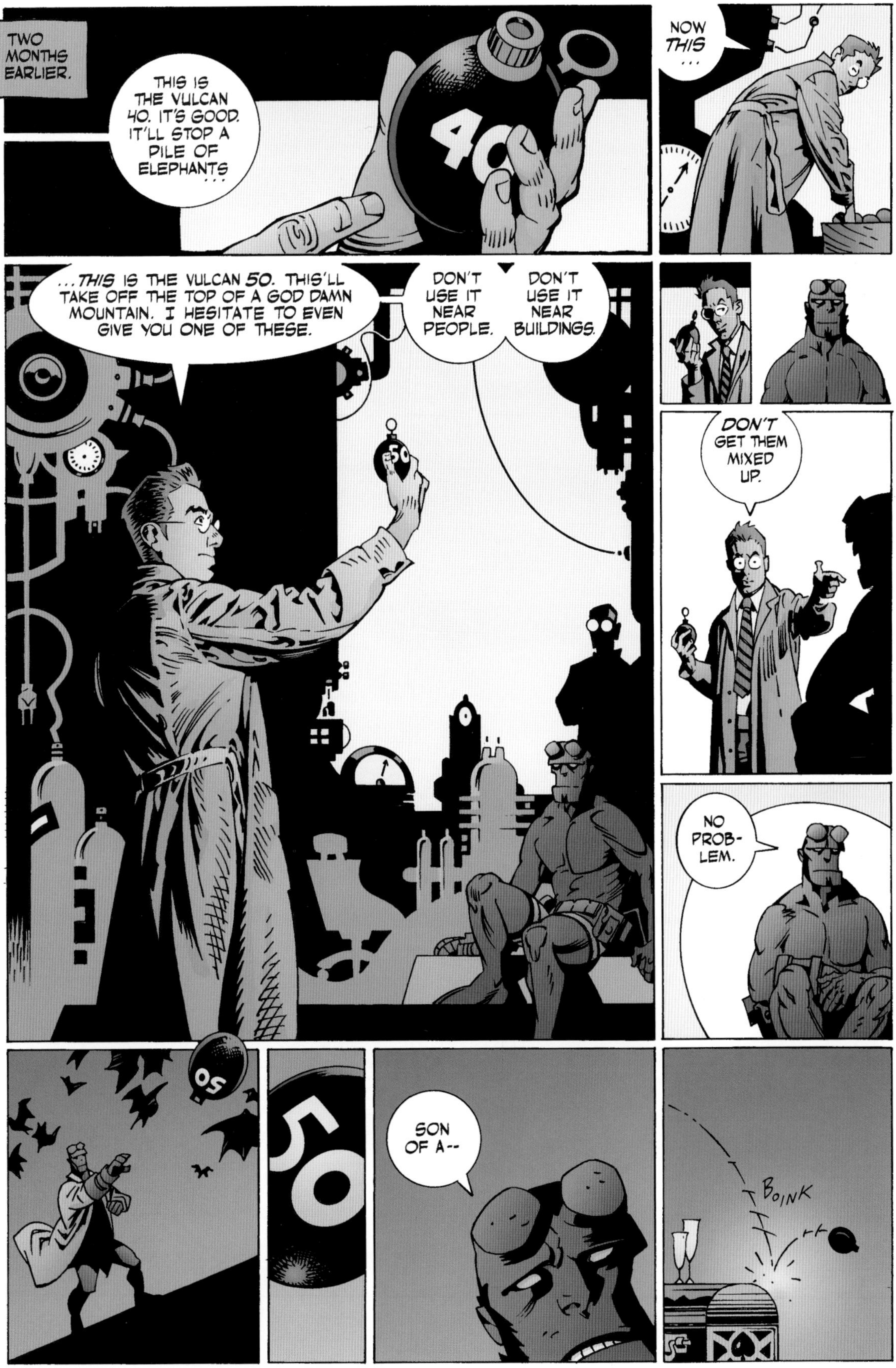

TWO MONTHS EARLIER.
THIS IS THE VULCAN 40. IT'S GOOD. IT'LL STOP A PILE OF ELEPHANTS . . .
NOW THIS . . .
. . . THIS IS THE VULCAN 50. THIS'LL TAKE OFF THE TOP OF A GOD DAMN MOUNTAIN. I HESITATE TO EVEN GIVE YOU ONE OF THESE.
DON'T USE IT NEAR PEOPLE.
DON'T USE IT NEAR BUILDINGS.
DON'T GET THEM MIXED UP.
NO PROB-LEM.
50
50
SON OF A--
BOINK

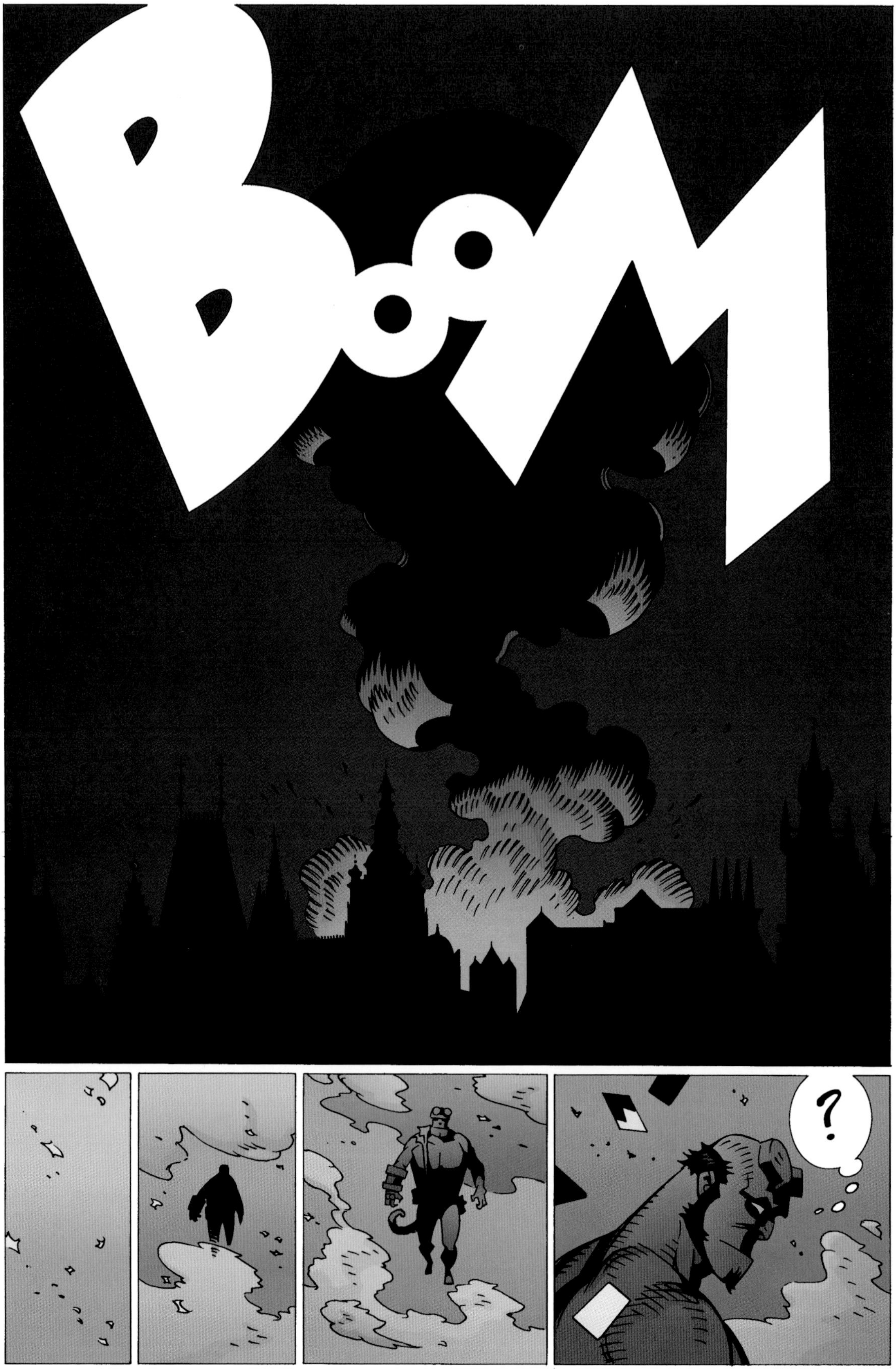
BOOM
?

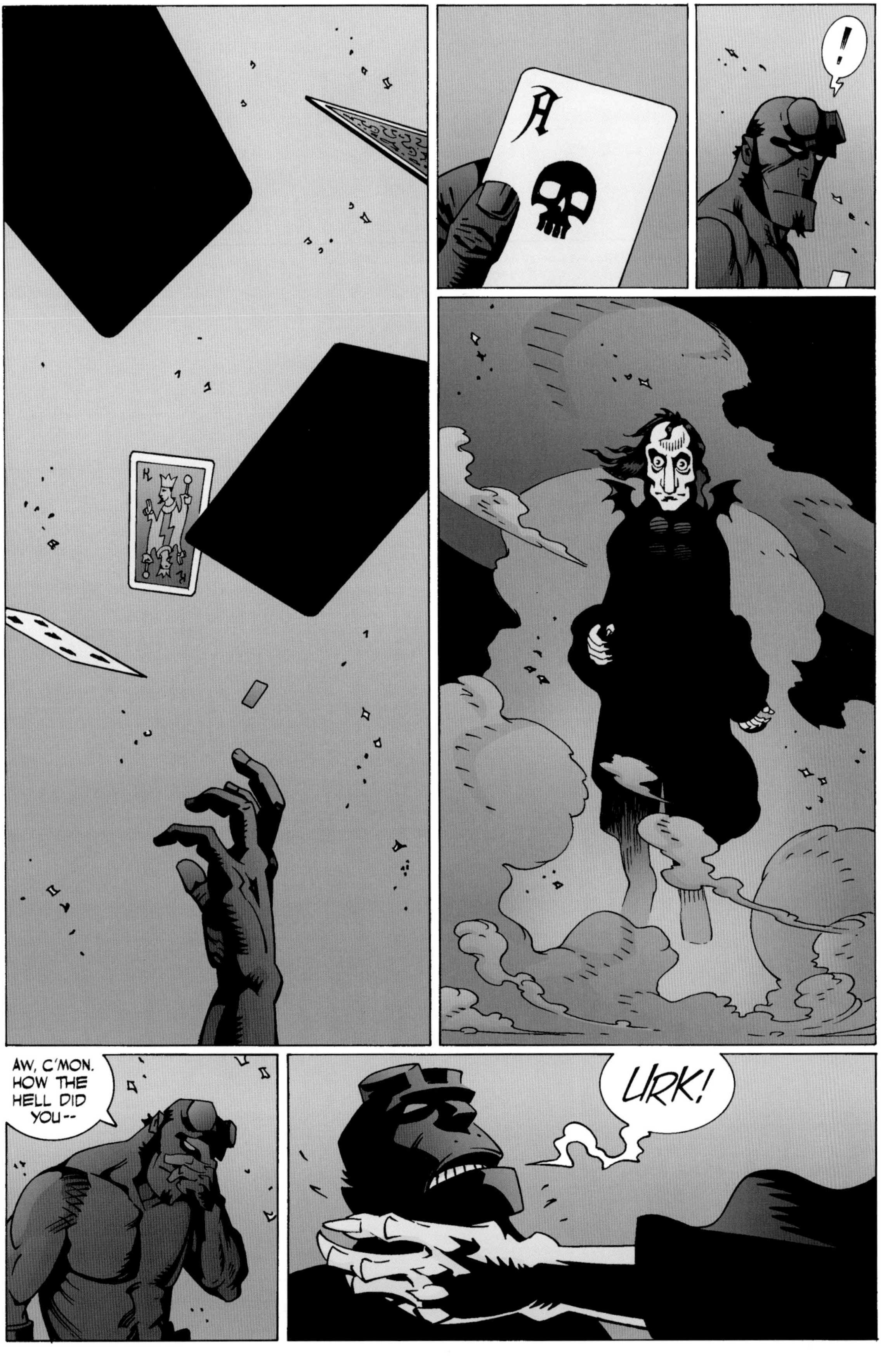
!
AW, C'MON. HOW THE HELL DID YOU --
URK!

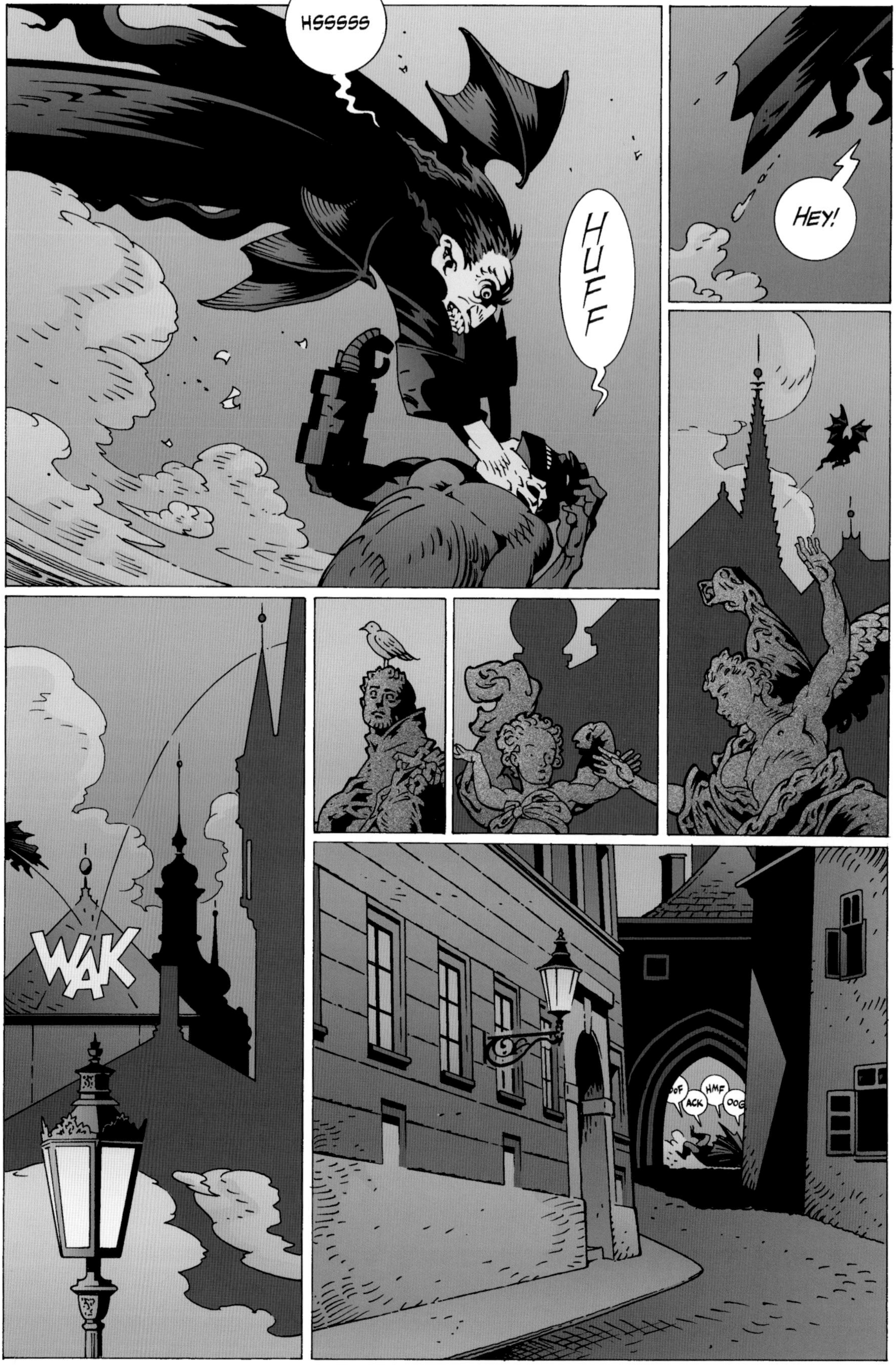
HSSSSS
HUFF
HEY!
WAK
OOF
ACK
HMF
OOG

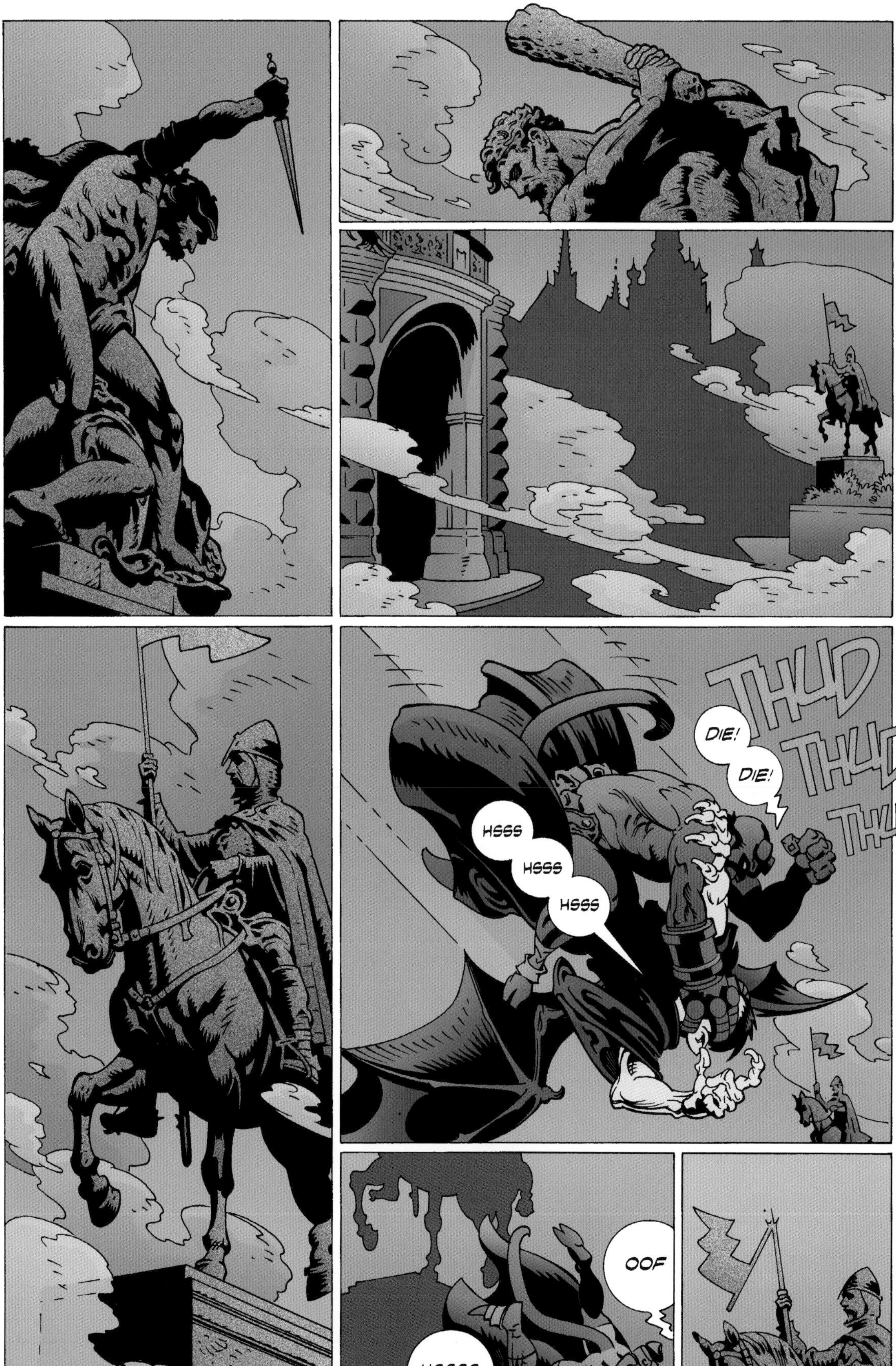
THUD
THUD
THUD
DIE!
DIE!
HSSS
HSSS
HSSS
OOF
HSSSS

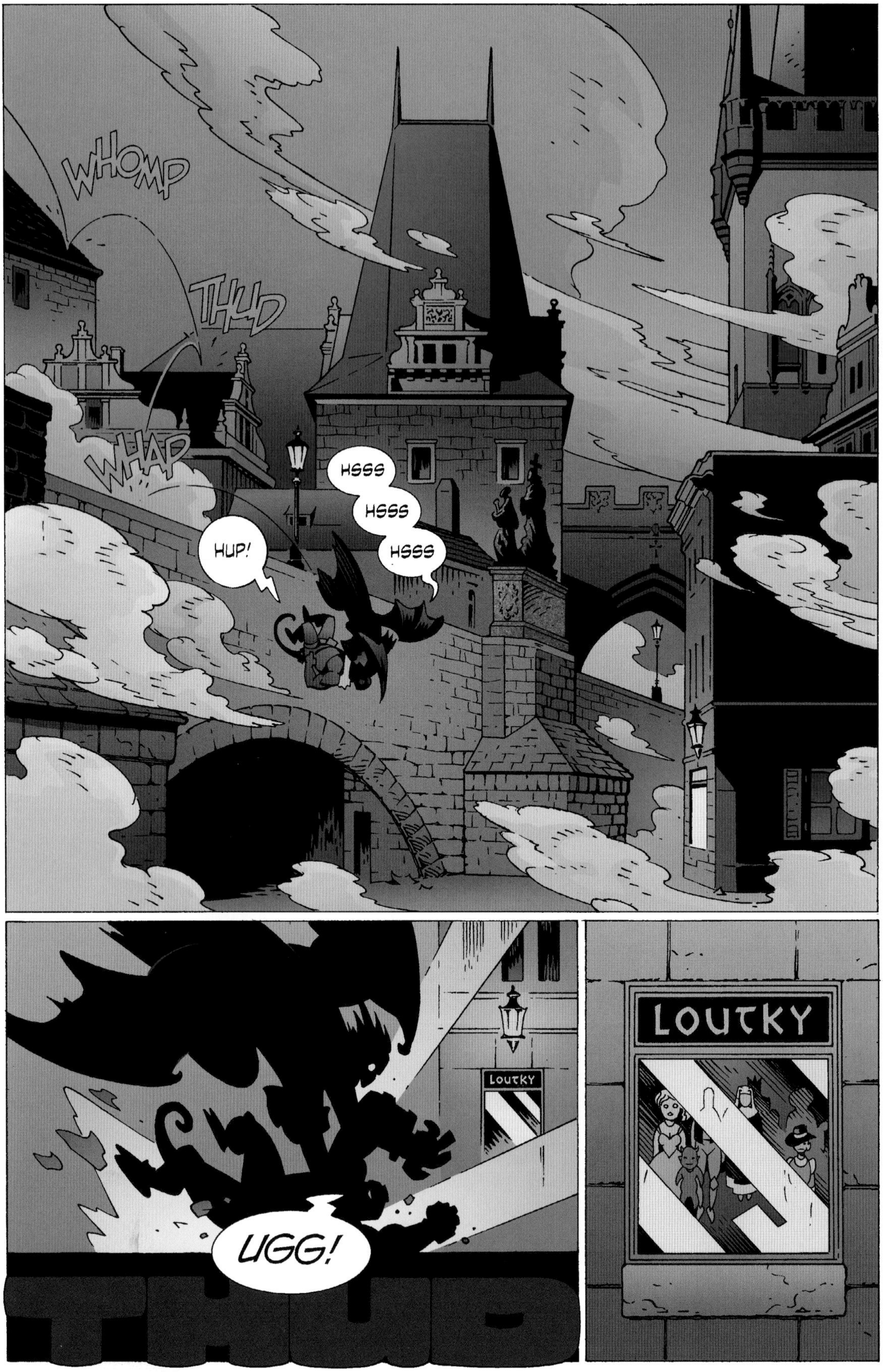
WHOMP
THUD
WHAP
HUP!
HSSS
HSSS
HSSS
LOUTKY
UGG!
THUD
LOUTKY

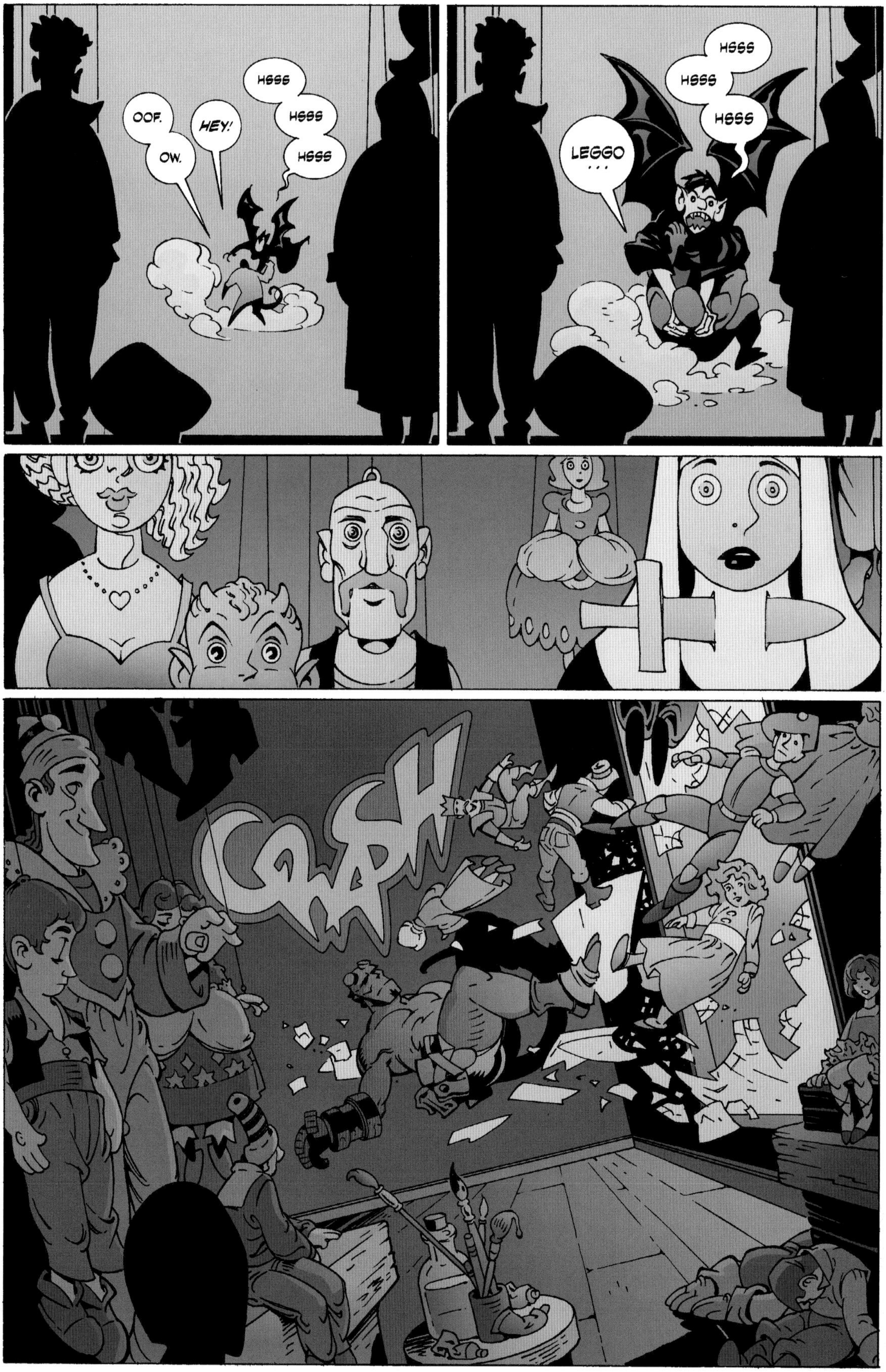
OOF.
OW.
HEY!
HSSS
HSSS
HSSS
LEGGO . . .
HSSS
HSSS
HSSS
CRASH

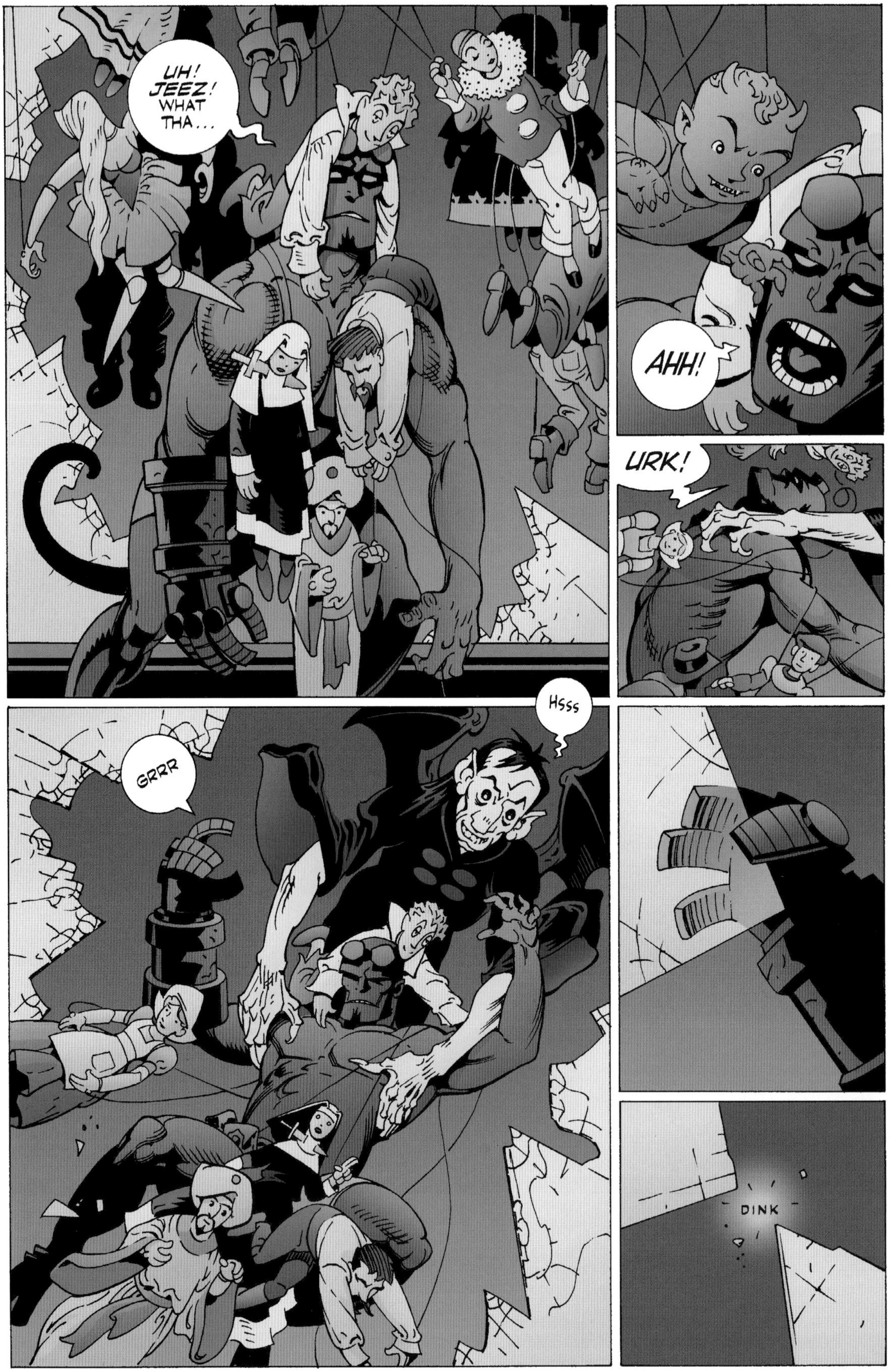
UH! JEEZ! WHAT THA...
AHH!
URK!
GRRR
HSSS
DINK

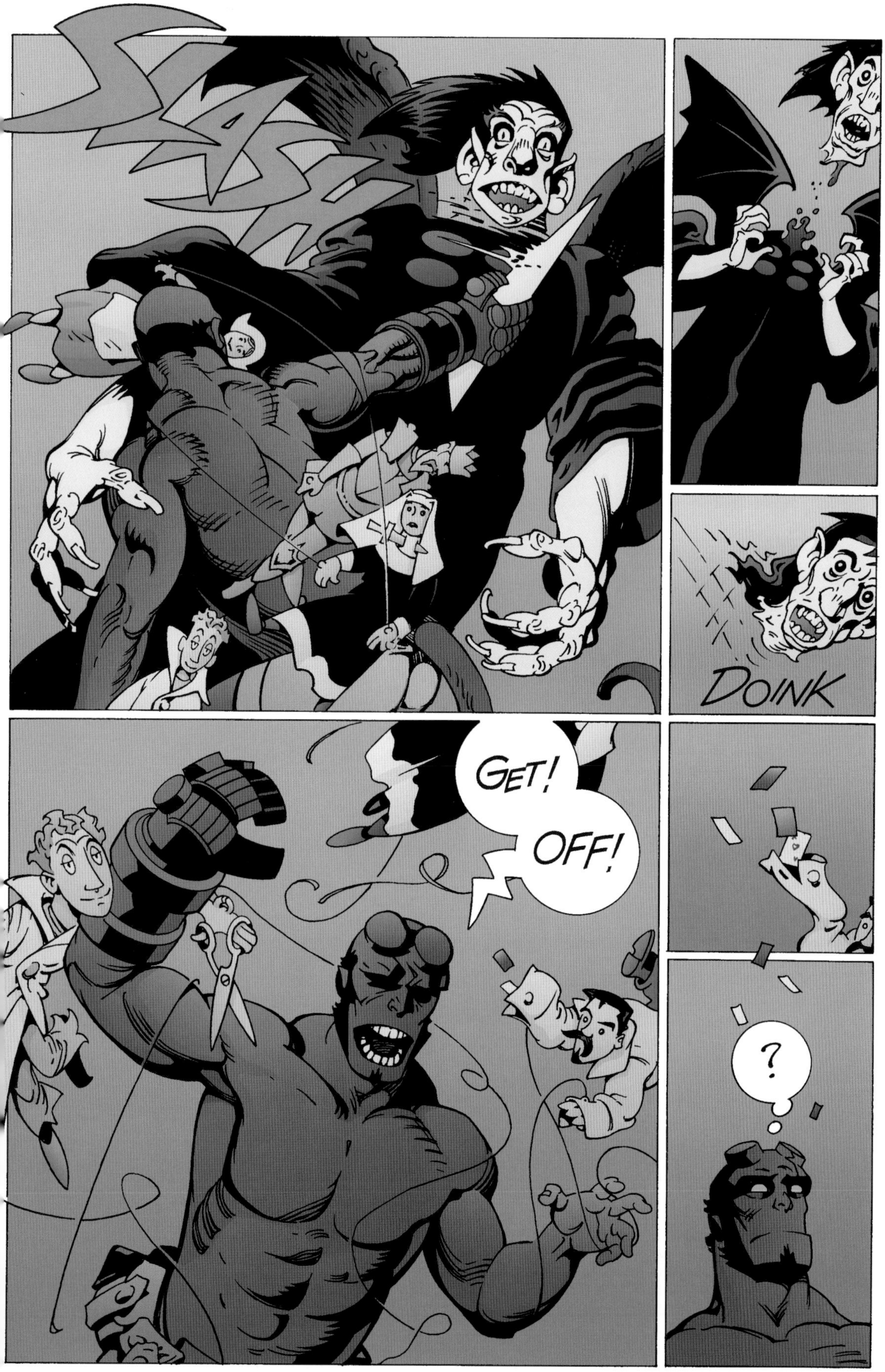
DOINK
GET!
OFF!
?

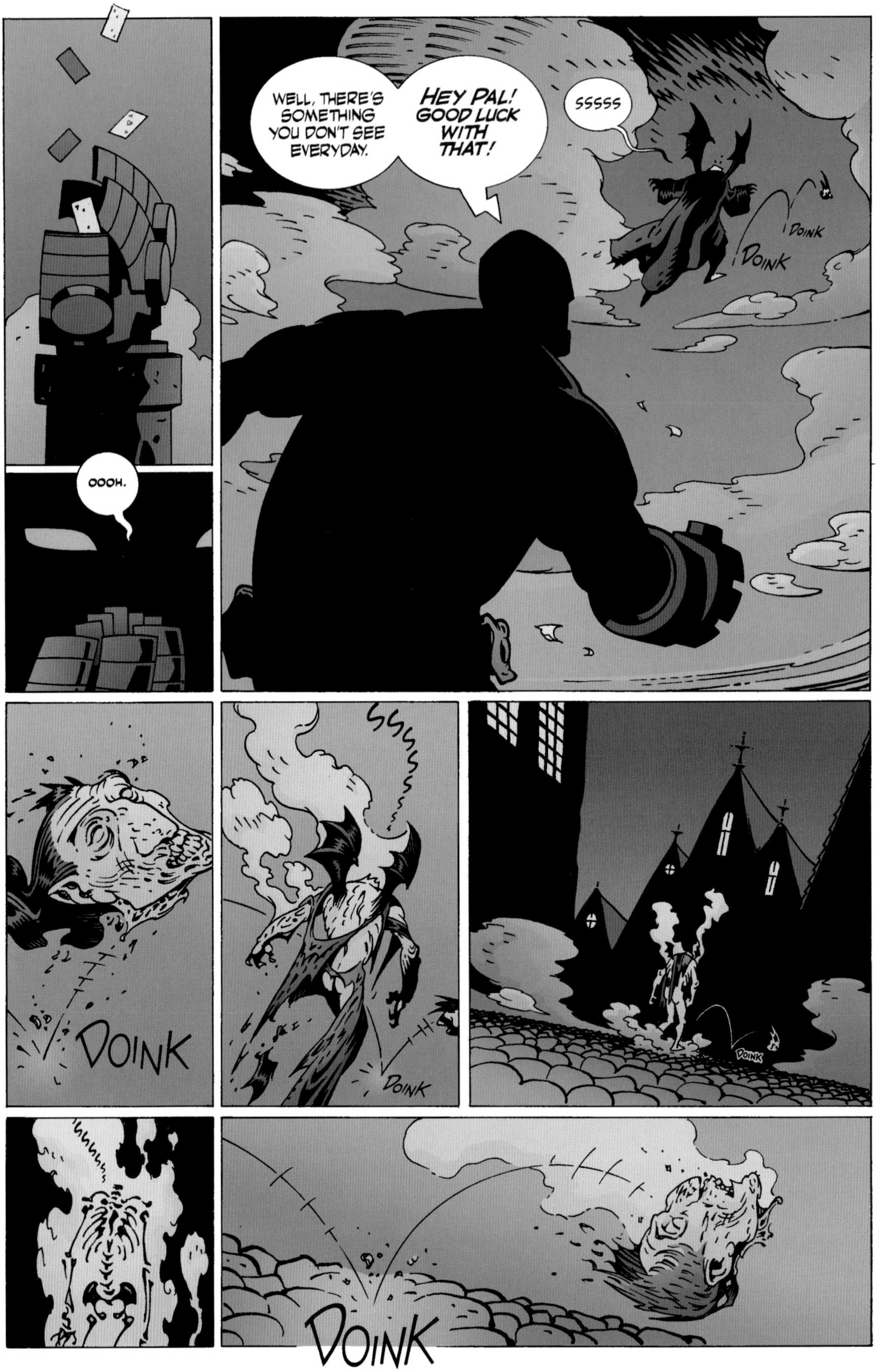
OOOH.
WELL, THERE'S SOMETHING YOU DON'T SEE EVERYDAY.
HEY PAL! GOOD LUCK WITH THAT!
SSSSS
DOINK
DOINK
DOINK
SSSSS
DOINK
DOINK
DOINK

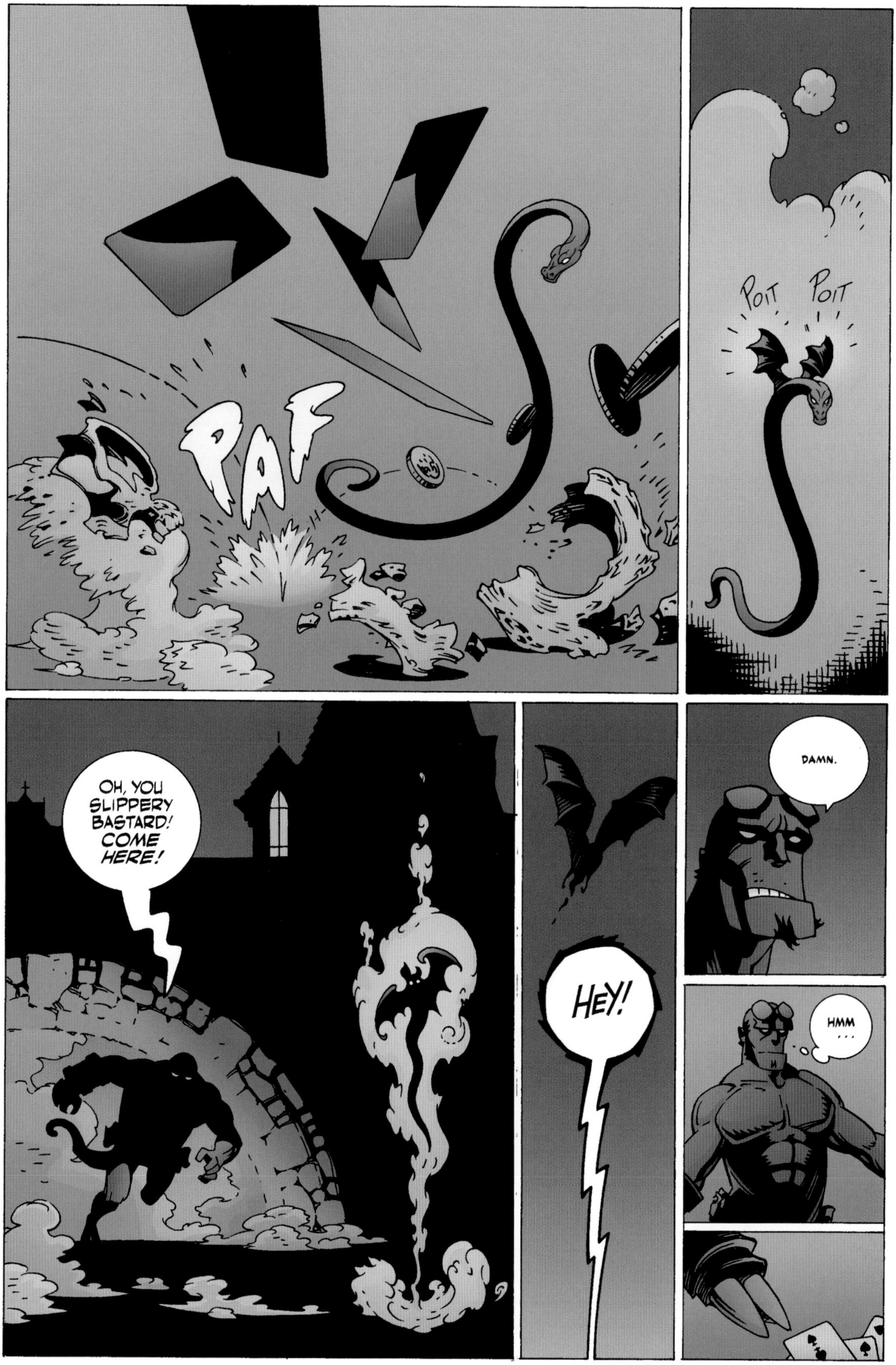
PAF
POIT POIT
OH, YOU SLIPPERY BASTARD! COME HERE!
HEY!
DAMN.
HMM . . .

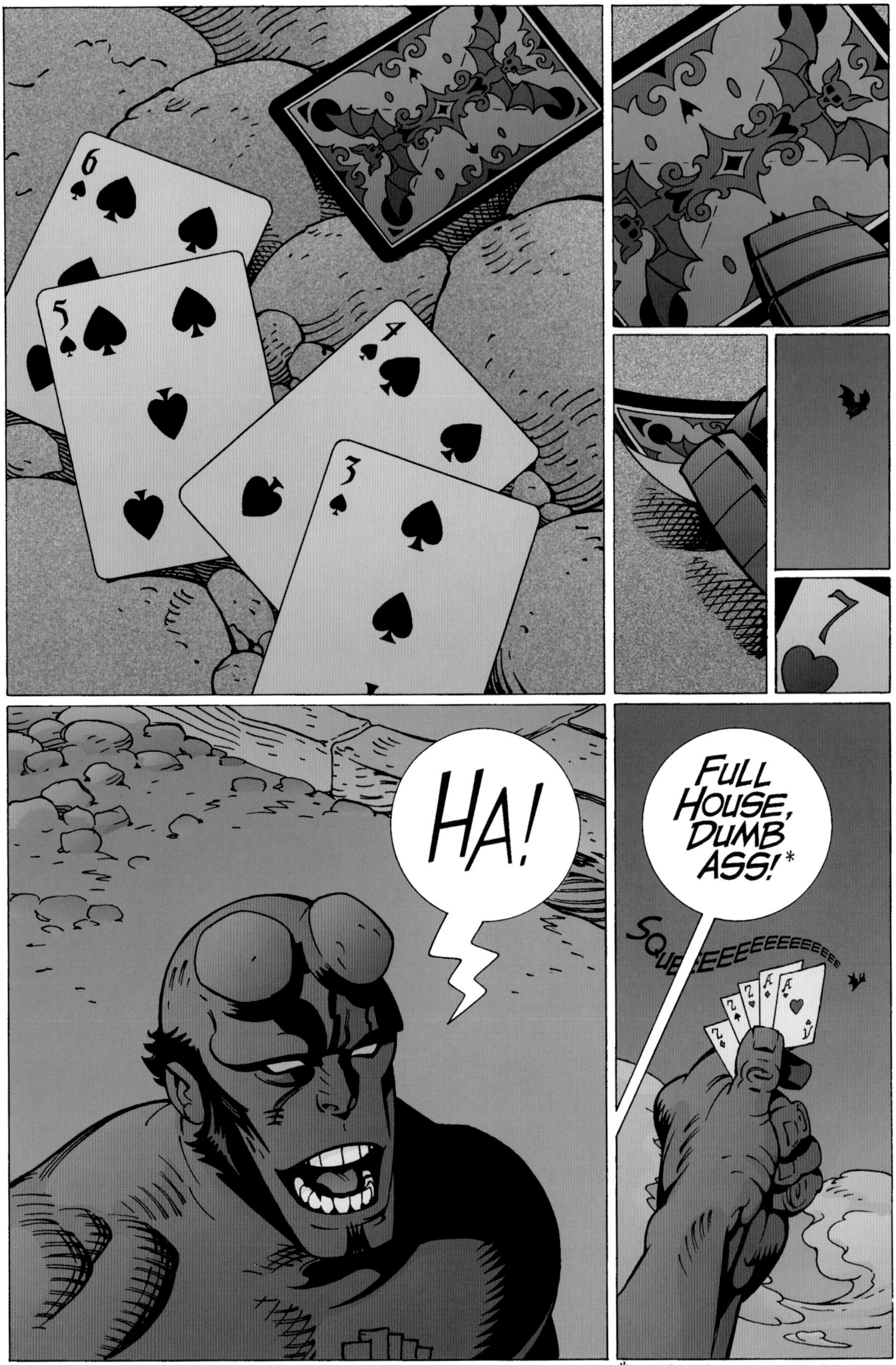
HA!
FULL HOUSE, DUMB ASS!*
SQUEEEEEEEEEEEEEE

* IN POKER, A FULL-HOUSE BEATS A STRAIGHT.

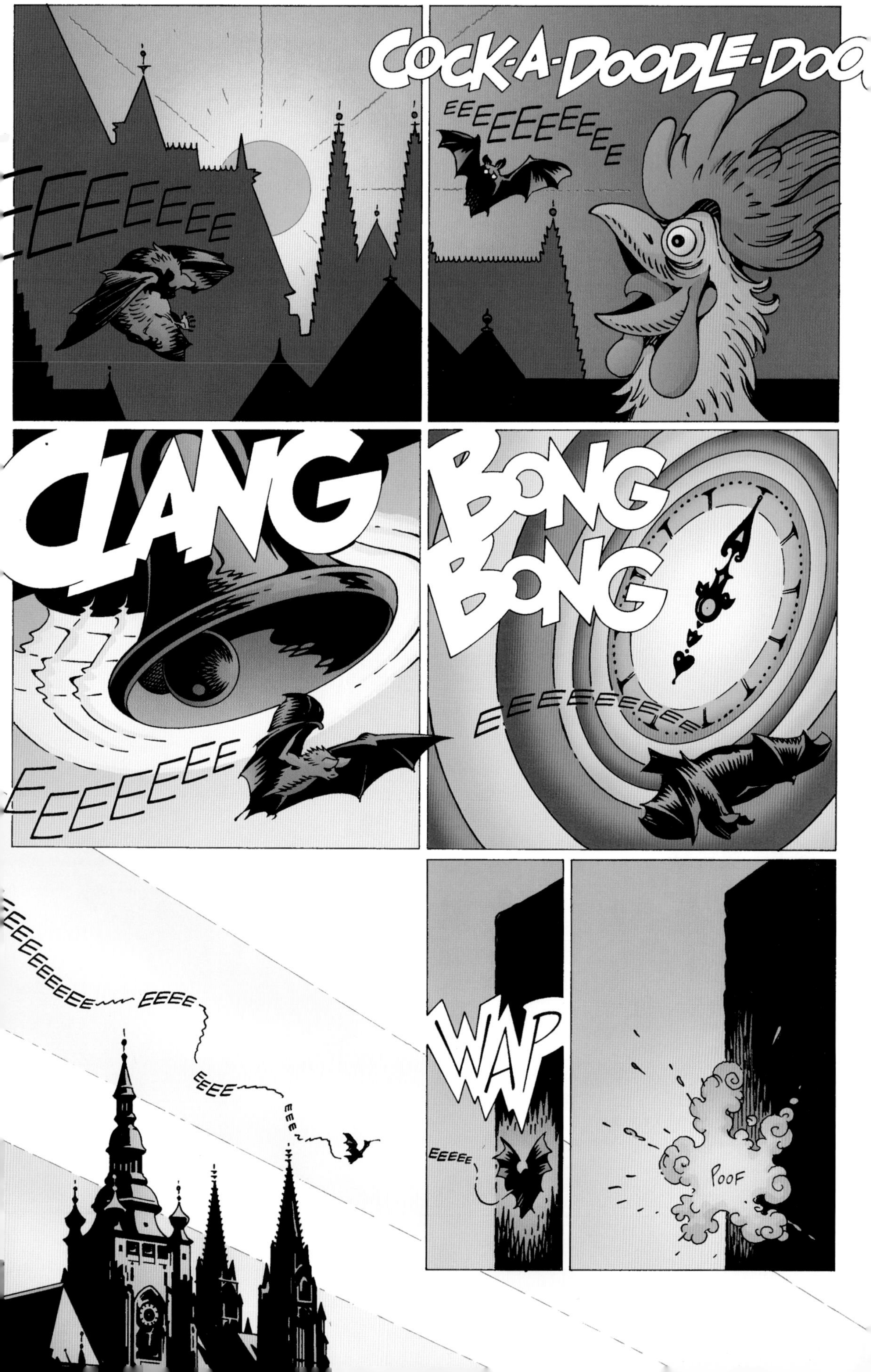

EEEEEEEEE
COCK-A-DOODLE-DOO
EEEEEEEEEEE
CLANG
EEEEEEEEE
BONG
BONG
EEEEEEEEEEE
EEEEEEEEE EEEE EEEE EEE
WAP
EEEEE
POOF

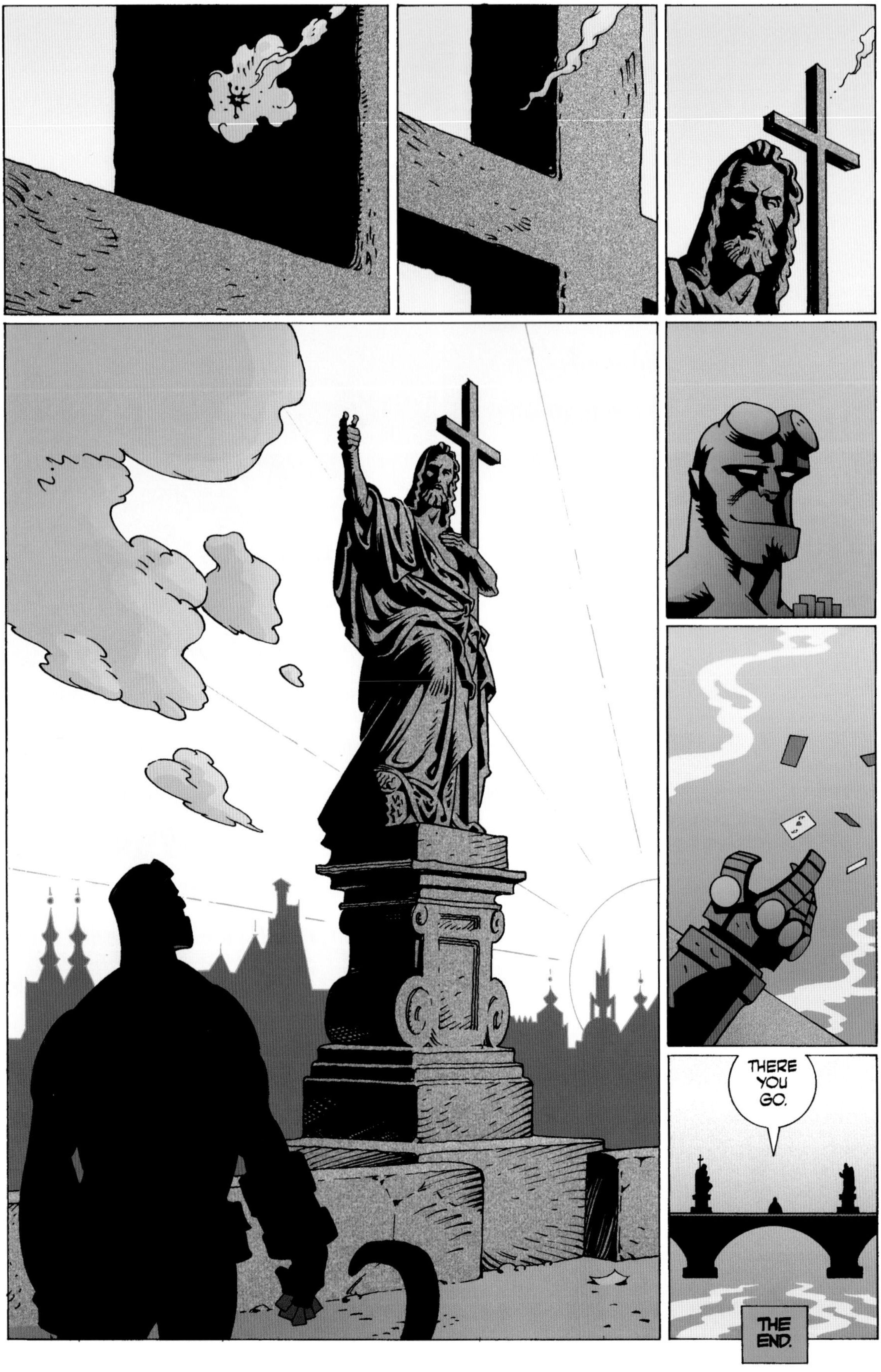
THERE YOU GO.
THE END.

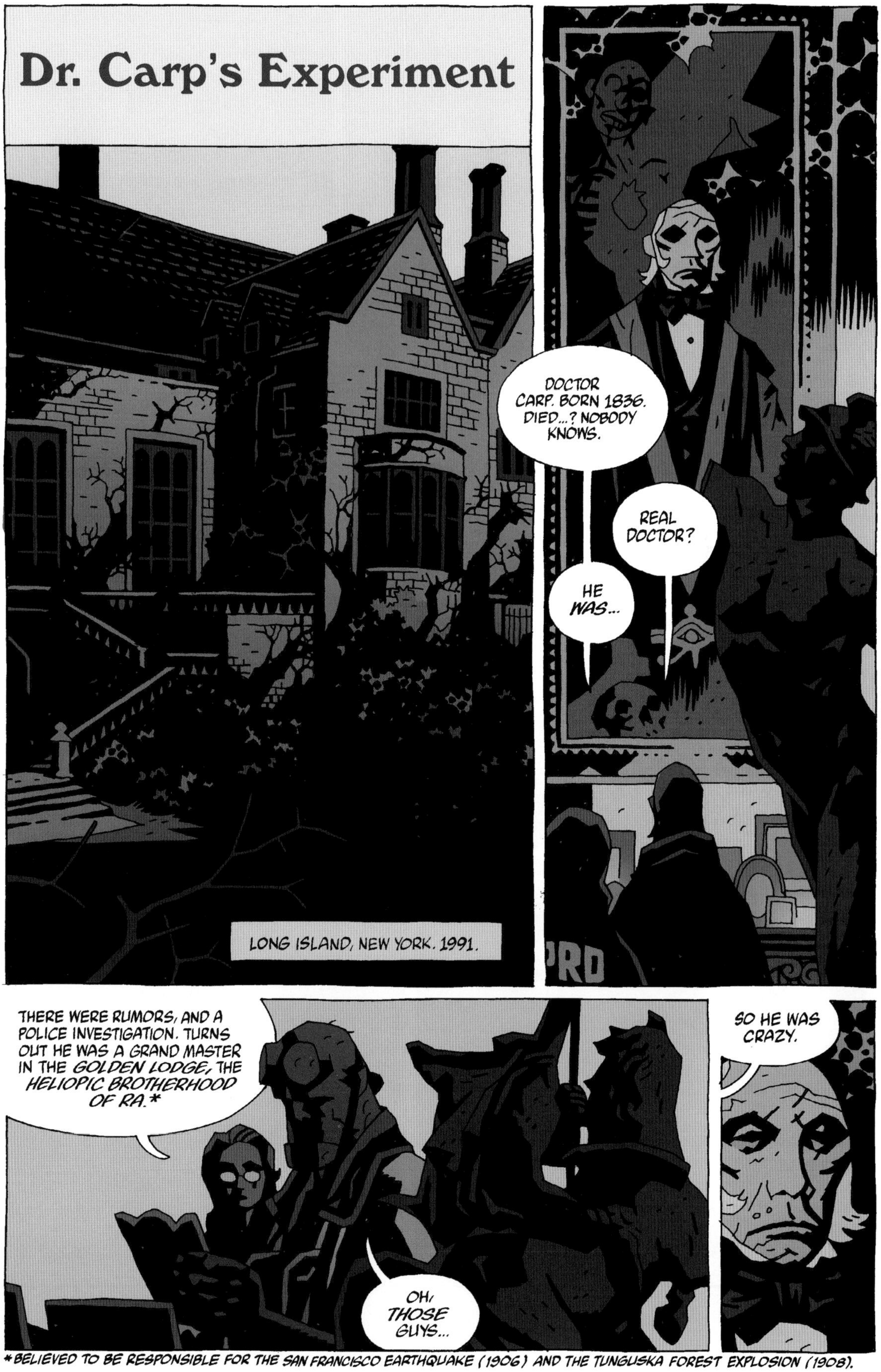
Dr. Carp's Experiment
LONG ISLAND, NEW YORK. 1991.
DOCTOR CARP. BORN 1836. DIED...? NOBODY KNOWS.
REAL DOCTOR?
HE WAS...
THERE WERE RUMORS, AND A POLICE INVESTIGATION. TURNS OUT HE WAS A GRAND MASTER IN THE GOLDEN LODGE, THE HELIOPIC BROTHERHOOD OF RA.*
OH, THOSE GUYS...
SO HE WAS CRAZY.

*BELIEVED TO BE RESPONSIBLE FOR THE SAN FRANCISCO EARTHQUAKE (1906) AND THE TUNGUSKA FOREST EXPLOSION (1908).

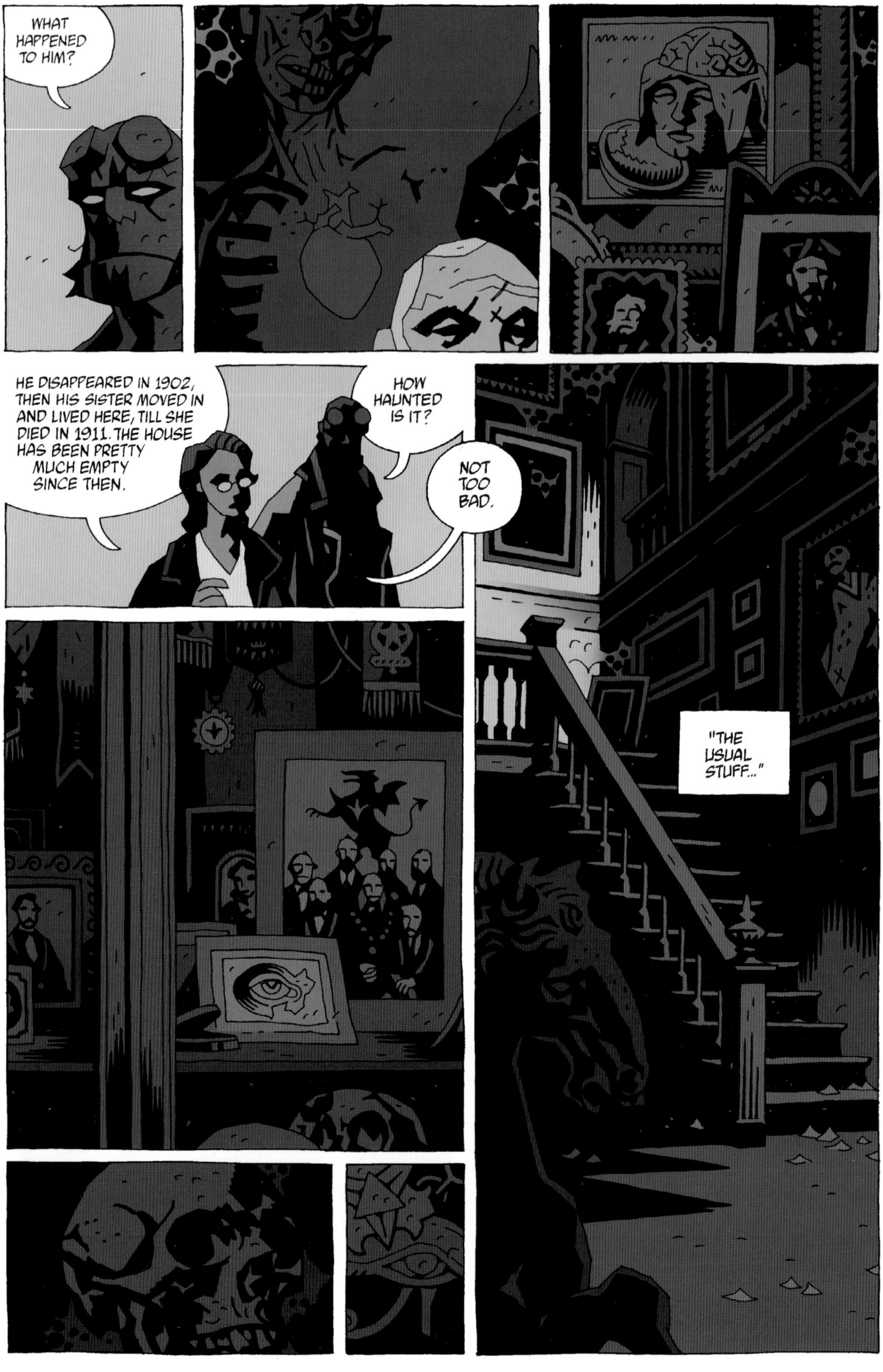
WHAT HAPPENED TO HIM?
HE DISAPPEARED IN 1902, THEN HIS SISTER MOVED IN AND LIVED HERE, TILL SHE DIED IN 1911. THE HOUSE HAS BEEN PRETTY MUCH EMPTY SINCE THEN.
HOW HAUNTED IS IT?
NOT TOO BAD.
"THE USUAL STUFF..."

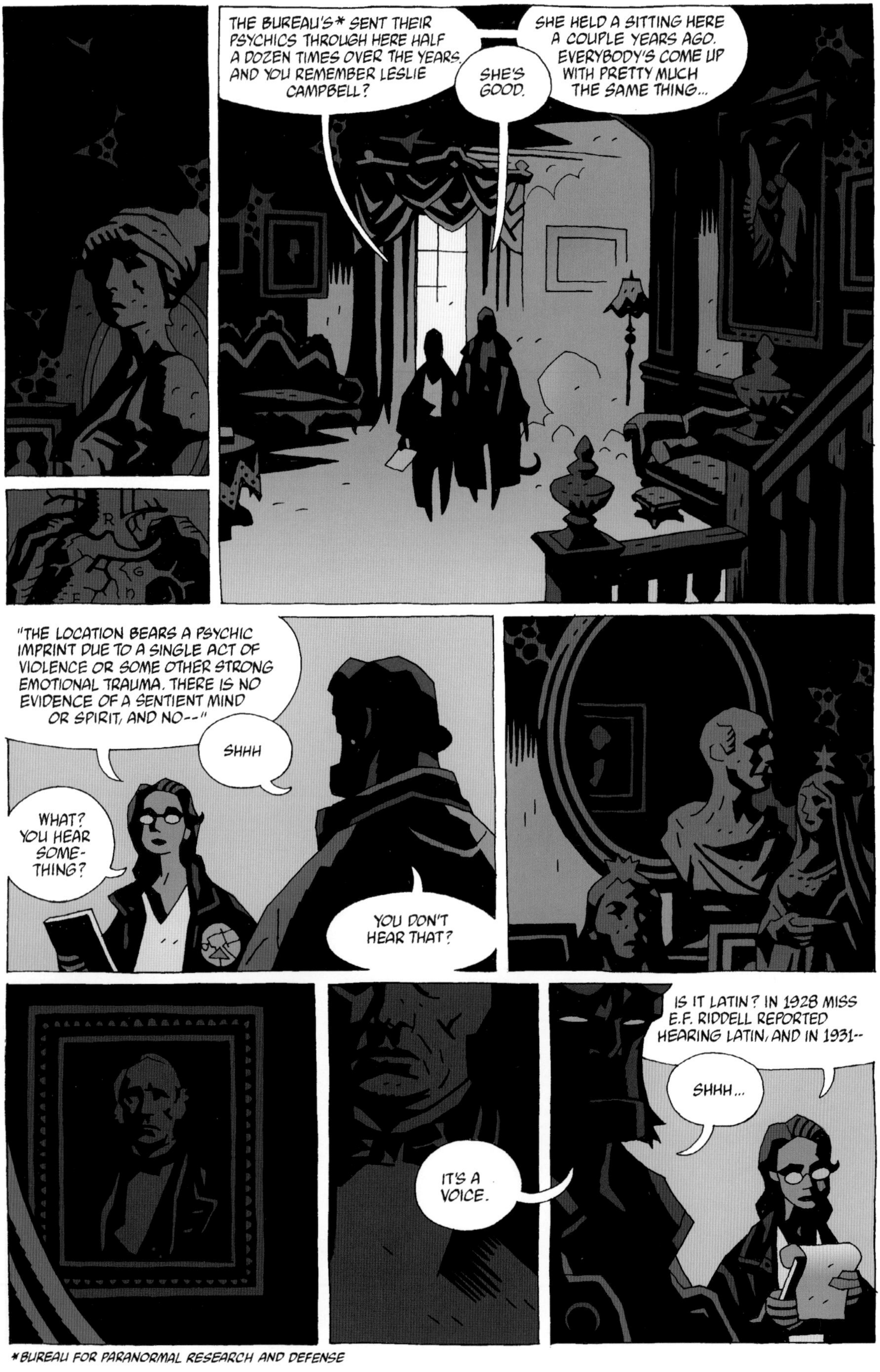
THE BUREAU'S* SENT THEIR PSYCHICS THROUGH HERE HALF A DOZEN TIMES OVER THE YEARS. AND YOU REMEMBER LESLIE CAMPBELL?
SHE'S GOOD.
SHE HELD A SITTING HERE A COUPLE YEARS AGO. EVERYBODY'S COME UP WITH PRETTY MUCH THE SAME THING...
"THE LOCATION BEARS A PSYCHIC IMPRINT DUE TO A SINGLE ACT OF VIOLENCE OR SOME OTHER STRONG EMOTIONAL TRAUMA. THERE IS NO EVIDENCE OF A SENTIENT MIND OR SPIRIT, AND NO--"
SHHH
WHAT? YOU HEAR SOME-THING?
YOU DON'T HEAR THAT?
IS IT LATIN? IN 1928 MISS E.F. RIDDELL REPORTED HEARING LATIN, AND IN 1931--
SHHH...
IT'S A VOICE.

*BUREAU FOR PARANORMAL RESEARCH AND DEFENSE

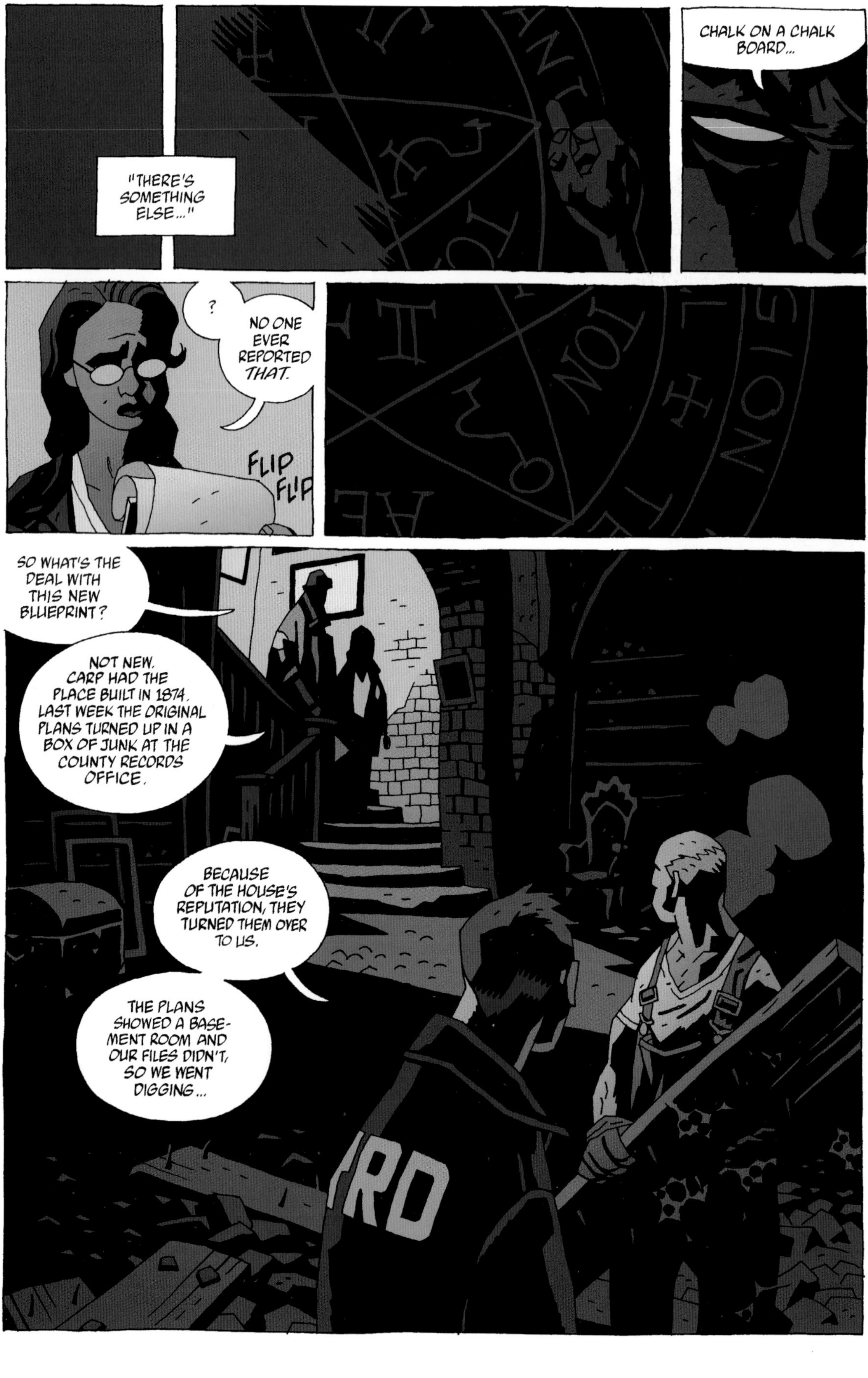

"THERE'S SOMETHING ELSE..."
CHALK ON A CHALK BOARD...
?
NO ONE EVER REPORTED THAT.
FLIP FLIP
SO WHAT'S THE DEAL WITH THIS NEW BLUEPRINT?
NOT NEW. CARP HAD THE PLACE BUILT IN 1874. LAST WEEK THE ORIGINAL PLANS TURNED UP IN A BOX OF JUNK AT THE COUNTY RECORDS OFFICE.
BECAUSE OF THE HOUSE'S REPUTATION, THEY TURNED THEM OVER TO US.
THE PLANS SHOWED A BASE-MENT ROOM AND OUR FILES DIDN'T, SO WE WENT DIGGING...

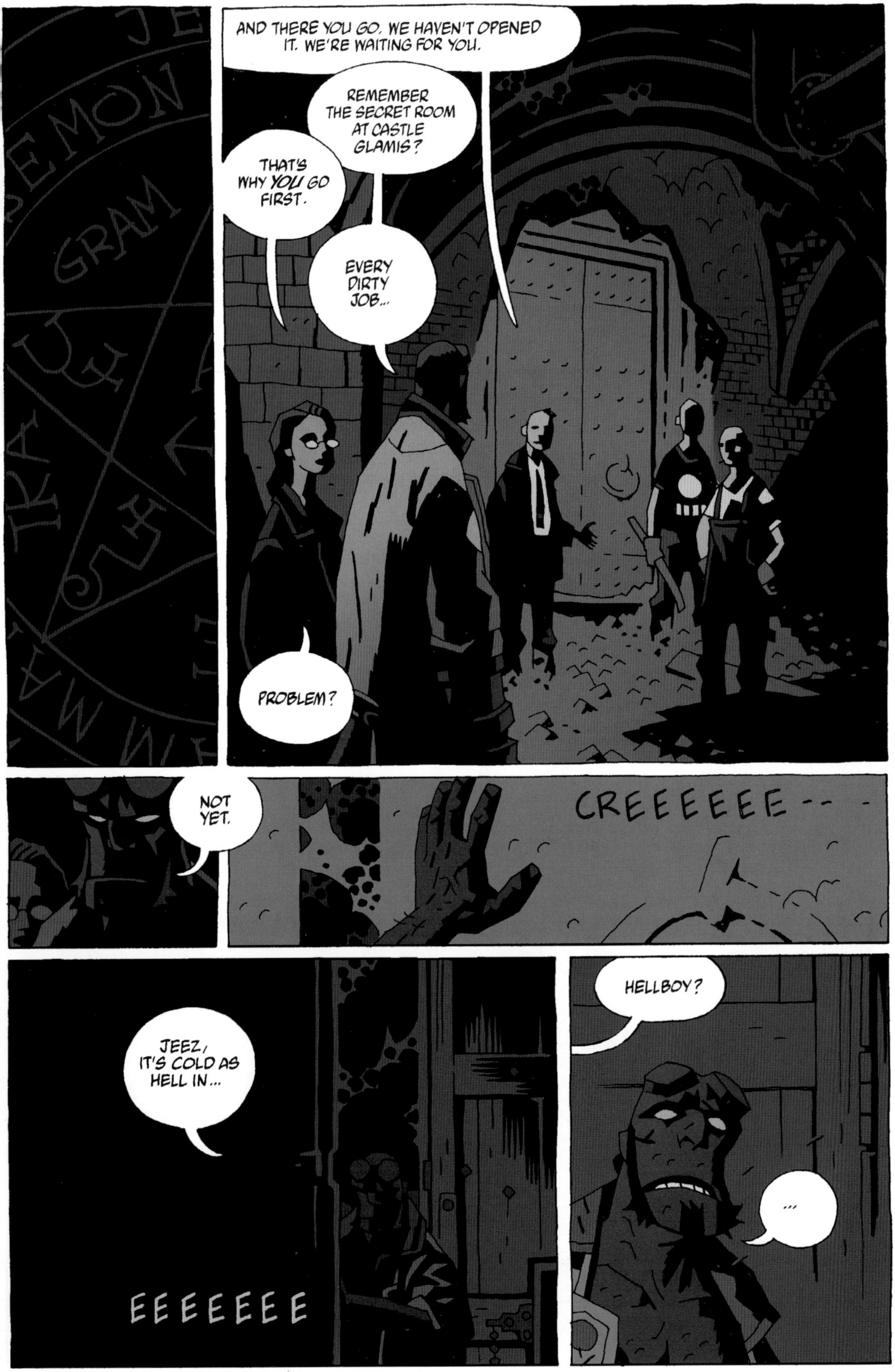

AND THERE YOU GO. WE HAVEN'T OPENED IT. WE'RE WAITING FOR YOU.
REMEMBER THE SECRET ROOM AT CASTLE GLAMIS?
THAT'S WHY *YOU* GO FIRST.
EVERY DIRTY JOB...
PROBLEM?
NOT YET.
CREEEEEEE
JEEZ, IT'S COLD AS HELL IN...
EEEEEEE
HELLBOY?
...

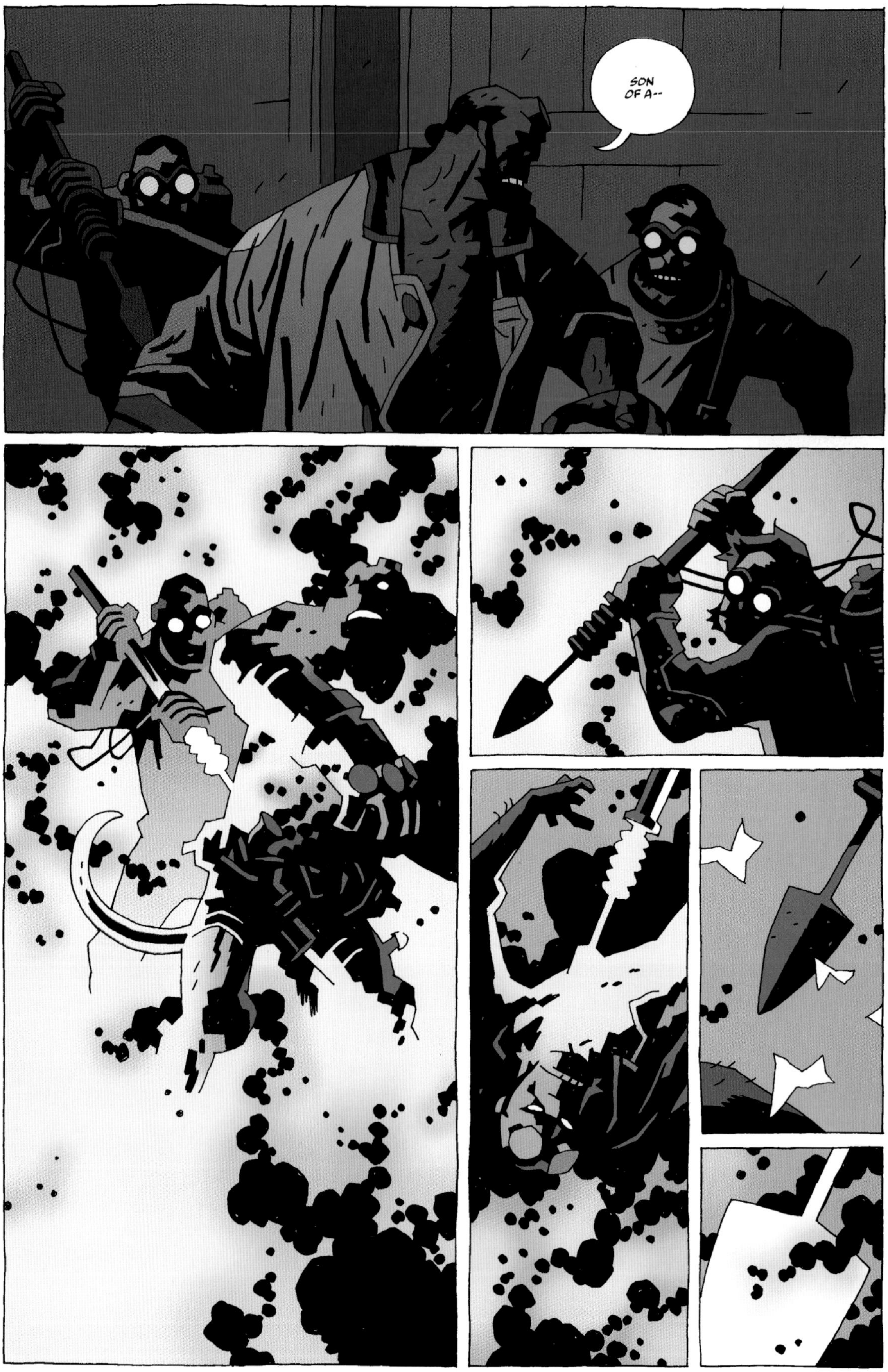
SON OF A--

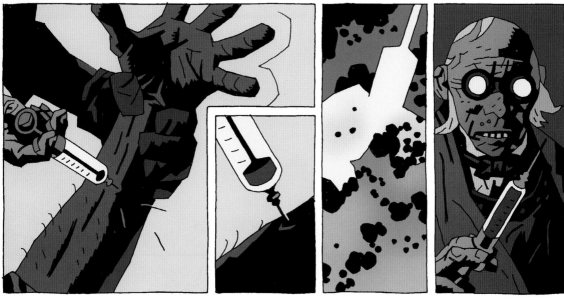

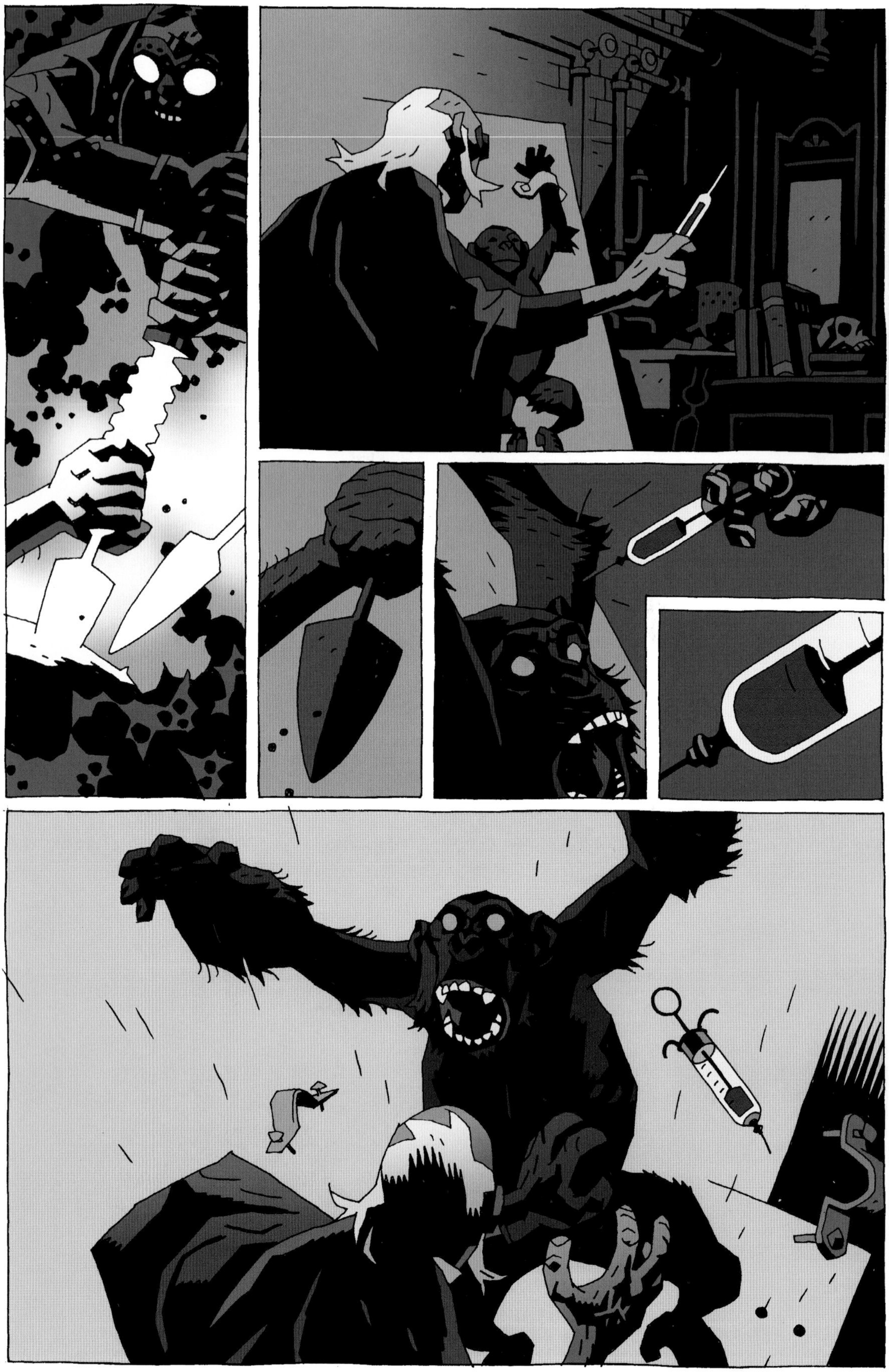

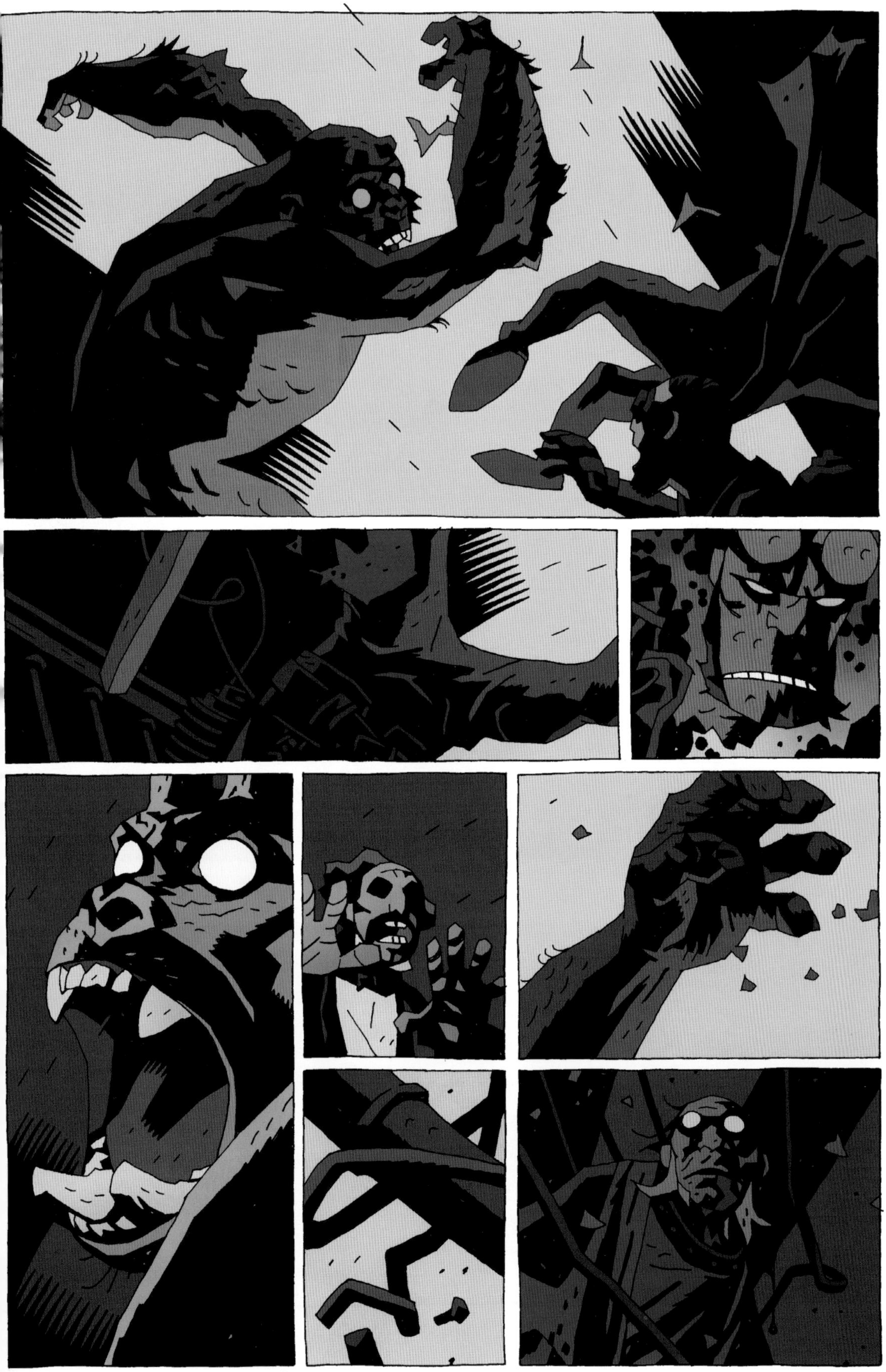

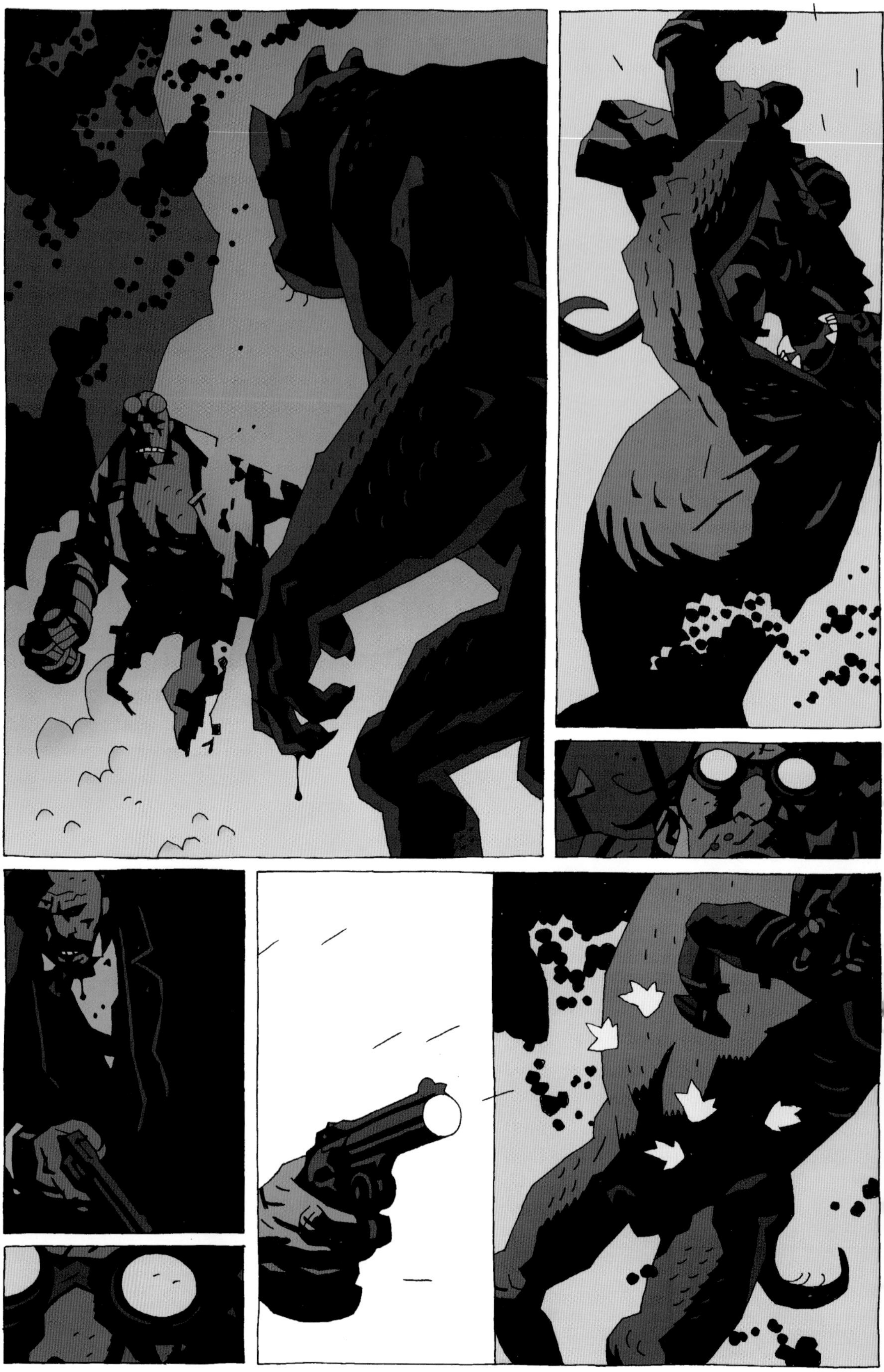

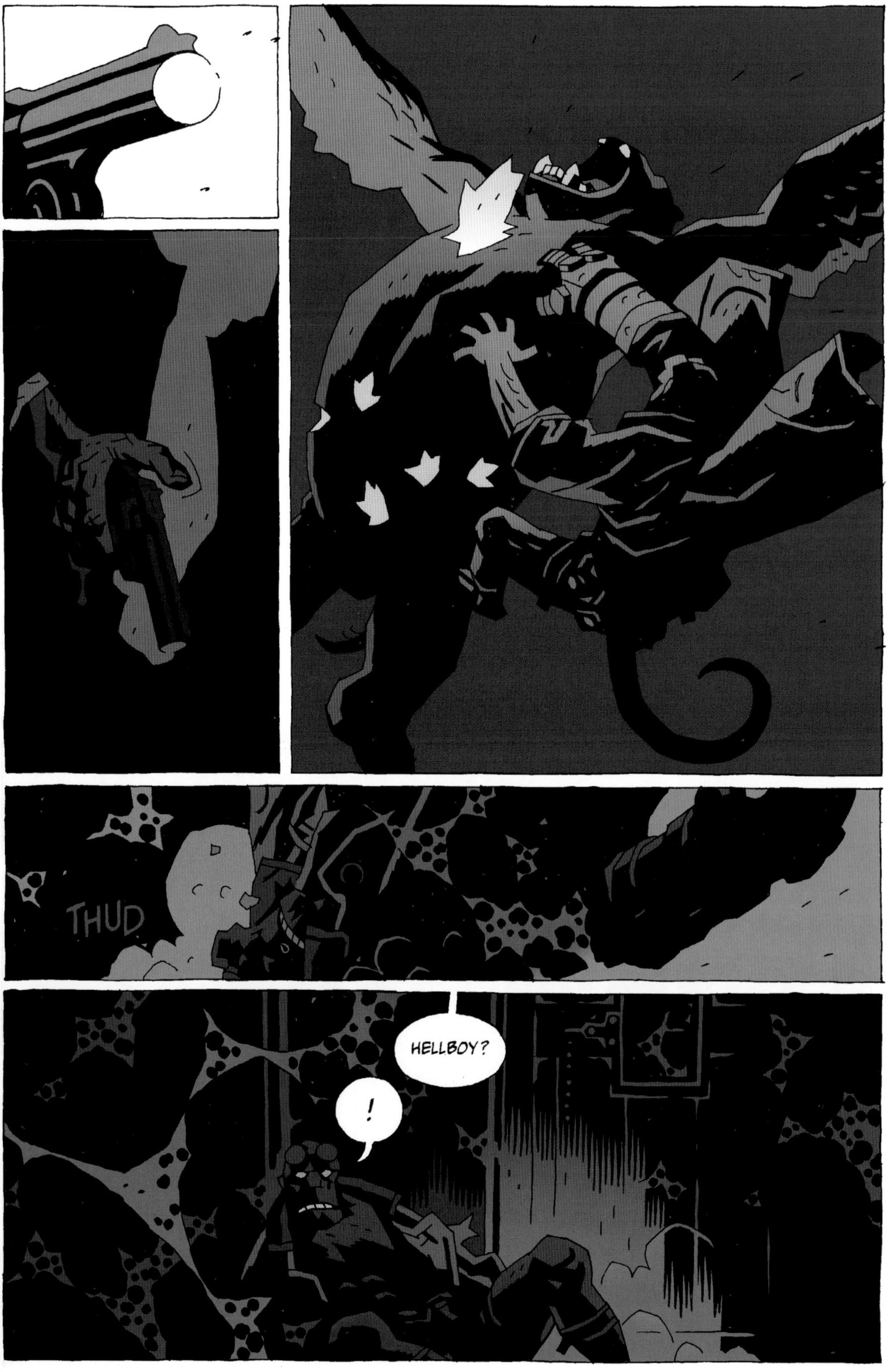
THUD
HELLBOY?
!

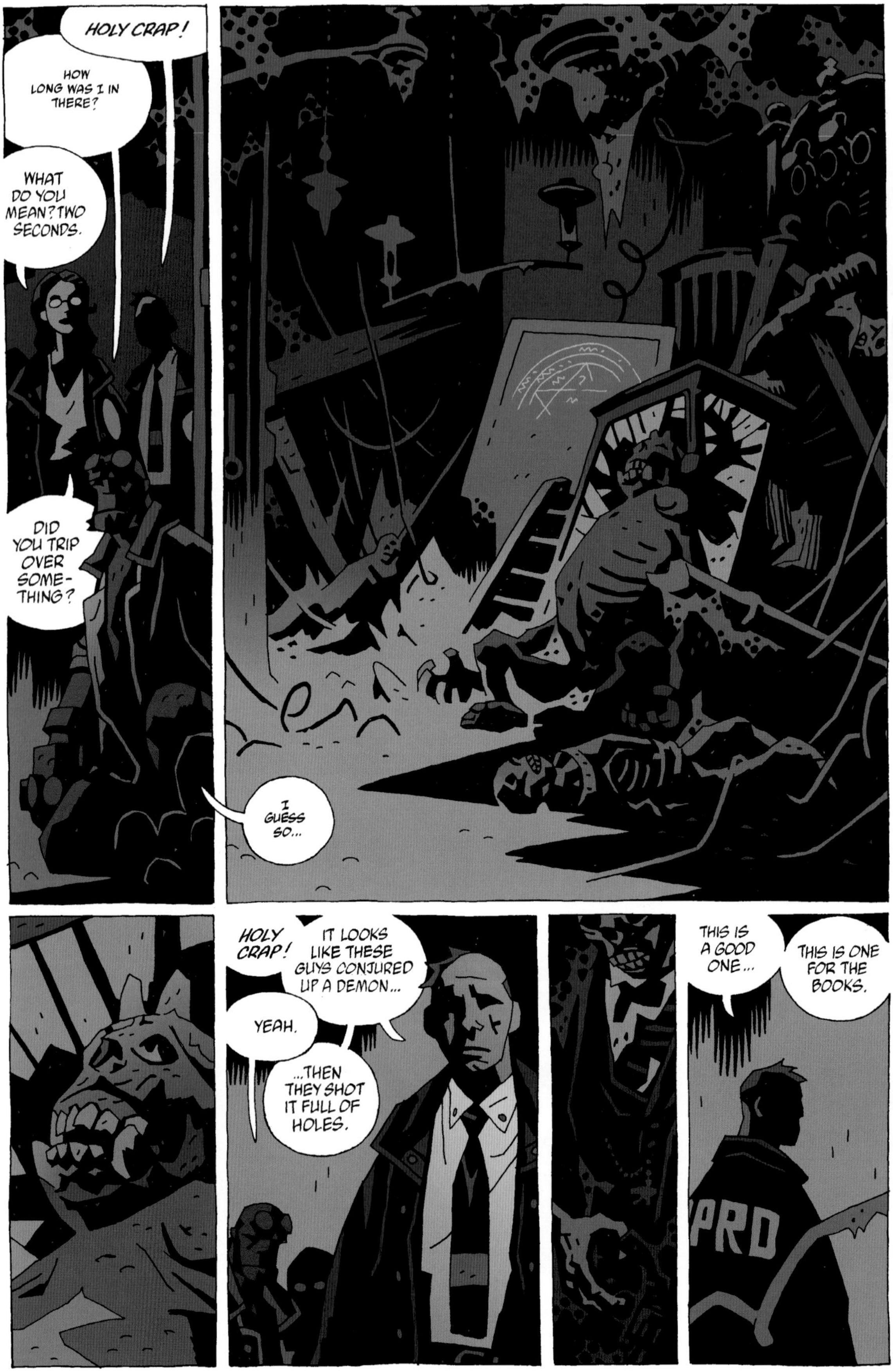
HOLY CRAP!
HOW LONG WAS I IN THERE?
WHAT DO YOU MEAN? TWO SECONDS.
DID YOU TRIP OVER SOME-THING?
I GUESS SO...
HOLY CRAP!
IT LOOKS LIKE THESE GUYS CONJURED UP A DEMON...
YEAH.
...THEN THEY SHOT IT FULL OF HOLES.
THIS IS A GOOD ONE...
THIS IS ONE FOR THE BOOKS.
PRD

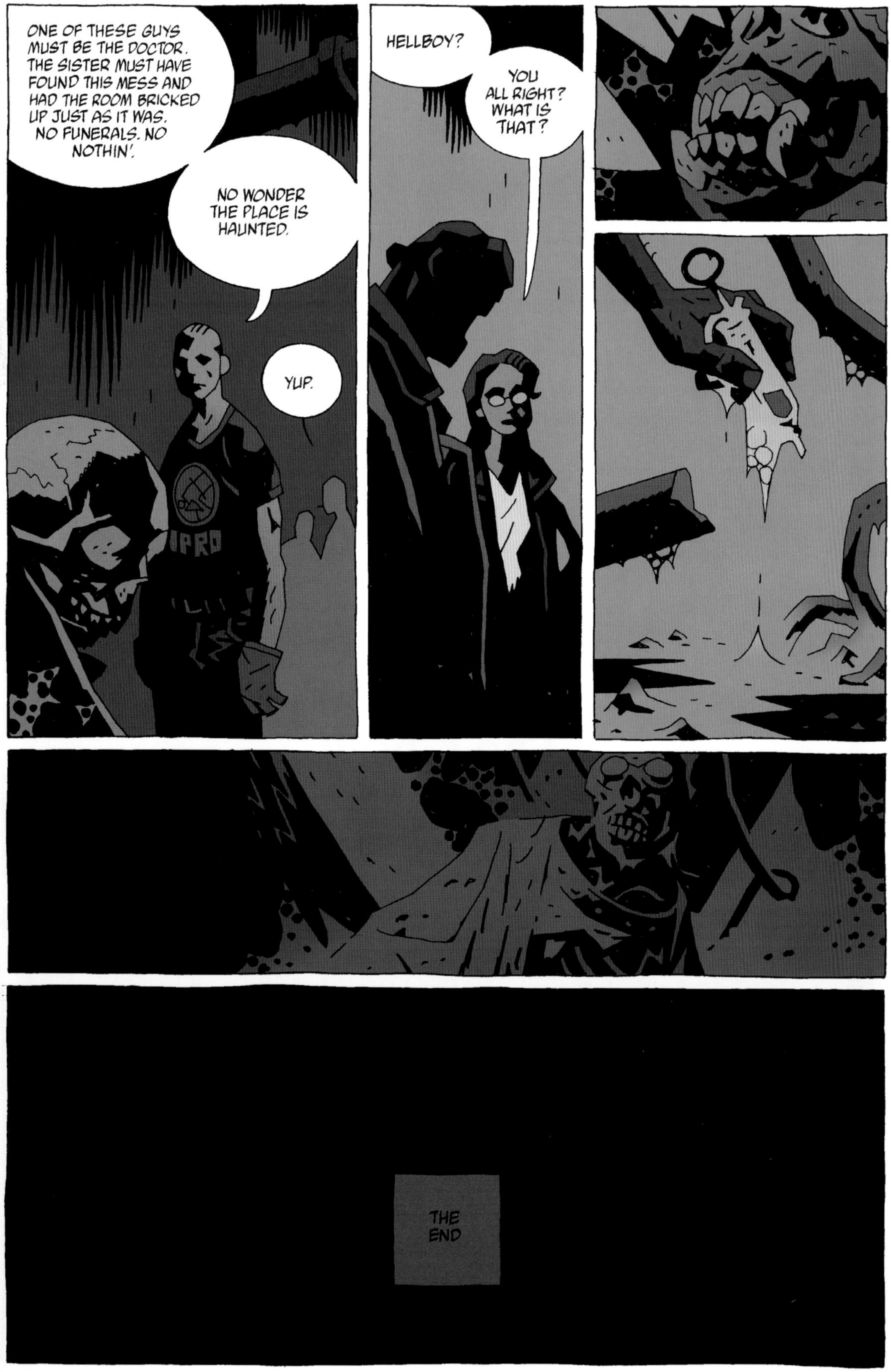

ONE OF THESE GUYS MUST BE THE DOCTOR. THE SISTER MUST HAVE FOUND THIS MESS AND HAD THE ROOM BRICKED UP JUST AS IT WAS. NO FUNERALS. NO NOTHIN'.
NO WONDER THE PLACE IS HAUNTED.
YUP.
HELLBOY?
YOU ALL RIGHT? WHAT IS THAT?
THE END

Dr. Carp's Experiment

THE BASIC IDEA OF THIS ONE—the time travel, the scientist, the monkey, and the blood—goes back a long time. It's probably one of the first Hellboy stories I thought of. I plotted and replotted it a bunch of different times over the years, setting it in a bunch of different locations. It was almost part of *Conqueror Worm* (it would have been in chapter three, instead of the cabinet full of heads), but for whatever reason I didn't get around to putting it on paper until 2003. Why this version instead of any of the others? I don't know. I think one day I realized I'd never done a haunted-house story and thought that doing something very subtle (old pictures and whispery voices) with something extremely unsubtle at the center of it (electric harpoons and a demon-monkey) would be sort of funny.

"Dr. Carp's Experiment" was published in *The Dark Horse Book of Hauntings*.

✠

The Ghoul

THIS IS ALMOST CERTAINLY the oddest Hellboy story I've done and, I'm afraid, it's not on too many readers' lists of favorites. That's okay. It was an experiment. It was inspired by that "how a king may go a progress through the guts of a beggar" bit from *Hamlet* (as beautiful a summing up of decomposition as I've ever read) and my love of old cemeteries. I am indebted to two tombs in particular (and what I saw there)—one in Oakland, California, and one in Prague. This story also, I think, owes a little to C. M. Eddy's short story, "The Loved Dead" (written in collaboration with H. P. Lovecraft), which made a pretty big impression on me as a kid.

I always knew the ghoul would speak in bits of poetry, but I drew the story first, *then* went looking for the specific poems to suit the mood of the specific panels. It was tough (thank you, internet, and my long-suffering wife) but that's what made it fun to do. I really like this one and, be warned, you readers, I'd love to do something like this again.

"The Ghoul" was published in 2005, in *The Dark Horse Book of the Dead*.

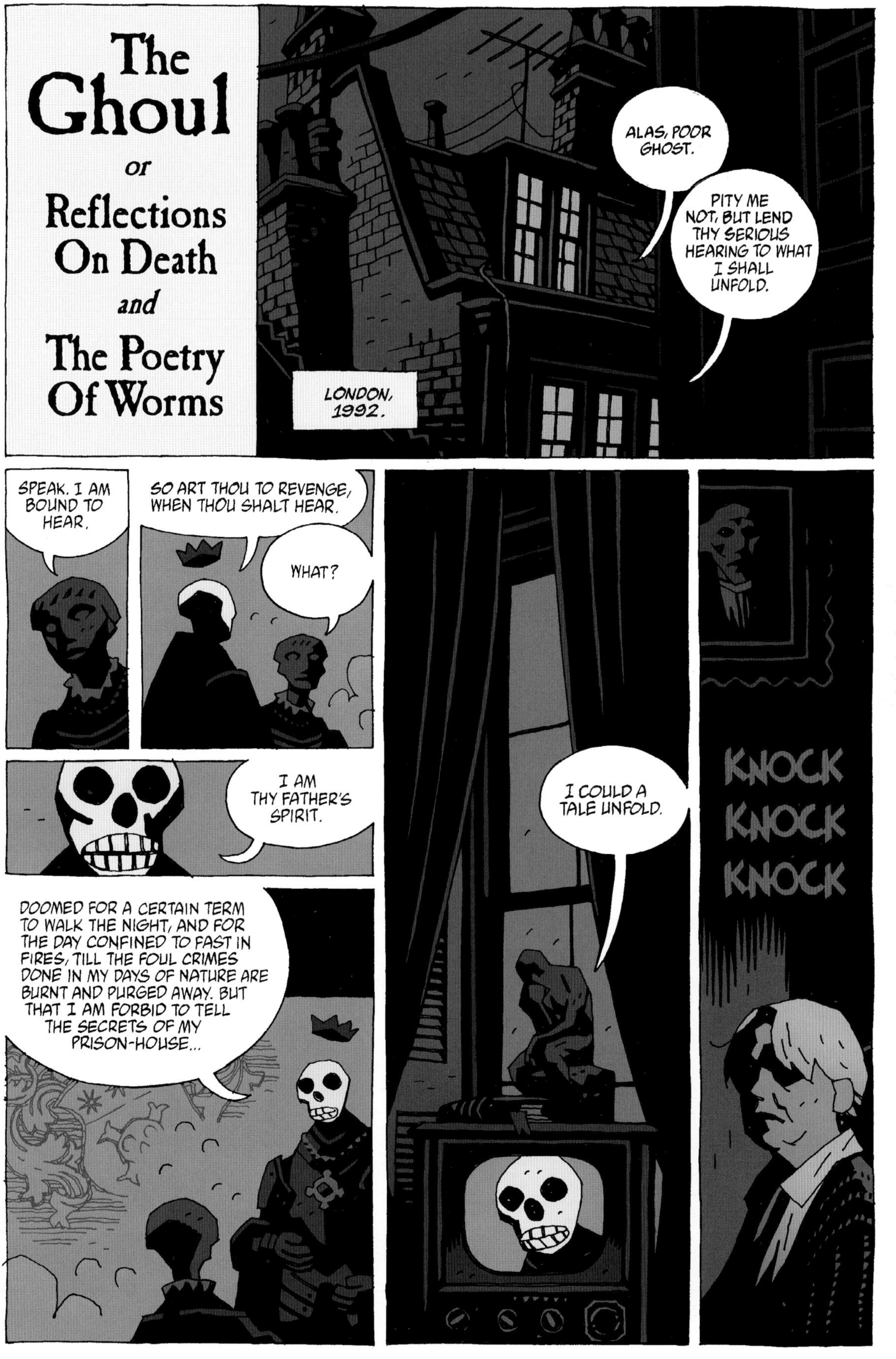
The Ghoul
or
Reflections On Death
and
The Poetry Of Worms
LONDON, 1992.
ALAS, POOR GHOST.
PITY ME NOT, BUT LEND THY SERIOUS HEARING TO WHAT I SHALL UNFOLD.
SPEAK. I AM BOUND TO HEAR.
SO ART THOU TO REVENGE, WHEN THOU SHALT HEAR.
WHAT?
I AM THY FATHER'S SPIRIT.
DOOMED FOR A CERTAIN TERM TO WALK THE NIGHT, AND FOR THE DAY CONFINED TO FAST IN FIRES, TILL THE FOUL CRIMES DONE IN MY DAYS OF NATURE ARE BURNT AND PURGED AWAY. BUT THAT I AM FORBID TO TELL THE SECRETS OF MY PRISON-HOUSE...
I COULD A TALE UNFOLD.
KNOCK
KNOCK
KNOCK

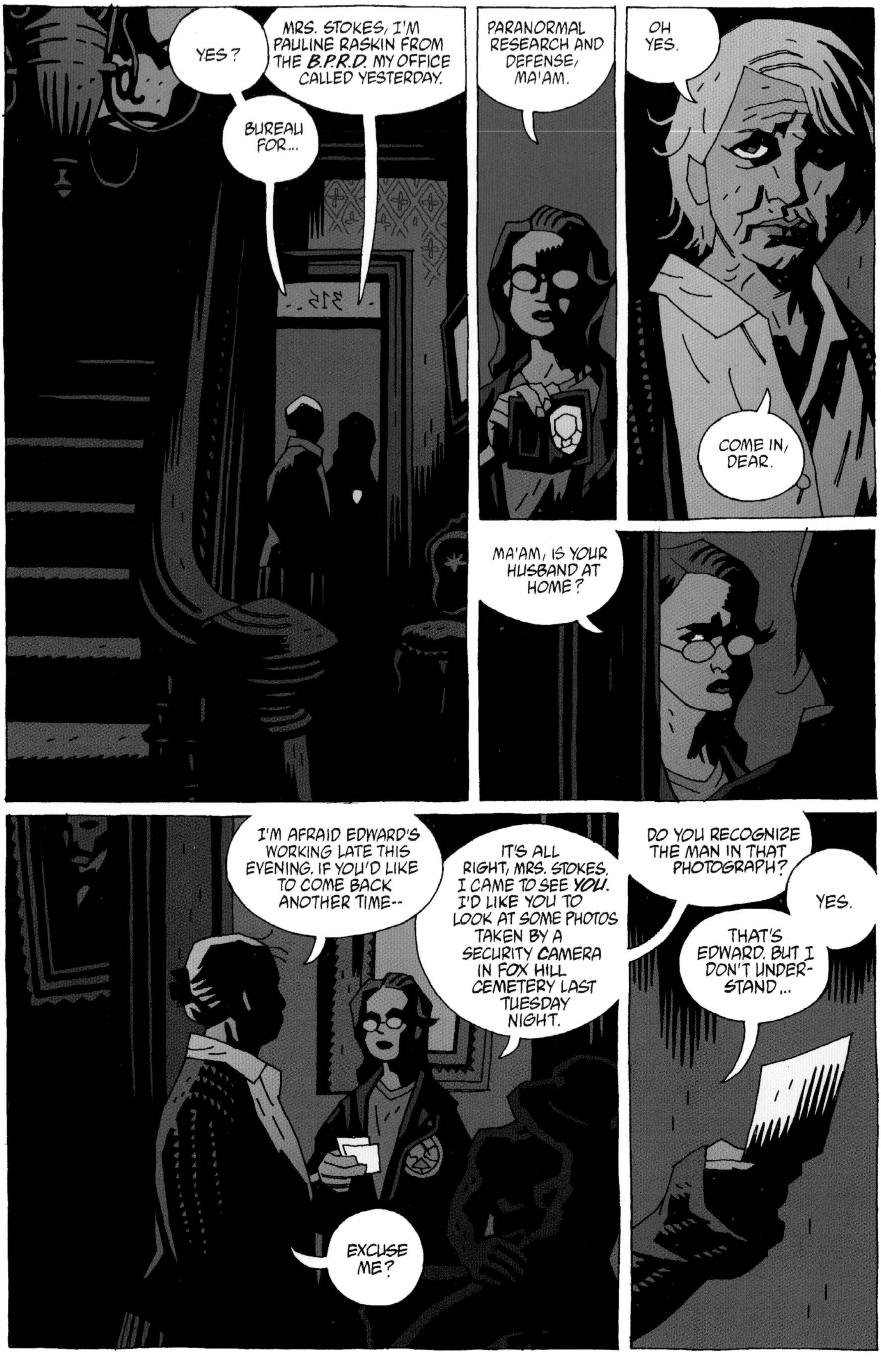
YES?
MRS. STOKES, I'M PAULINE RASKIN FROM THE B.P.R.D. MY OFFICE CALLED YESTERDAY.
BUREAU FOR...
315
PARANORMAL RESEARCH AND DEFENSE, MA'AM.
OH YES.
COME IN, DEAR.
MA'AM, IS YOUR HUSBAND AT HOME?
I'M AFRAID EDWARD'S WORKING LATE THIS EVENING. IF YOU'D LIKE TO COME BACK ANOTHER TIME--
EXCUSE ME?
IT'S ALL RIGHT, MRS. STOKES. I CAME TO SEE YOU. I'D LIKE YOU TO LOOK AT SOME PHOTOS TAKEN BY A SECURITY CAMERA IN FOX HILL CEMETERY LAST TUESDAY NIGHT.
DO YOU RECOGNIZE THE MAN IN THAT PHOTOGRAPH?
YES.
THAT'S EDWARD. BUT I DON'T UNDERSTAND...

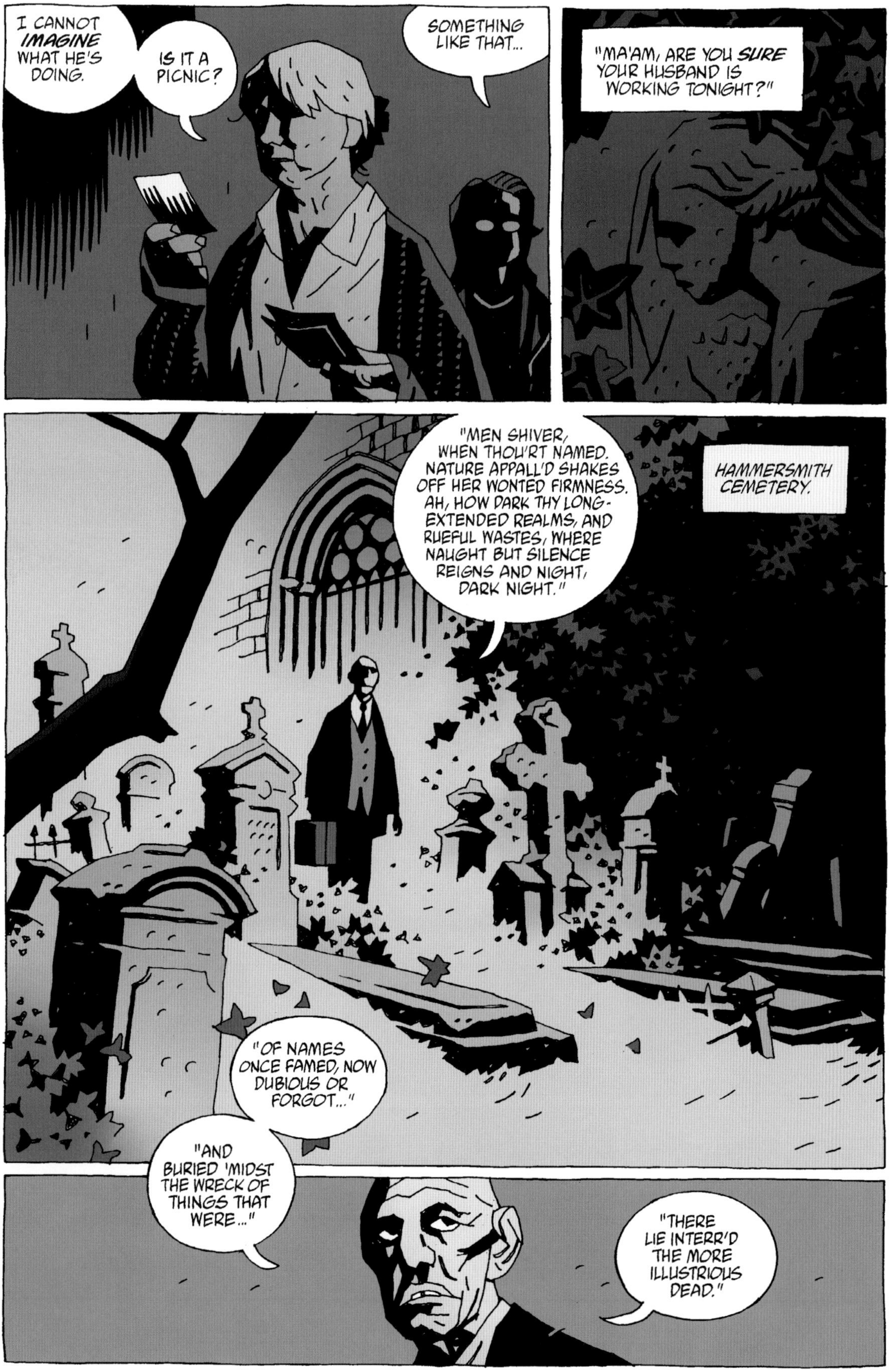
I CANNOT IMAGINE WHAT HE'S DOING.
IS IT A PICNIC?
SOMETHING LIKE THAT...
"MA'AM, ARE YOU SURE YOUR HUSBAND IS WORKING TONIGHT?"
HAMMERSMITH CEMETERY.
"MEN SHIVER, WHEN THOU'RT NAMED. NATURE APPALL'D SHAKES OFF HER WONTED FIRMNESS. AH, HOW DARK THY LONG-EXTENDED REALMS, AND RUEFUL WASTES, WHERE NAUGHT BUT SILENCE REIGNS AND NIGHT, DARK NIGHT."
"OF NAMES ONCE FAMED, NOW DUBIOUS OR FORGOT..."
"AND BURIED 'MIDST THE WRECK OF THINGS THAT WERE..."
"THERE LIE INTERR'D THE MORE ILLUSTRIOUS DEAD."

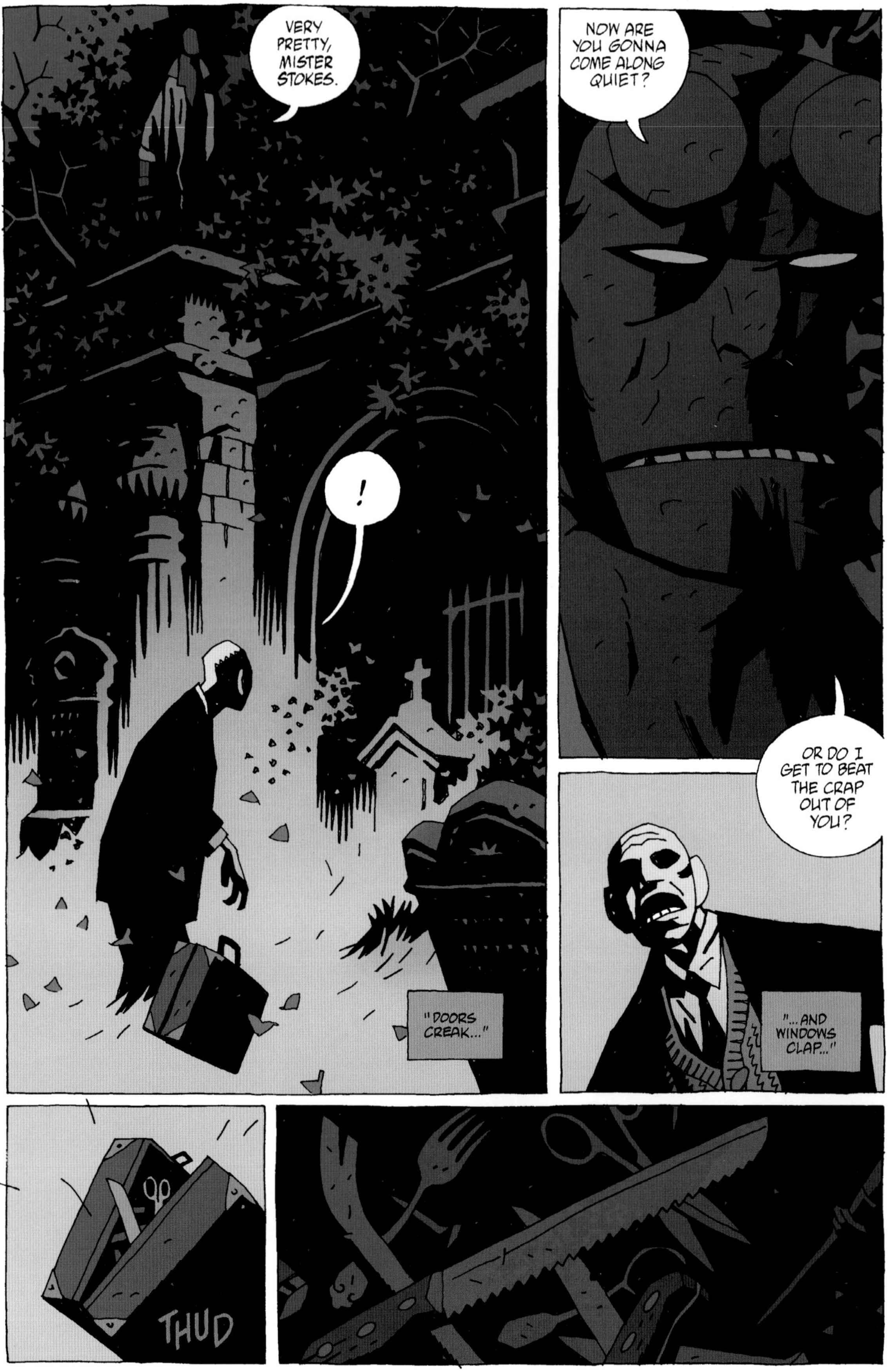
VERY PRETTY, MISTER STOKES.
!
"DOORS CREAK..."
NOW ARE YOU GONNA COME ALONG QUIET?
OR DO I GET TO BEAT THE CRAP OUT OF YOU?
"...AND WINDOWS CLAP..."
THUD

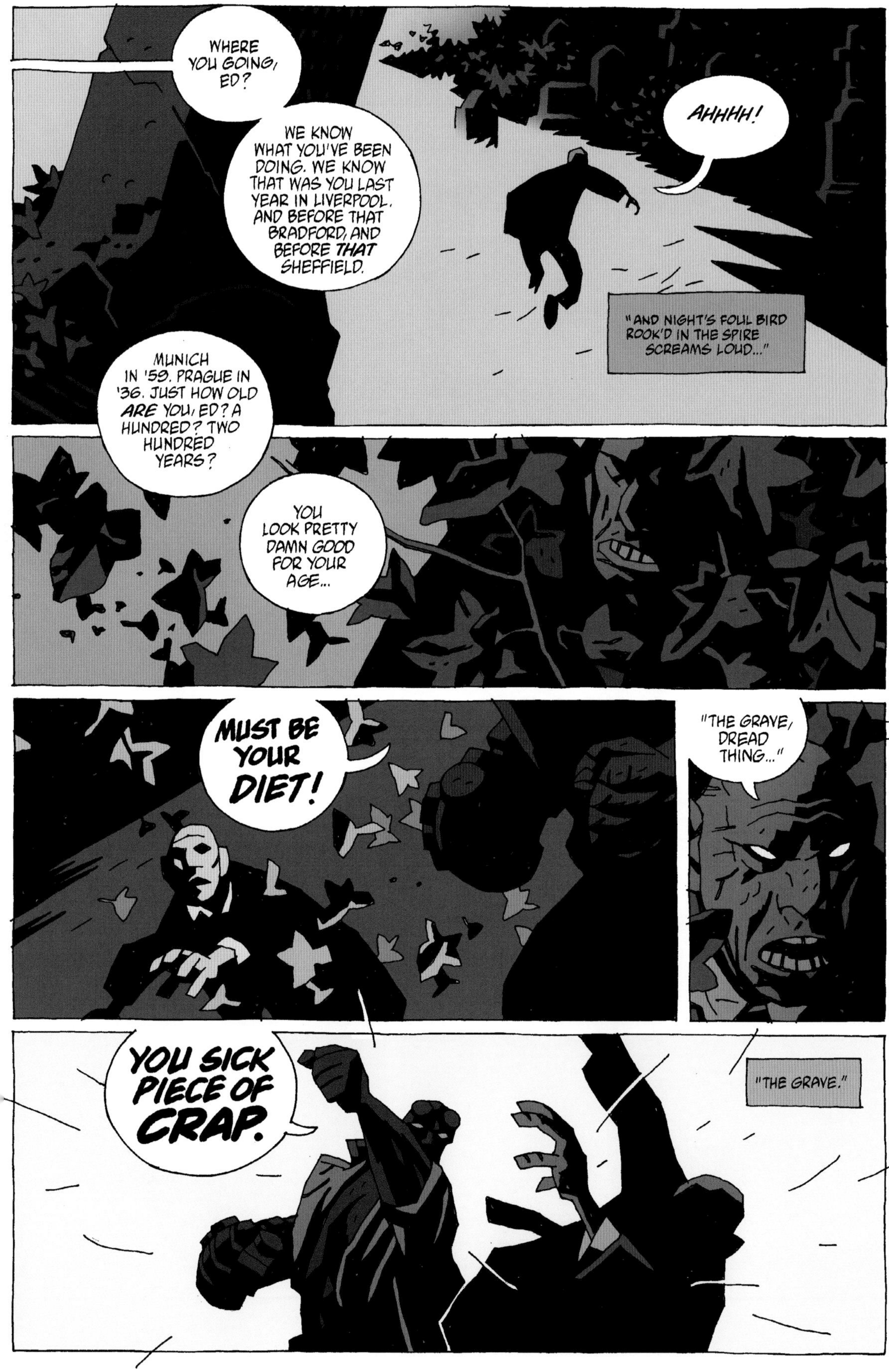
WHERE YOU GOING, ED?
WE KNOW WHAT YOU'VE BEEN DOING. WE KNOW THAT WAS YOU LAST YEAR IN LIVERPOOL, AND BEFORE THAT BRADFORD, AND BEFORE THAT SHEFFIELD.
AHHHH!
"AND NIGHT'S FOUL BIRD ROOK'D IN THE SPIRE SCREAMS LOUD..."
MUNICH IN '59. PRAGUE IN '36. JUST HOW OLD ARE YOU, ED? A HUNDRED? TWO HUNDRED YEARS?
YOU LOOK PRETTY DAMN GOOD FOR YOUR AGE...
MUST BE YOUR DIET!
"THE GRAVE, DREAD THING..."
YOU SICK PIECE OF CRAP.
"THE GRAVE."

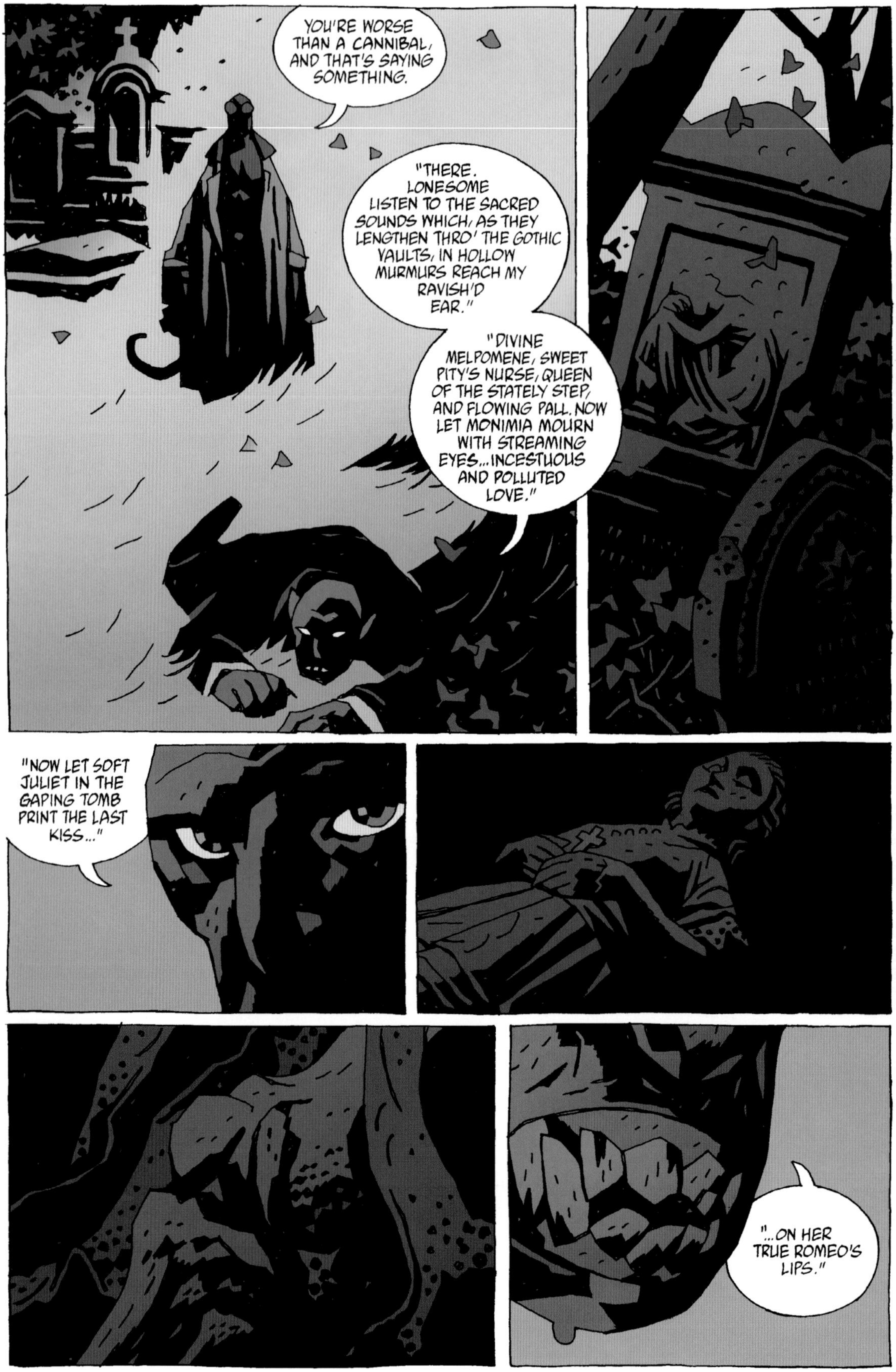
YOU'RE WORSE THAN A CANNIBAL, AND THAT'S SAYING SOMETHING.
"THERE. LONESOME LISTEN TO THE SACRED SOUNDS WHICH, AS THEY LENGTHEN THRO' THE GOTHIC VAULTS, IN HOLLOW MURMURS REACH MY RAVISH'D EAR."
"DIVINE MELPOMENE, SWEET PITY'S NURSE, QUEEN OF THE STATELY STEP, AND FLOWING PALL. NOW LET MONIMIA MOURN WITH STREAMING EYES... INCESTUOUS AND POLLUTED LOVE."
"NOW LET SOFT JULIET IN THE GAPING TOMB PRINT THE LAST KISS..."
"...ON HER TRUE ROMEO'S LIPS."

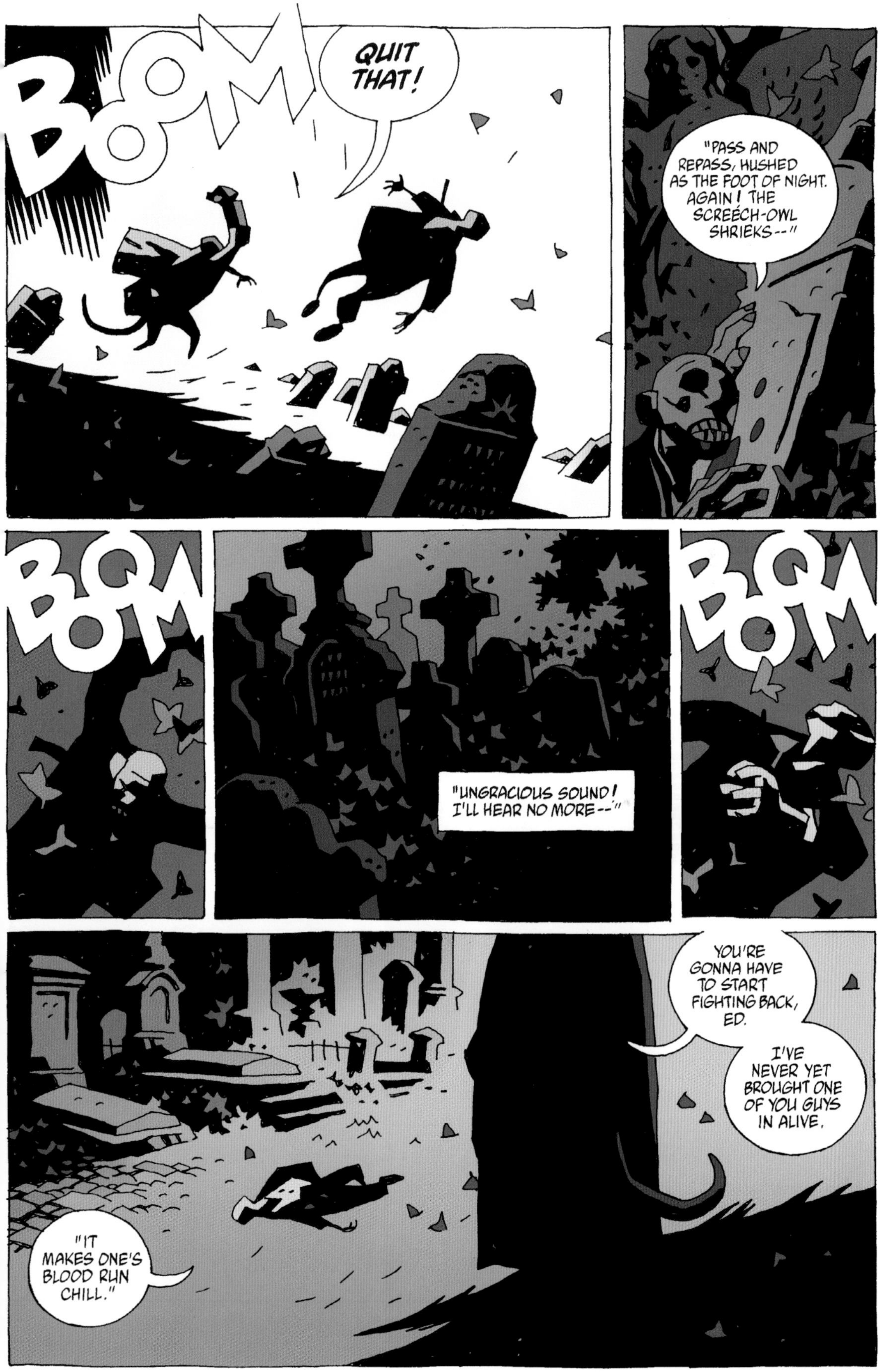
BOOM
QUIT THAT!
"PASS AND REPASS, HUSHED AS THE FOOT OF NIGHT. AGAIN! THE SCREECH-OWL SHRIEKS--"
BOOM
"UNGRACIOUS SOUND! I'LL HEAR NO MORE--"
BOOM
YOU'RE GONNA HAVE TO START FIGHTING BACK, ED.
I'VE NEVER YET BROUGHT ONE OF YOU GUYS IN ALIVE.
"IT MAKES ONE'S BLOOD RUN CHILL."

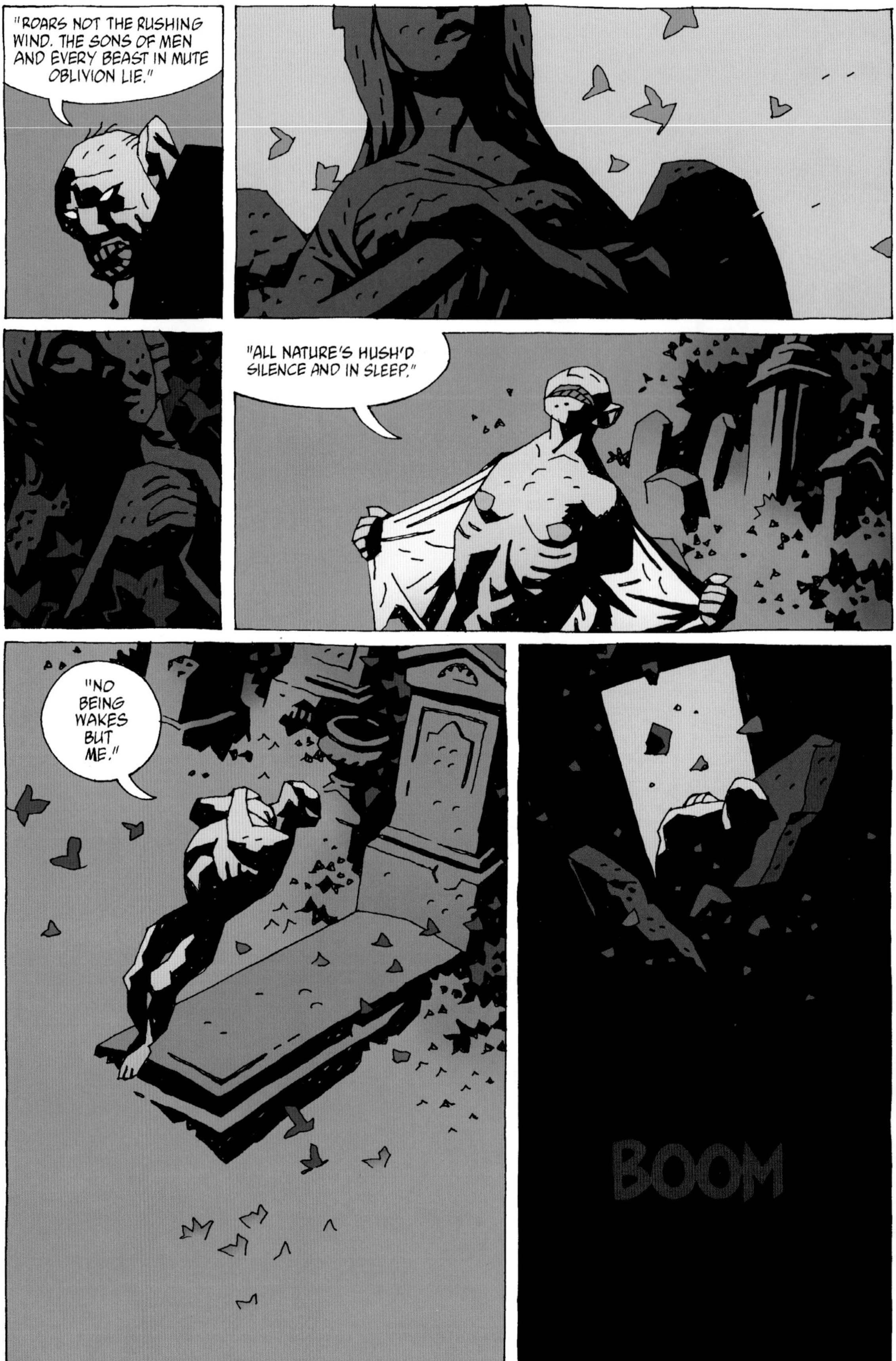
"ROARS NOT THE RUSHING WIND. THE SONS OF MEN AND EVERY BEAST IN MUTE OBLIVION LIE."
"ALL NATURE'S HUSH'D SILENCE AND IN SLEEP."
"NO BEING WAKES BUT ME."
BOOM

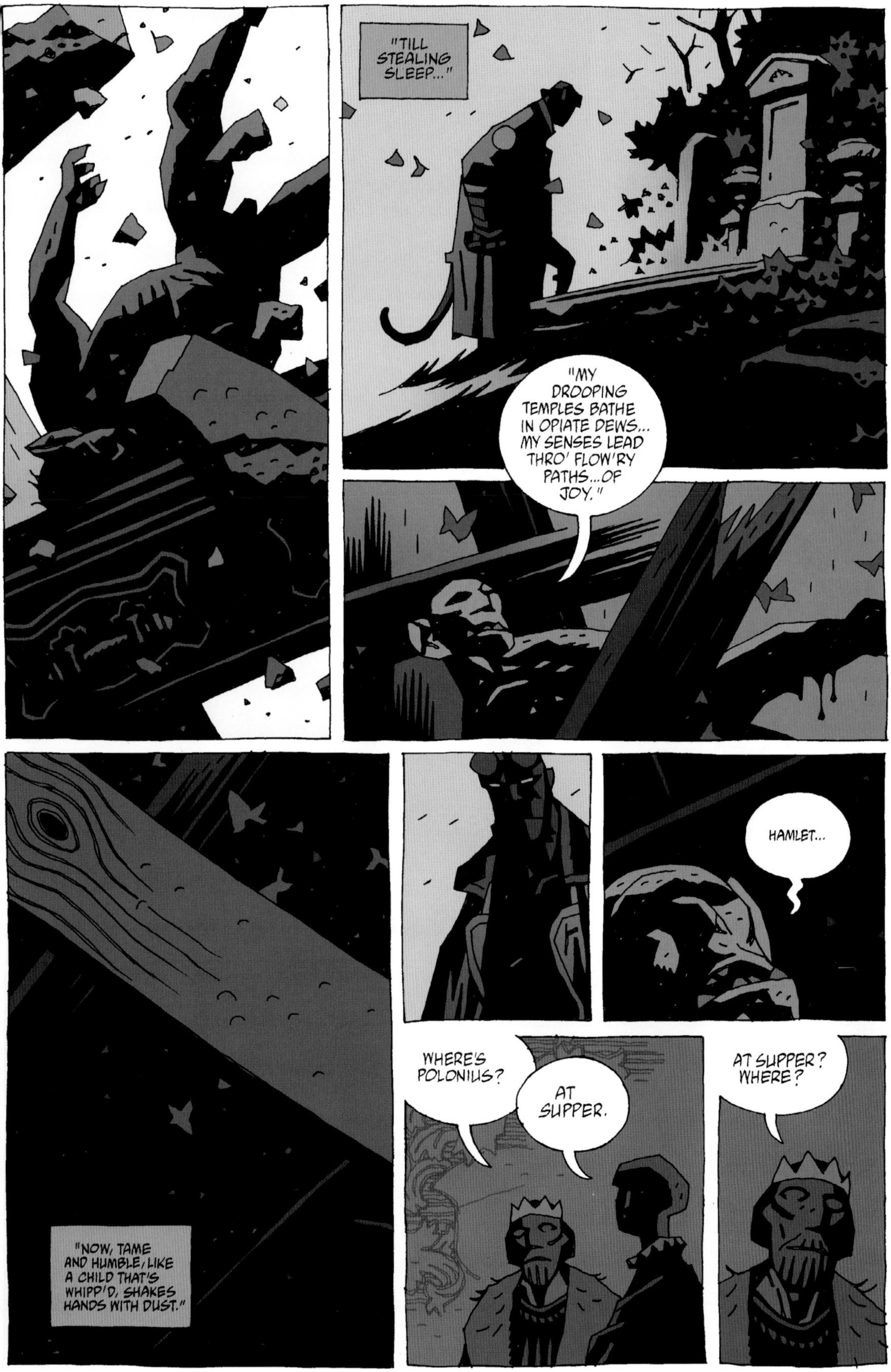
"TILL STEALING SLEEP..."
"MY DROOPING TEMPLES BATHE IN OPIATE DEWS... MY SENSES LEAD THRO' FLOW'RY PATHS...OF JOY."
"NOW, TAME AND HUMBLE, LIKE A CHILD THAT'S WHIPP'D, SHAKES HANDS WITH DUST."
HAMLET...
WHERE'S POLONIUS?
AT SUPPER.
AT SUPPER? WHERE?

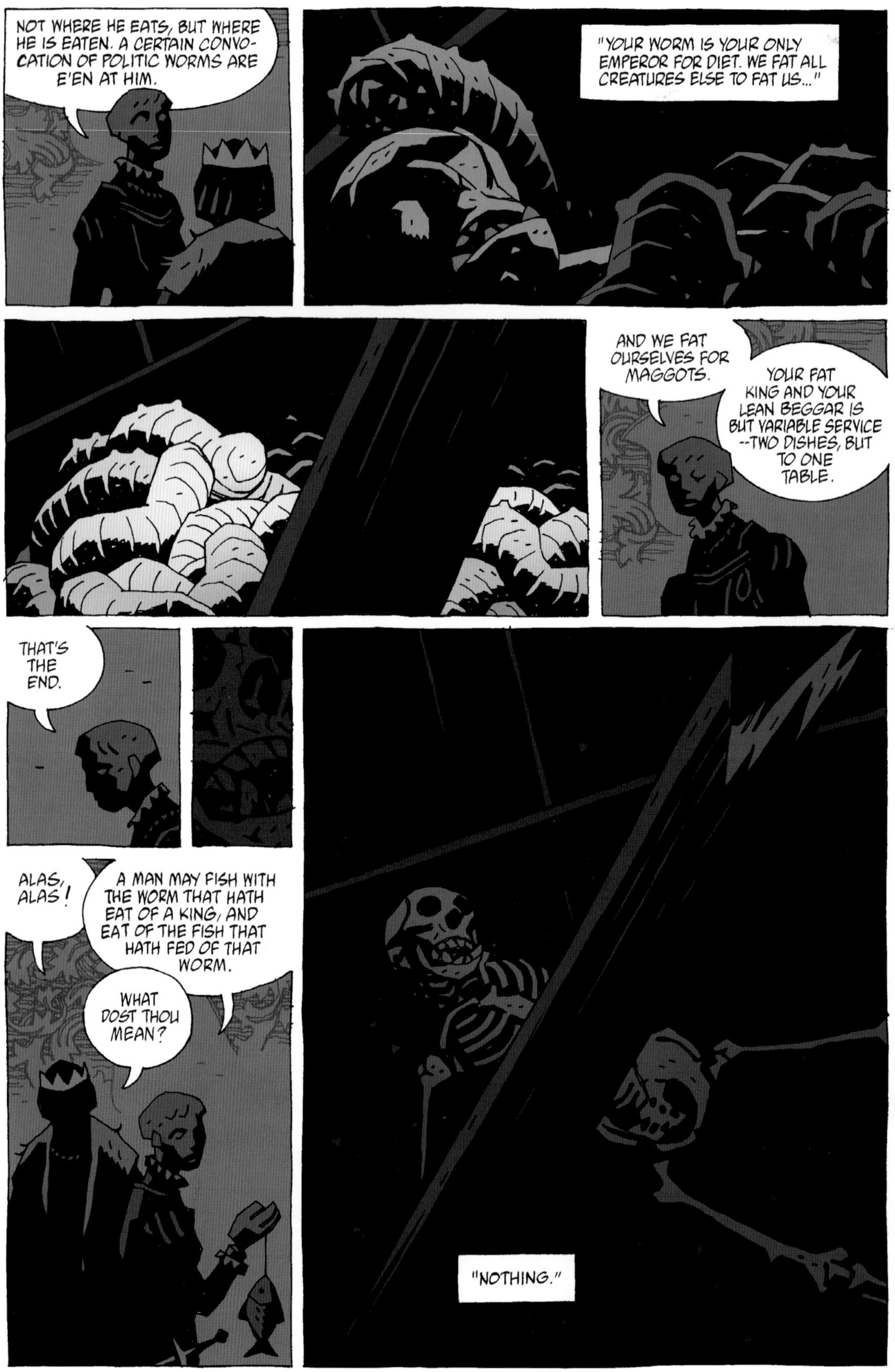
NOT WHERE HE EATS, BUT WHERE HE IS EATEN. A CERTAIN CONVOCATION OF POLITIC WORMS ARE E'EN AT HIM.
"YOUR WORM IS YOUR ONLY EMPEROR FOR DIET. WE FAT ALL CREATURES ELSE TO FAT US..."
AND WE FAT OURSELVES FOR MAGGOTS.
YOUR FAT KING AND YOUR LEAN BEGGAR IS BUT VARIABLE SERVICE --TWO DISHES, BUT TO ONE TABLE.
THAT'S THE END.
ALAS, ALAS!
A MAN MAY FISH WITH THE WORM THAT HATH EAT OF A KING, AND EAT OF THE FISH THAT HATH FED OF THAT WORM.
WHAT DOST THOU MEAN?
"NOTHING."

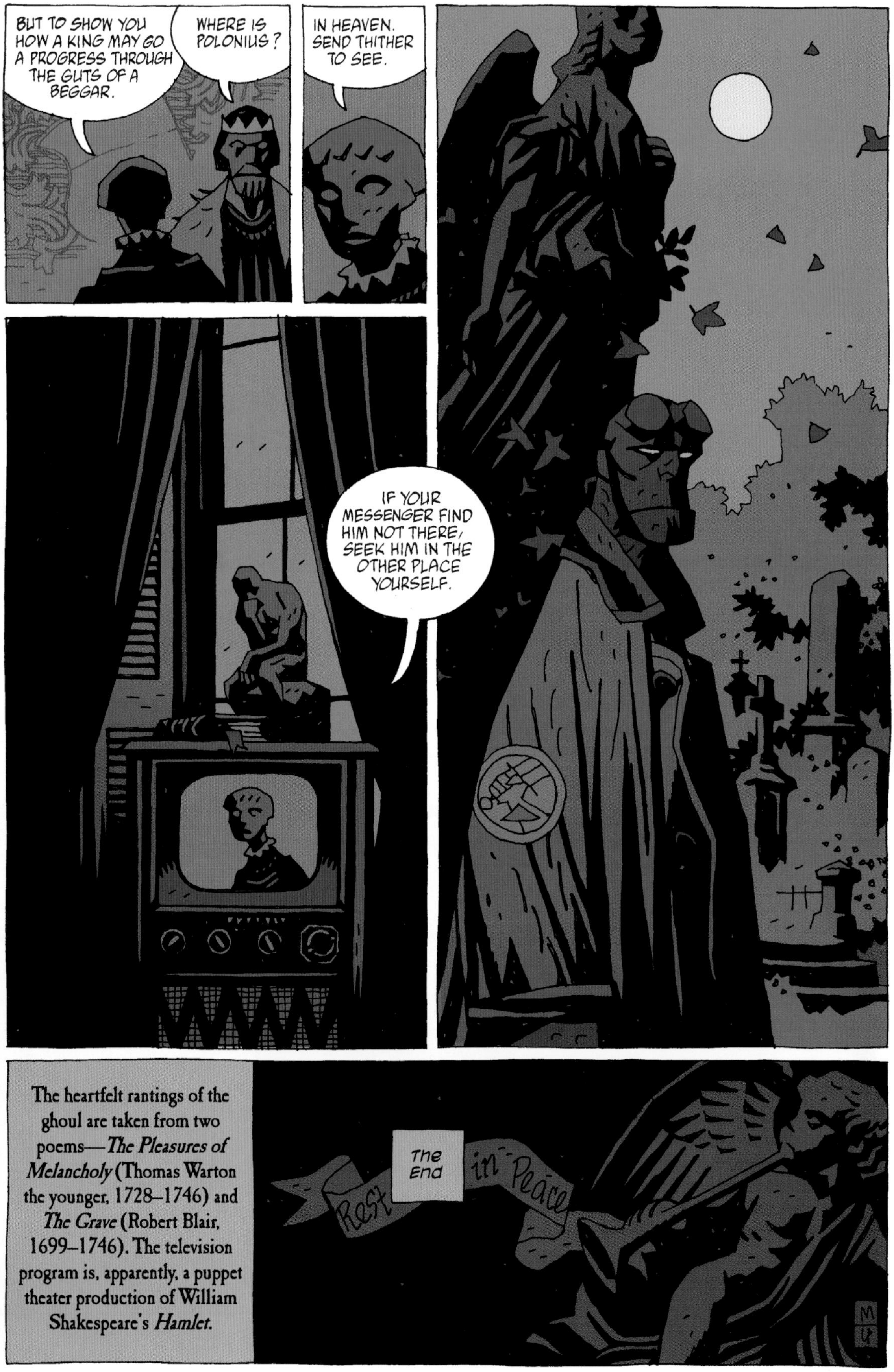
BUT TO SHOW YOU HOW A KING MAY GO A PROGRESS THROUGH THE GUTS OF A BEGGAR.
WHERE IS POLONIUS?
IN HEAVEN. SEND THITHER TO SEE.
IF YOUR MESSENGER FIND HIM NOT THERE, SEEK HIM IN THE OTHER PLACE YOURSELF.
The heartfelt rantings of the ghoul are taken from two poems—*The Pleasures of Melancholy* (Thomas Warton the younger, 1728–1746) and *The Grave* (Robert Blair, 1699–1746). The television program is, apparently, a puppet theater production of William Shakespeare's *Hamlet*.
Rest in Peace
The End
MM

Makoma

HERE'S ANOTHER ODD ONE.

I stumbled across the story of Makoma and the giants in one of those Andrew Lang Fairy Books (I don't remember which color) and fell in love with it instantly. For years I planned to do a more or less straight adaptation of it, but I just couldn't get away from the parallels to what I was doing (or planning to do) in Hellboy. This thing wanted to be a Hellboy story. Eventually I gave in and put it on that crowded mental Hellboy shelf. I knew I *would* do it. It was just a question of when.

Jump ahead a few years. I'm exchanging e-mails with the legendary Richard Corben and he's saying some very nice things about Hellboy. I work up the nerve to ask if he'd ever consider drawing a Hellboy story and (much to my joy and amazement) he says yes. There you go. I immediately grabbed Makoma off that mental shelf, blew the dust off, added some stuff to the second half (I wanted to see Richard drawing singing corpses and ant-men), and came up with a framing sequence to root the story in Hellboy continuity and give myself something to draw. Richard got to do the fun stuff, but I'm not complaining.

I have been in awe of Richard Corben for a very long time, from *Den*, *Mutant World*, *Bloodstar*, and *Sinbad* to *House on the Borderland* (maybe my personal favorite) and the recent pseudo-adaptations of Edgar Allan Poe stories for Marvel. He is one of the most unique storytellers working in comics today, and one of the best draftsmen to *ever* work in comics. And he keeps getting better. As with P. Craig Russell, it was a great and unexpected pleasure to work with him. Hopefully we'll get to do it again one of these days.

"Makoma" was originally published as a two-issue miniseries in February and March of 2006. While nothing has been added to the story here, I have added a new pinup page following the story—my chance to finally draw the fun stuff.

Mike Mignola

Mike Mignola
Somewhere in Southern California

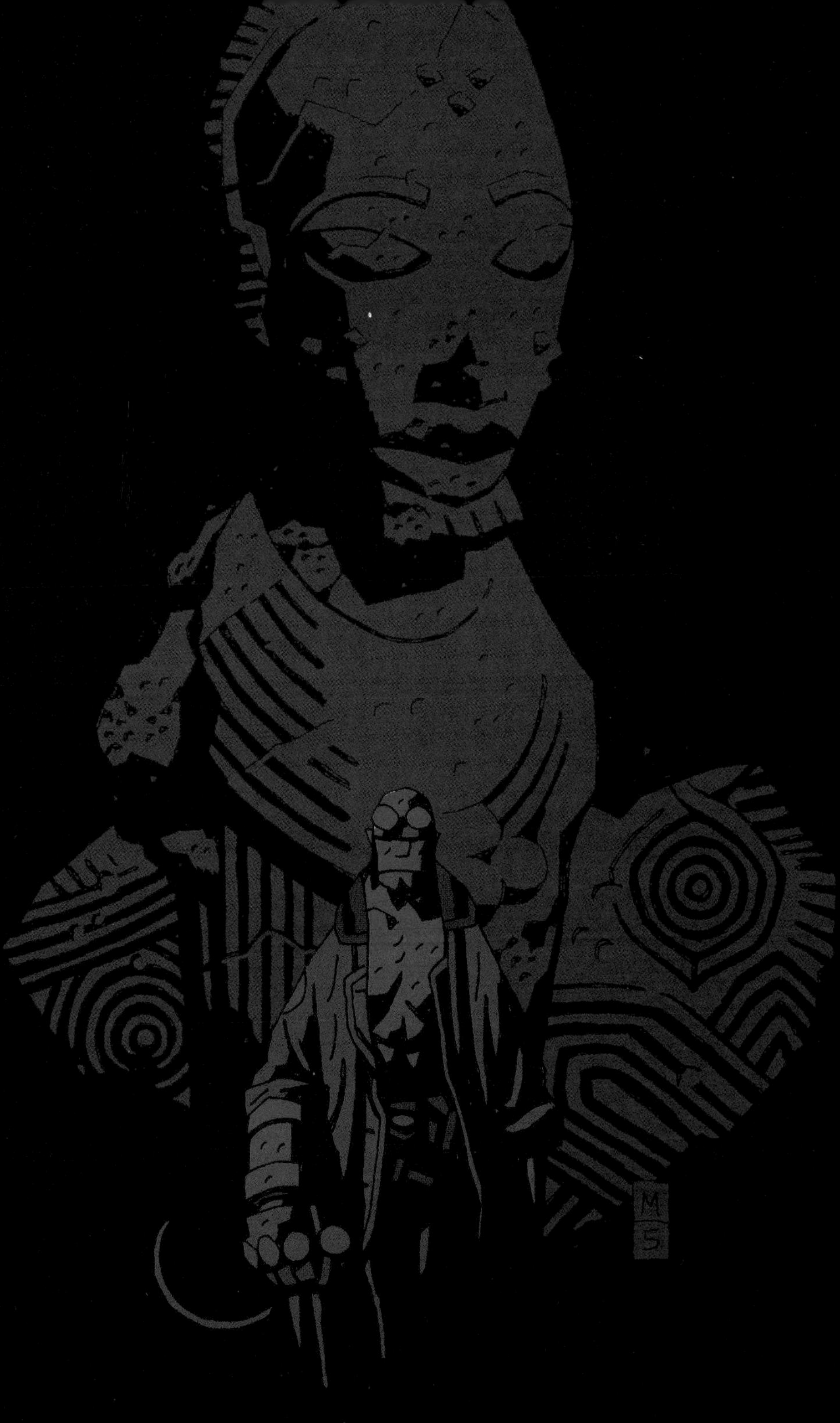

Makoma

or, A TALE TOLD BY A MUMMY IN THE NEW YORK CITY EXPLORERS' CLUB ON AUGUST 16, 1993

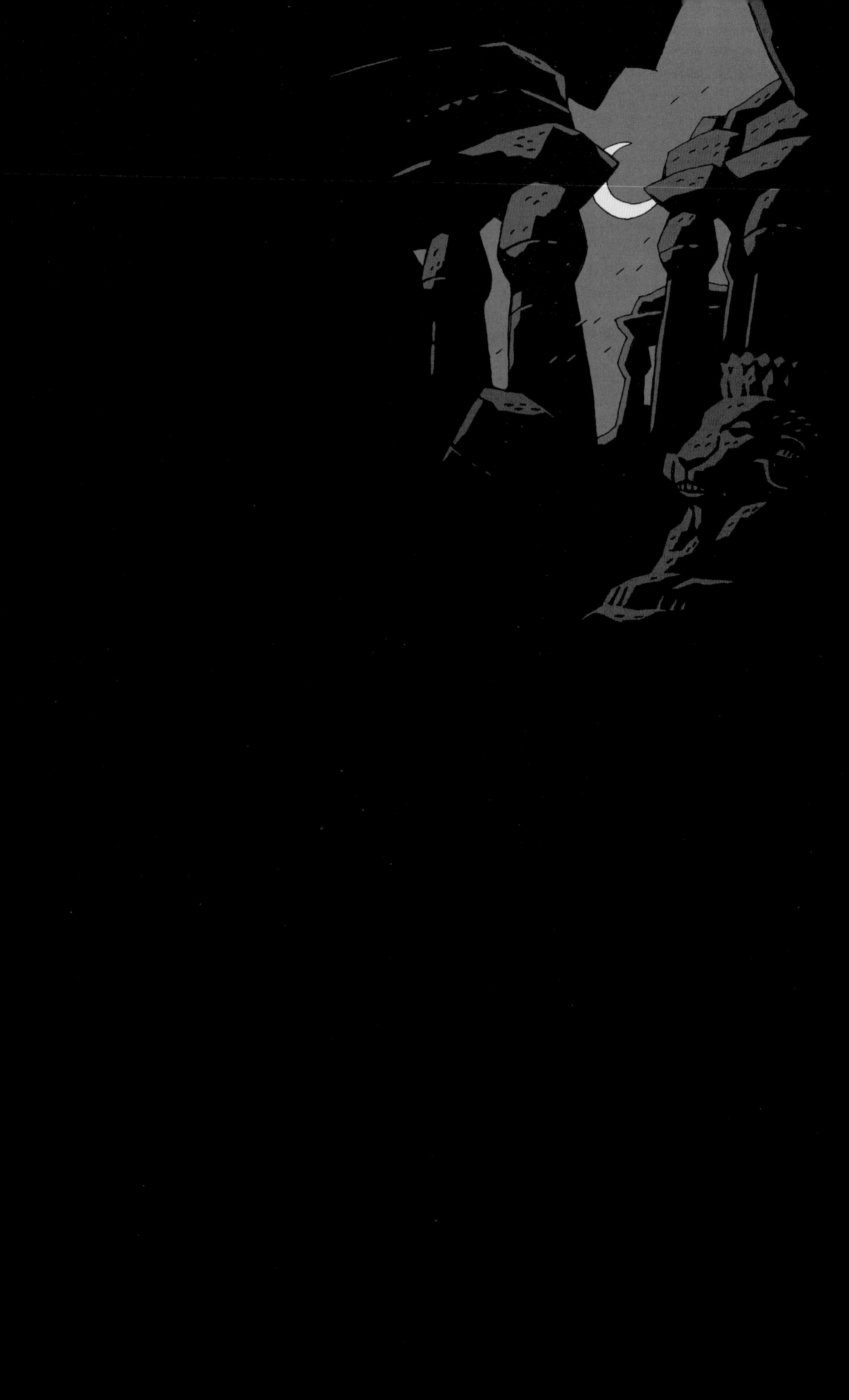

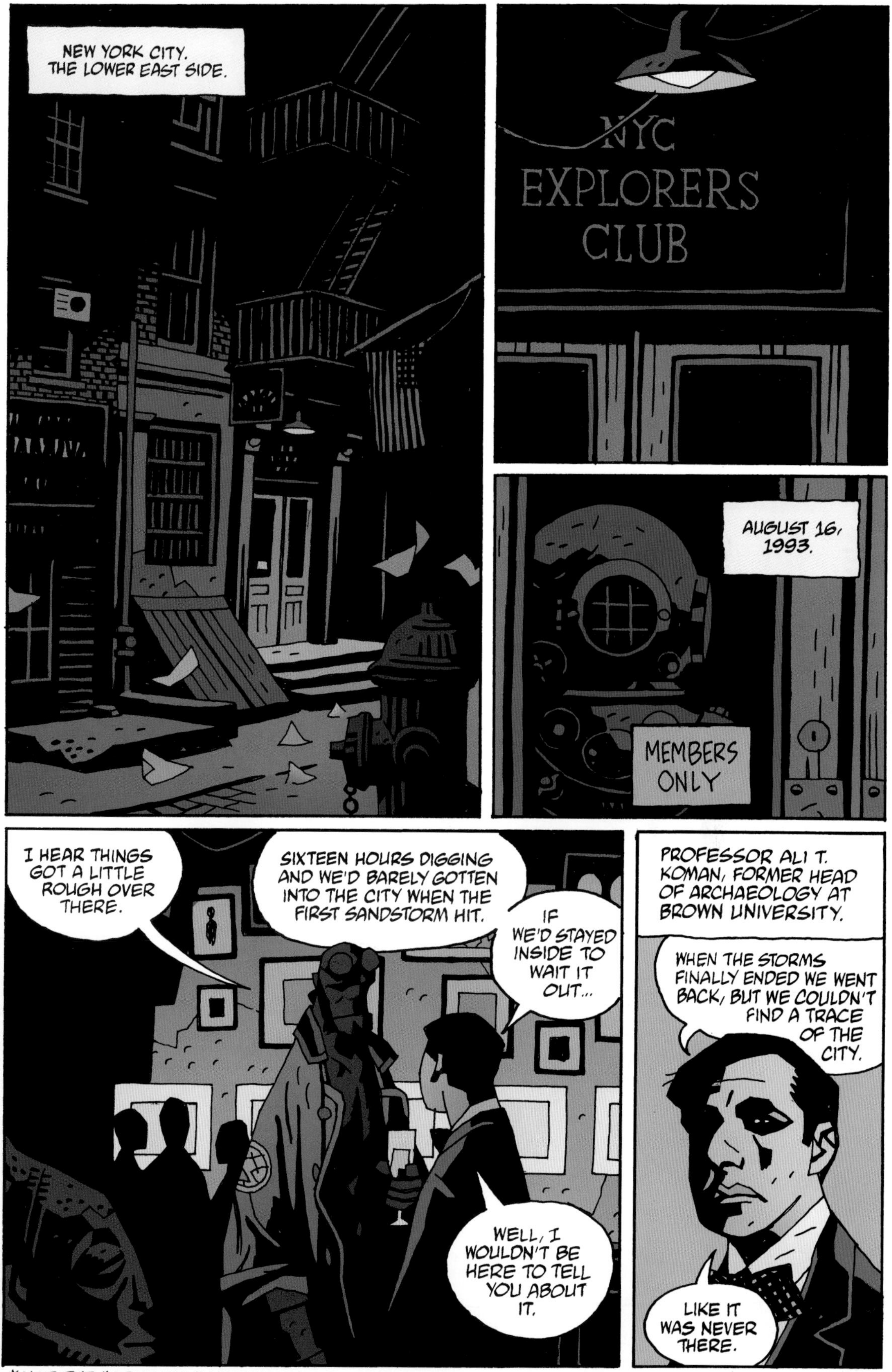
NEW YORK CITY. THE LOWER EAST SIDE.
NYC EXPLORERS CLUB
AUGUST 16, 1993.
MEMBERS ONLY
I HEAR THINGS GOT A LITTLE ROUGH OVER THERE.
SIXTEEN HOURS DIGGING AND WE'D BARELY GOTTEN INTO THE CITY WHEN THE FIRST SANDSTORM HIT.
IF WE'D STAYED INSIDE TO WAIT IT OUT...
WELL, I WOULDN'T BE HERE TO TELL YOU ABOUT IT.
PROFESSOR ALI T. KOMAN, FORMER HEAD OF ARCHAEOLOGY AT BROWN UNIVERSITY.
WHEN THE STORMS FINALLY ENDED WE WENT BACK, BUT WE COULDN'T FIND A TRACE OF THE CITY.
LIKE IT WAS NEVER THERE.

*NOT THE "ORIGINAL" NEW YORK CITY EXPLORERS' CLUB, BUT THE ONE FOUNDED BY THEOSOPHIST ALDEN ALBERT KERN IN 1929.

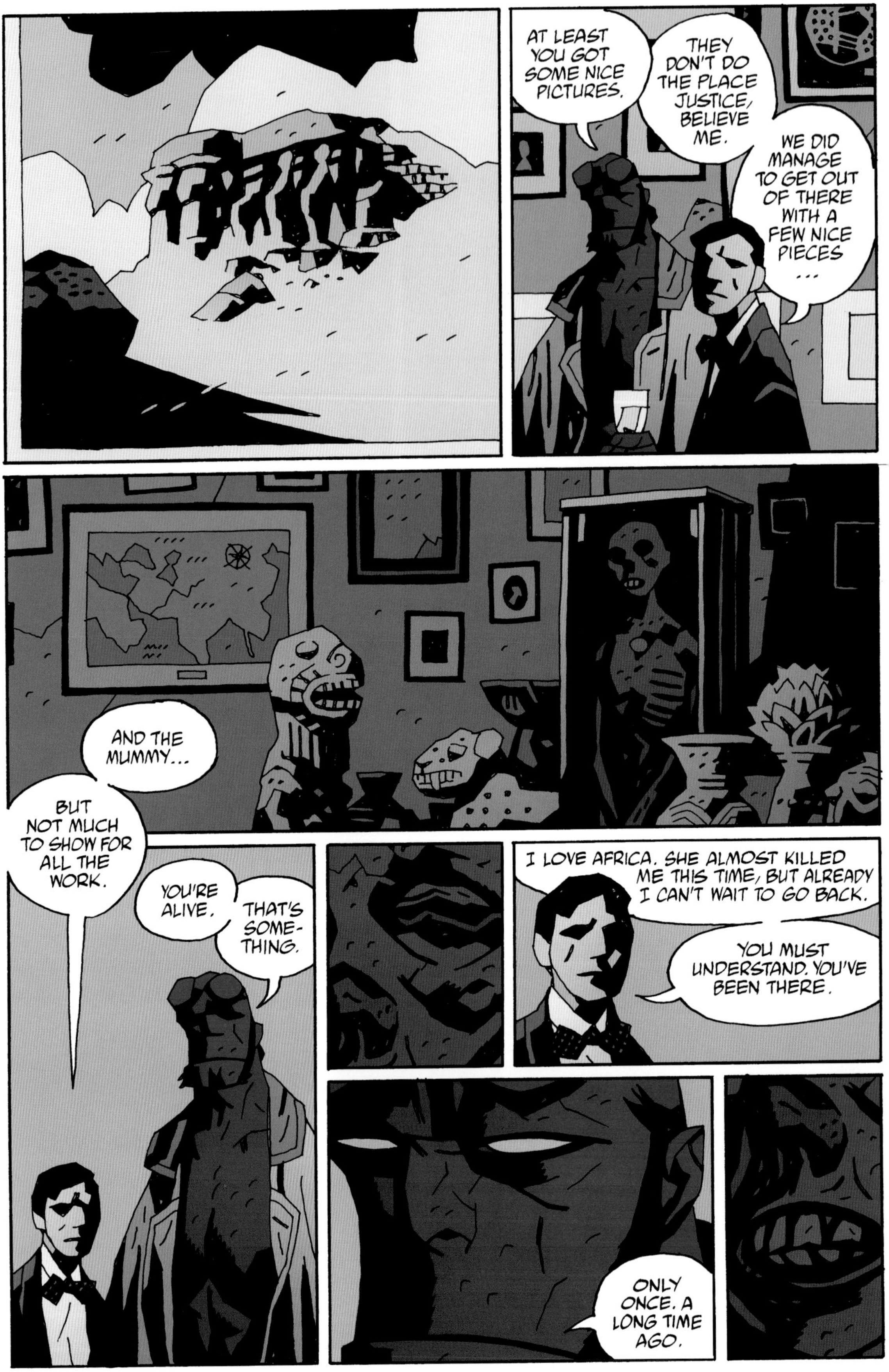
AT LEAST YOU GOT SOME NICE PICTURES.
THEY DON'T DO THE PLACE JUSTICE, BELIEVE ME.
WE DID MANAGE TO GET OUT OF THERE WITH A FEW NICE PIECES . . .
AND THE MUMMY...
BUT NOT MUCH TO SHOW FOR ALL THE WORK.
YOU'RE ALIVE.
THAT'S SOME-THING.
I LOVE AFRICA. SHE ALMOST KILLED ME THIS TIME, BUT ALREADY I CAN'T WAIT TO GO BACK.
YOU MUST UNDERSTAND. YOU'VE BEEN THERE.
ONLY ONCE. A LONG TIME AGO.

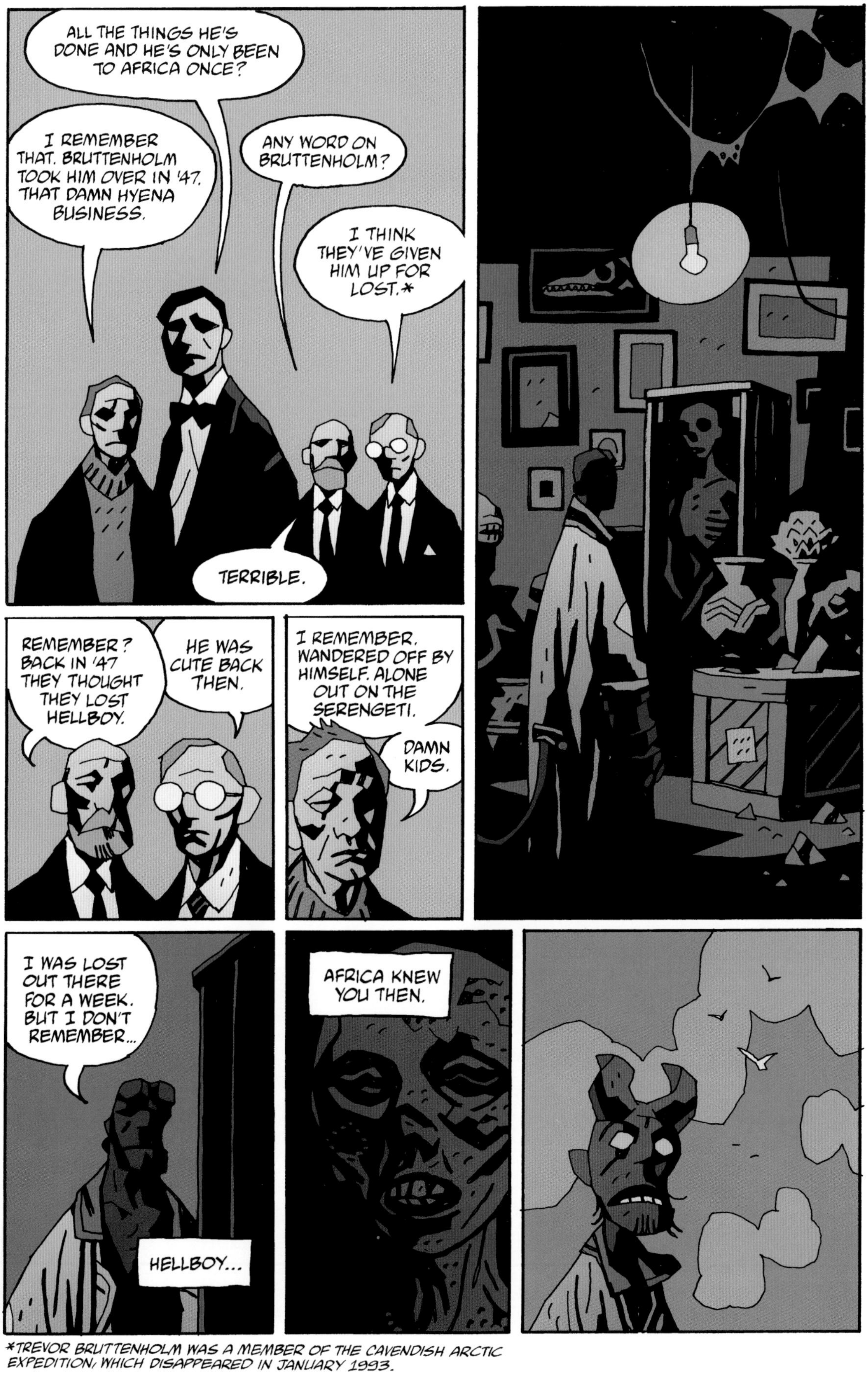

ALL THE THINGS HE'S DONE AND HE'S ONLY BEEN TO AFRICA ONCE?
I REMEMBER THAT. BRUTTENHOLM TOOK HIM OVER IN '47. THAT DAMN HYENA BUSINESS.
ANY WORD ON BRUTTENHOLM?
I THINK THEY'VE GIVEN HIM UP FOR LOST.*
TERRIBLE.
REMEMBER? BACK IN '47 THEY THOUGHT THEY LOST HELLBOY.
HE WAS CUTE BACK THEN.
I REMEMBER. WANDERED OFF BY HIMSELF. ALONE OUT ON THE SERENGETI.
DAMN KIDS.
I WAS LOST OUT THERE FOR A WEEK. BUT I DON'T REMEMBER...
HELLBOY...
AFRICA KNEW YOU THEN.

*TREVOR BRUTTENHOLM WAS A MEMBER OF THE CAVENDISH ARCTIC EXPEDITION, WHICH DISAPPEARED IN JANUARY 1993.

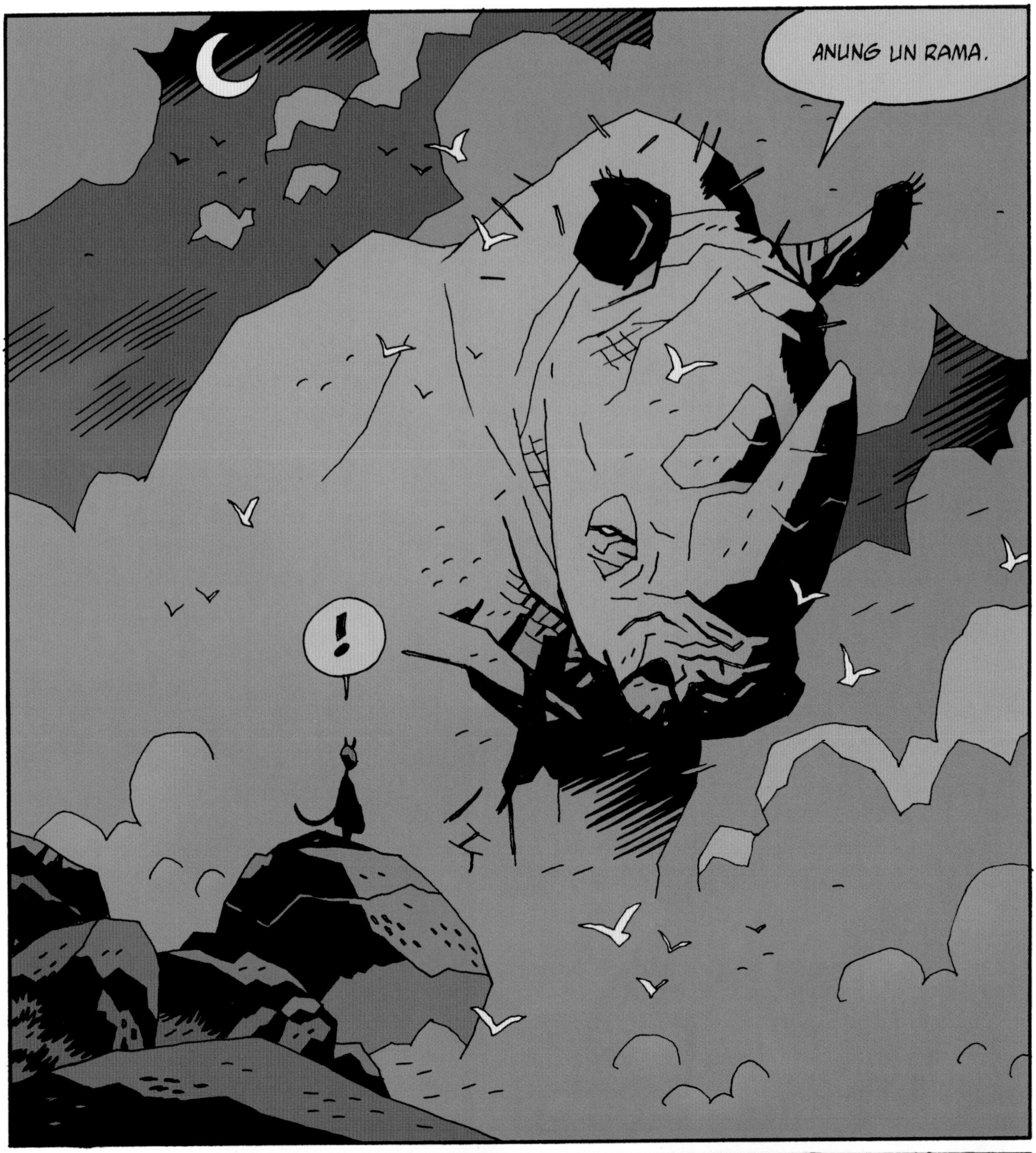
ANUNG UN RAMA.
!

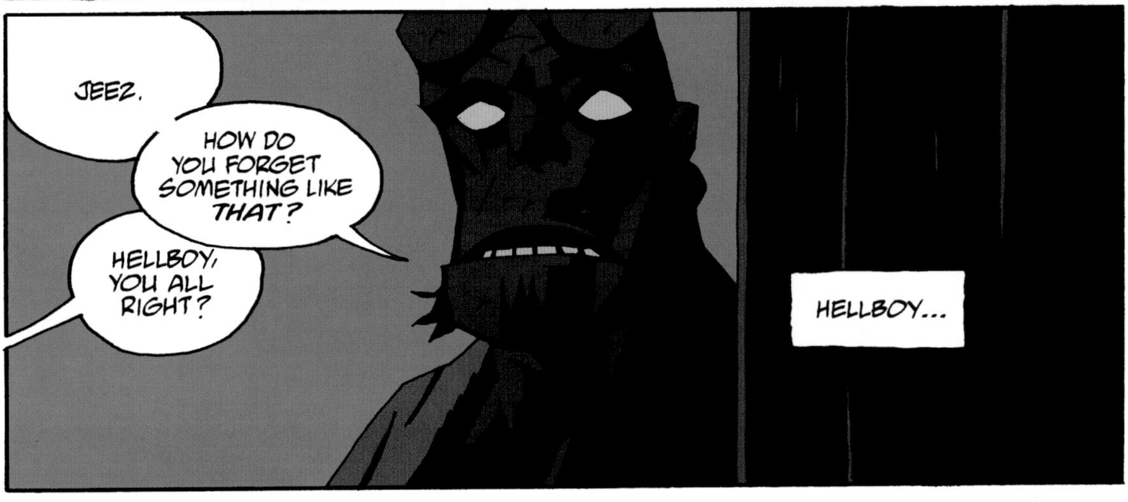
JEEZ.
HOW DO YOU FORGET SOMETHING LIKE THAT?
HELLBOY, YOU ALL RIGHT?
HELLBOY...

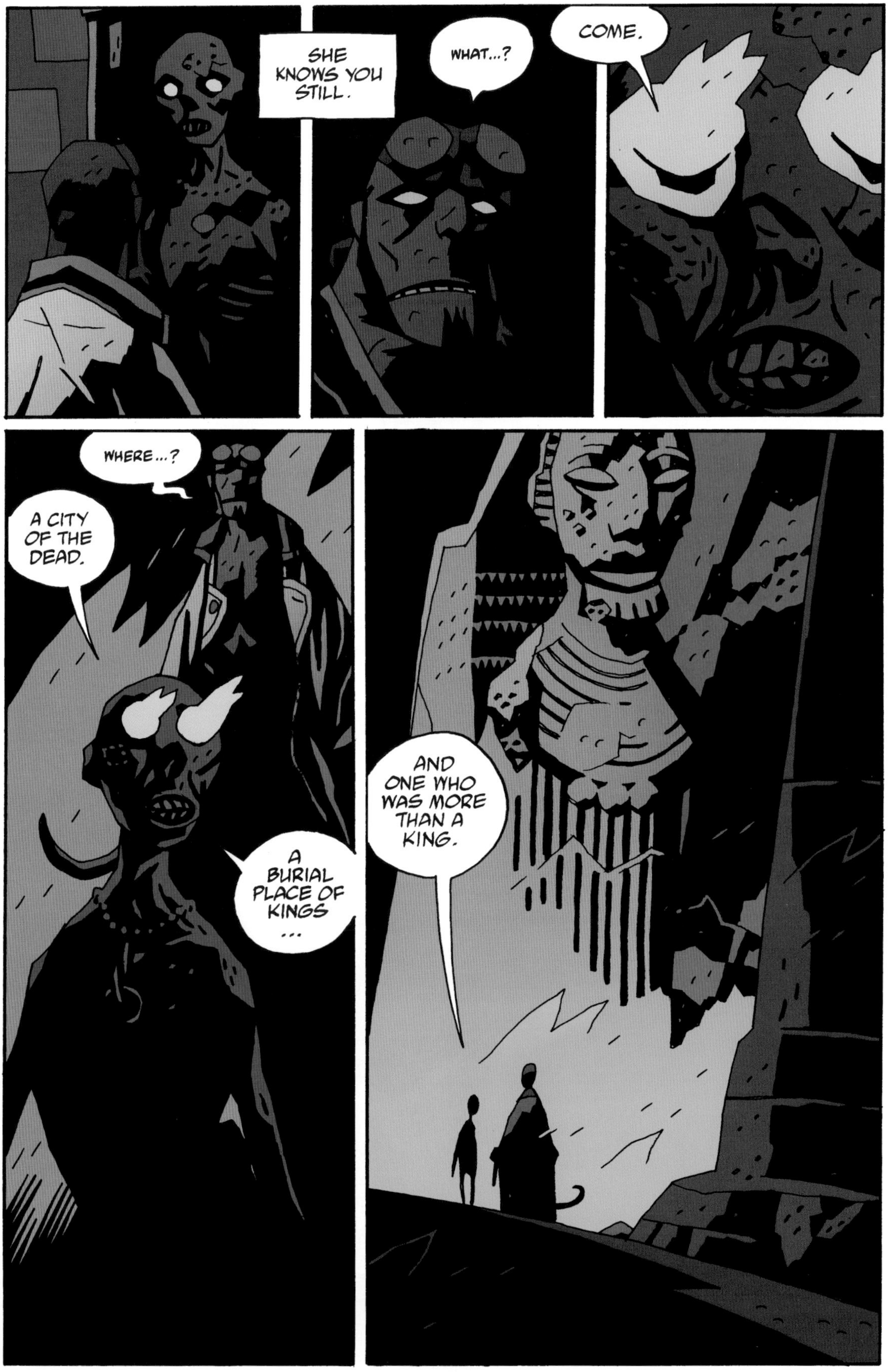
SHE KNOWS YOU STILL.
WHAT...?
COME.
WHERE...?
A CITY OF THE DEAD.
A BURIAL PLACE OF KINGS ...
AND ONE WHO WAS MORE THAN A KING.

MAKOMA

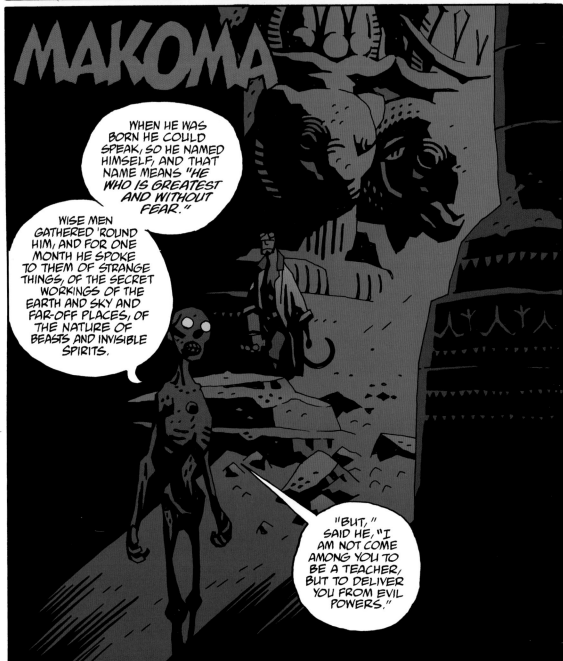

WHEN HE WAS BORN HE COULD SPEAK, SO HE NAMED HIMSELF, AND THAT NAME MEANS *"HE WHO IS GREATEST AND WITHOUT FEAR."*

WISE MEN GATHERED 'ROUND HIM, AND FOR ONE MONTH HE SPOKE TO THEM OF STRANGE THINGS, OF THE SECRET WORKINGS OF THE EARTH AND SKY AND FAR-OFF PLACES, OF THE NATURE OF BEASTS AND INVISIBLE SPIRITS.

"BUT," SAID HE, *"I AM NOT COME AMONG YOU TO BE A TEACHER, BUT TO DELIVER YOU FROM EVIL POWERS."*

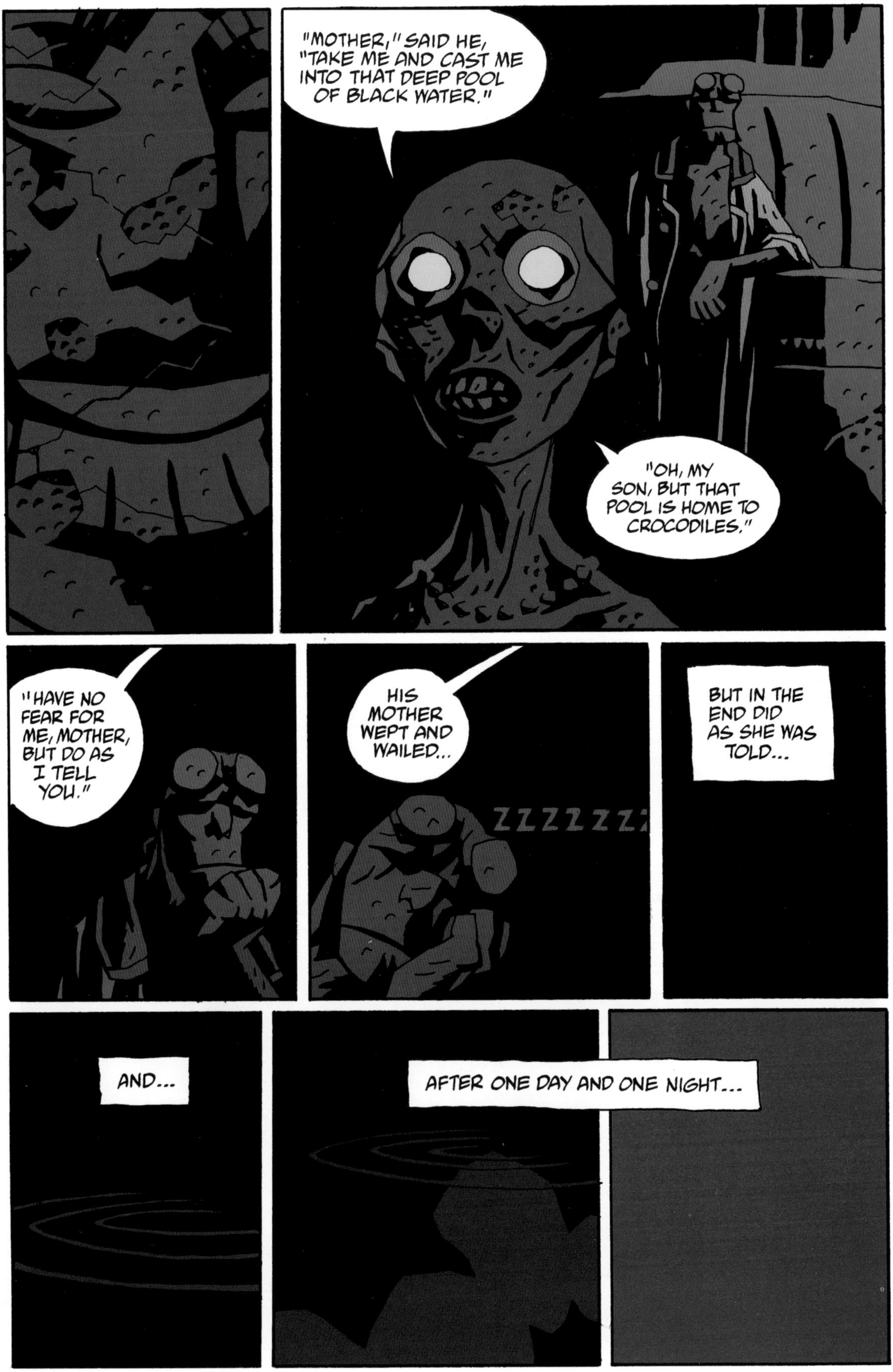
"MOTHER," SAID HE, "TAKE ME AND CAST ME INTO THAT DEEP POOL OF BLACK WATER."
"OH, MY SON, BUT THAT POOL IS HOME TO CROCODILES."
"HAVE NO FEAR FOR ME, MOTHER, BUT DO AS I TELL YOU."
HIS MOTHER WEPT AND WAILED...
ZZZZZZZ
BUT IN THE END DID AS SHE WAS TOLD...
AND...
AFTER ONE DAY AND ONE NIGHT...

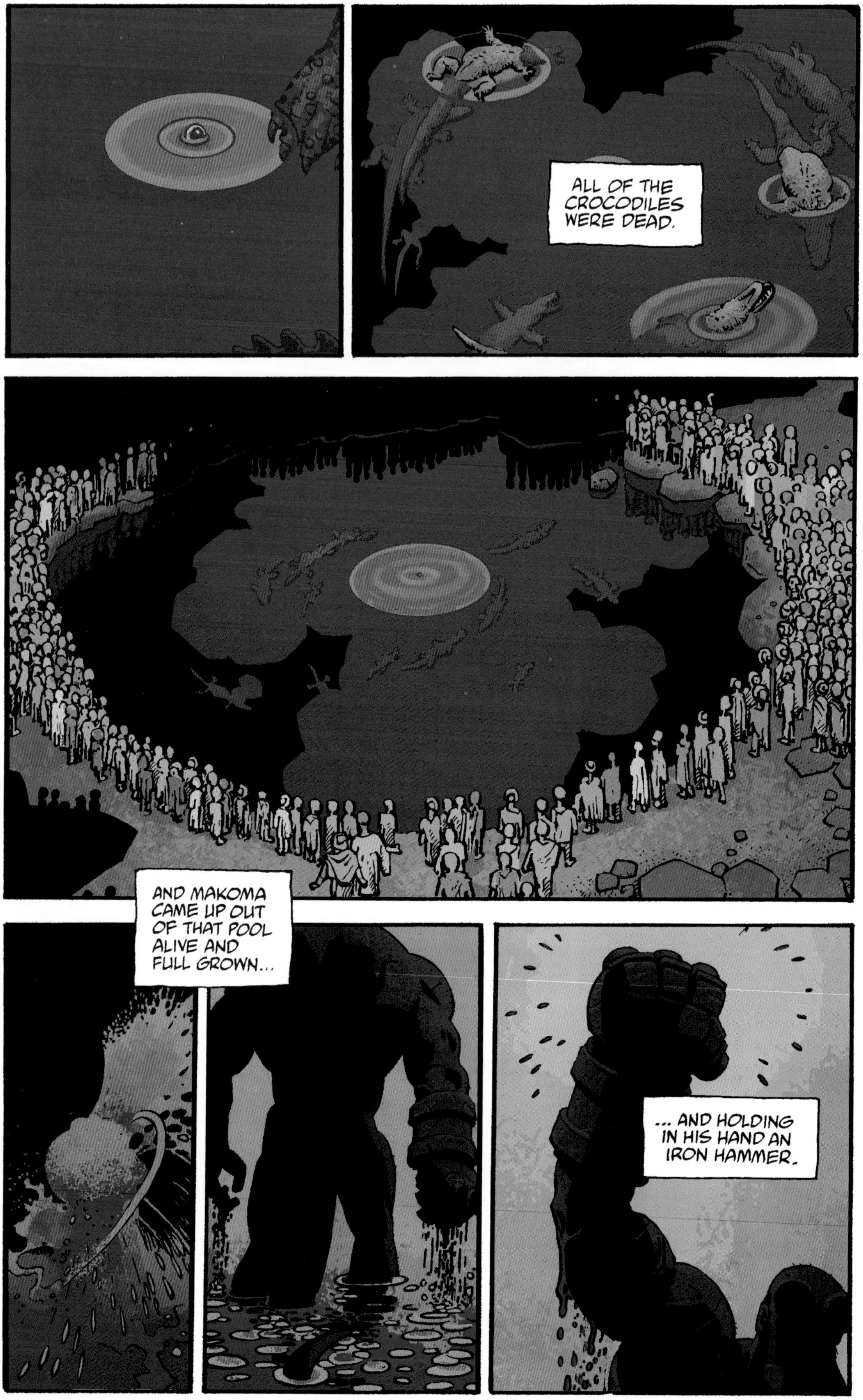
ALL OF THE CROCODILES WERE DEAD.
AND MAKOMA CAME UP OUT OF THAT POOL ALIVE AND FULL GROWN...
... AND HOLDING IN HIS HAND AN IRON HAMMER.

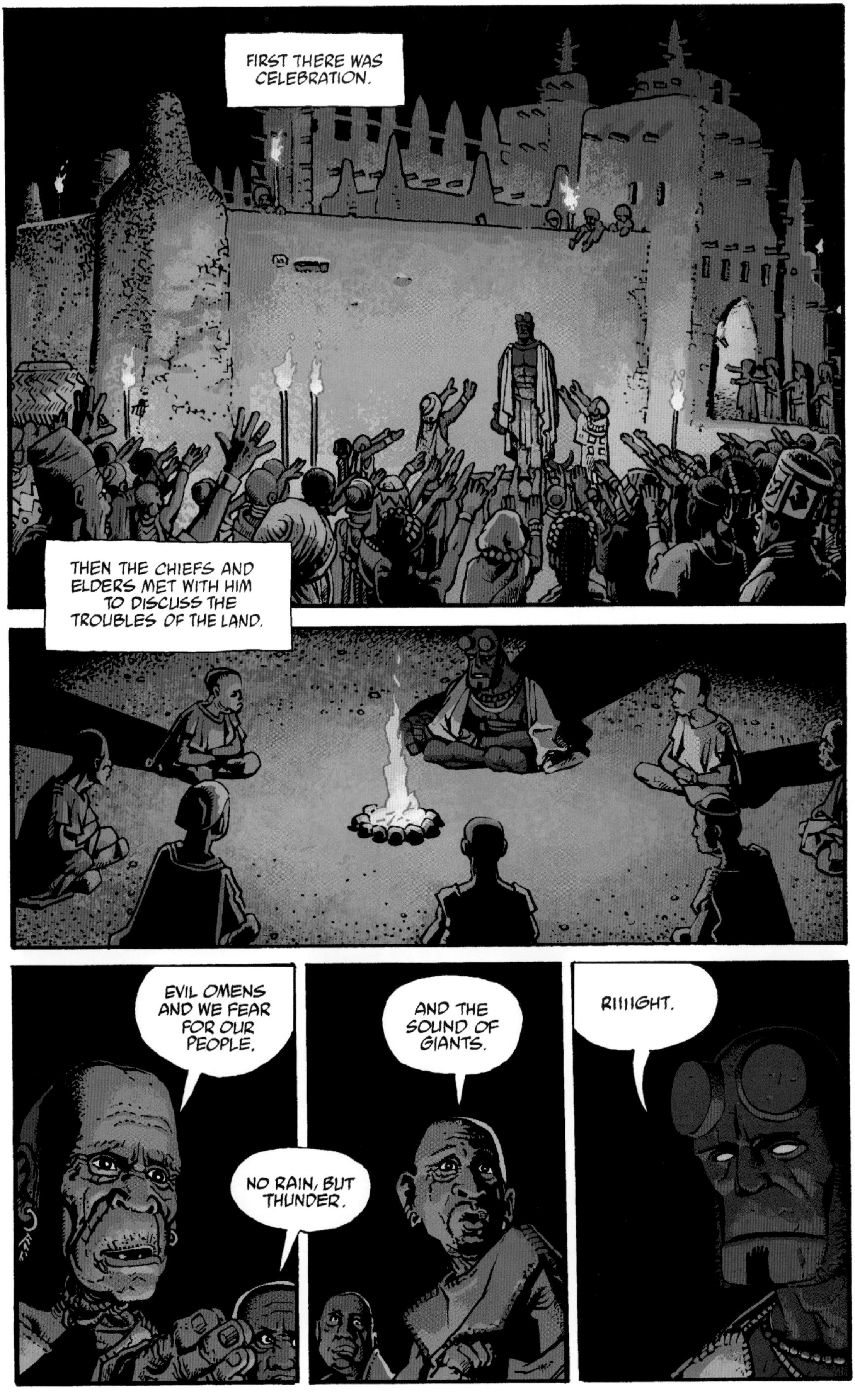

FIRST THERE WAS CELEBRATION.
THEN THE CHIEFS AND ELDERS MET WITH HIM TO DISCUSS THE TROUBLES OF THE LAND.
EVIL OMENS AND WE FEAR FOR OUR PEOPLE.
NO RAIN, BUT THUNDER.
AND THE SOUND OF GIANTS.
RIIIIGHT.

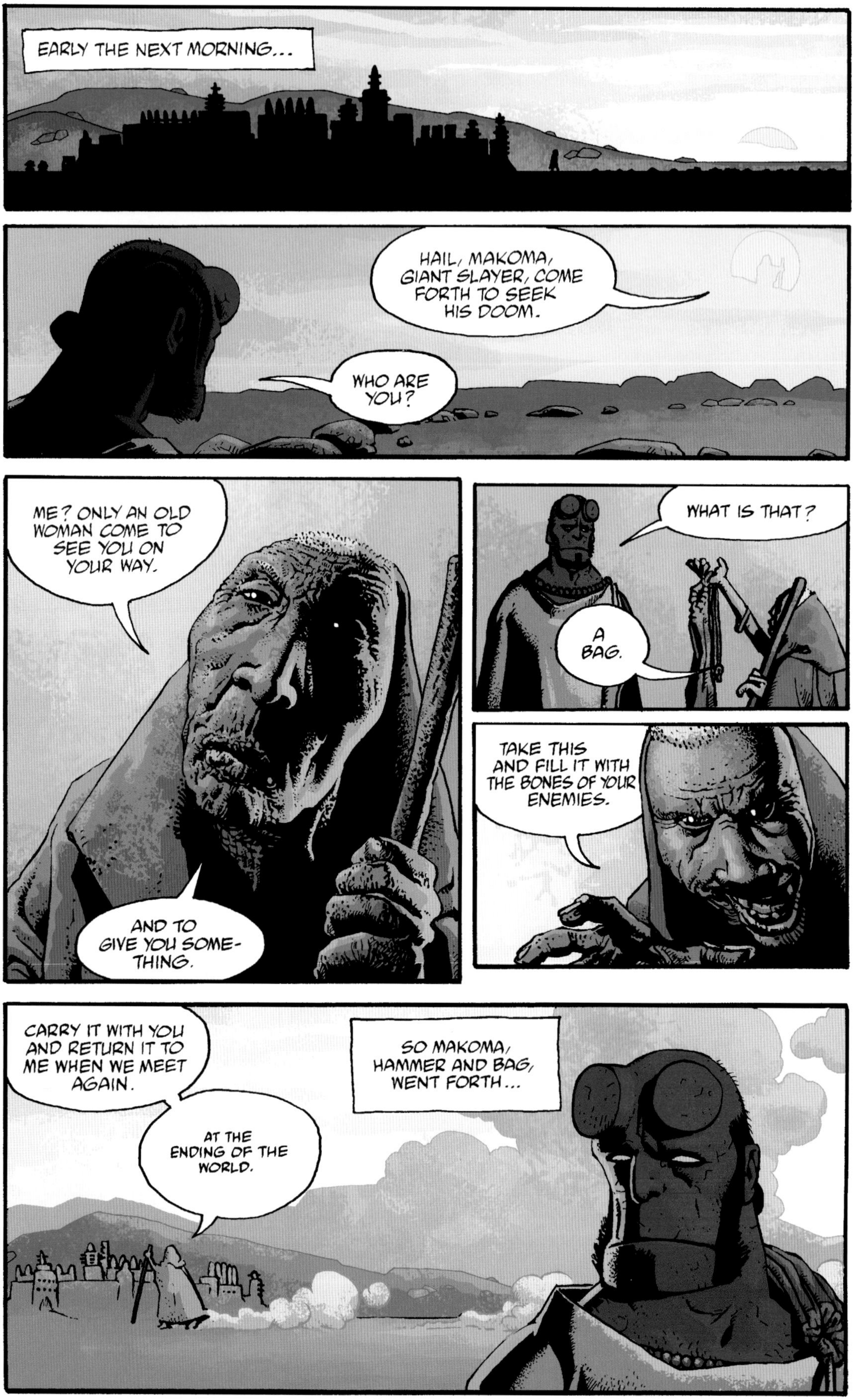
EARLY THE NEXT MORNING...
HAIL, MAKOMA, GIANT SLAYER, COME FORTH TO SEEK HIS DOOM.
WHO ARE YOU?
ME? ONLY AN OLD WOMAN COME TO SEE YOU ON YOUR WAY.
AND TO GIVE YOU SOME-THING.
WHAT IS THAT?
A BAG.
TAKE THIS AND FILL IT WITH THE BONES OF YOUR ENEMIES.
CARRY IT WITH YOU AND RETURN IT TO ME WHEN WE MEET AGAIN.
AT THE ENDING OF THE WORLD.
SO MAKOMA, HAMMER AND BAG, WENT FORTH...

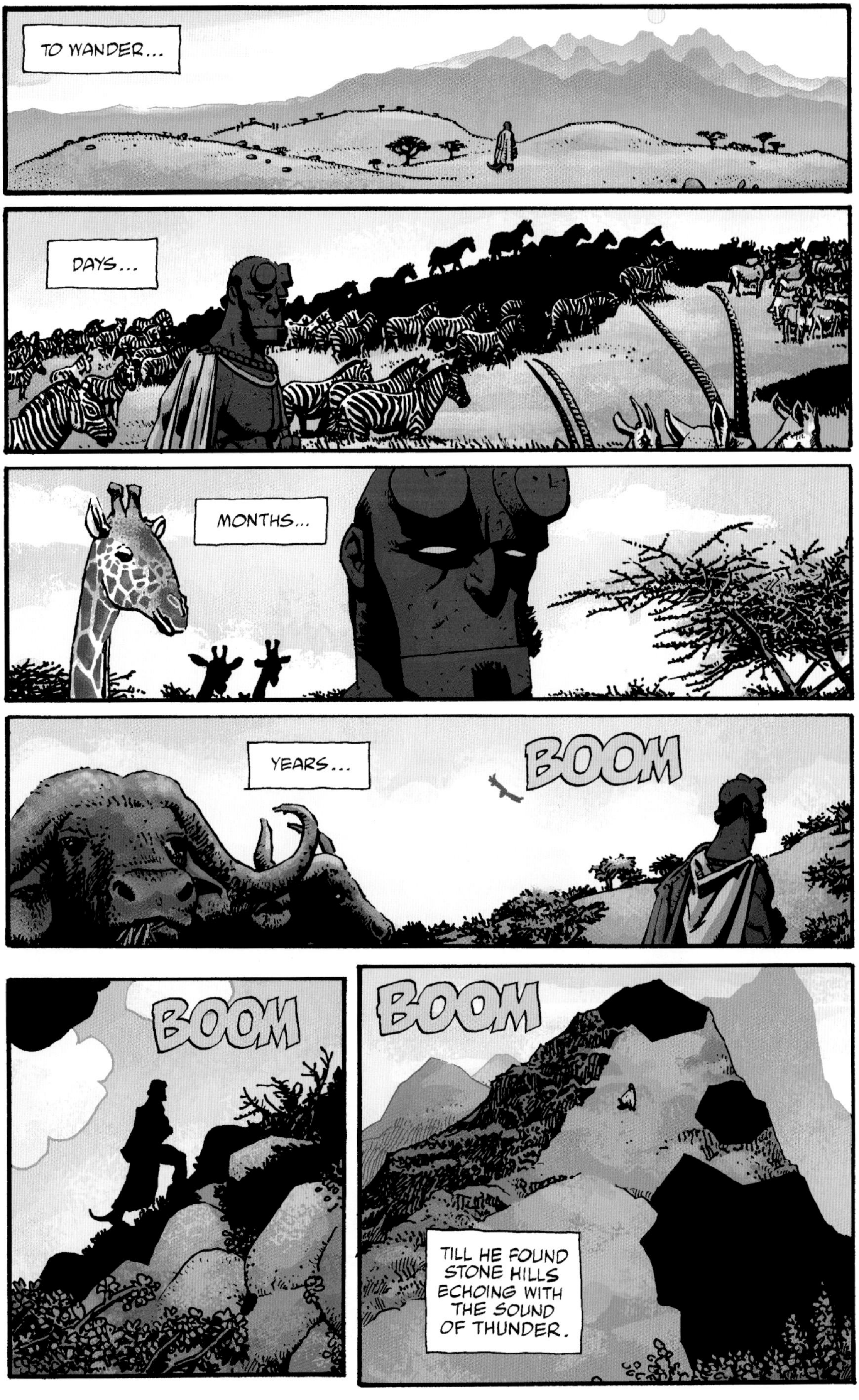
TO WANDER...
DAYS...
MONTHS...
YEARS...
BOOM
BOOM
BOOM
TILL HE FOUND STONE HILLS ECHOING WITH THE SOUND OF THUNDER.

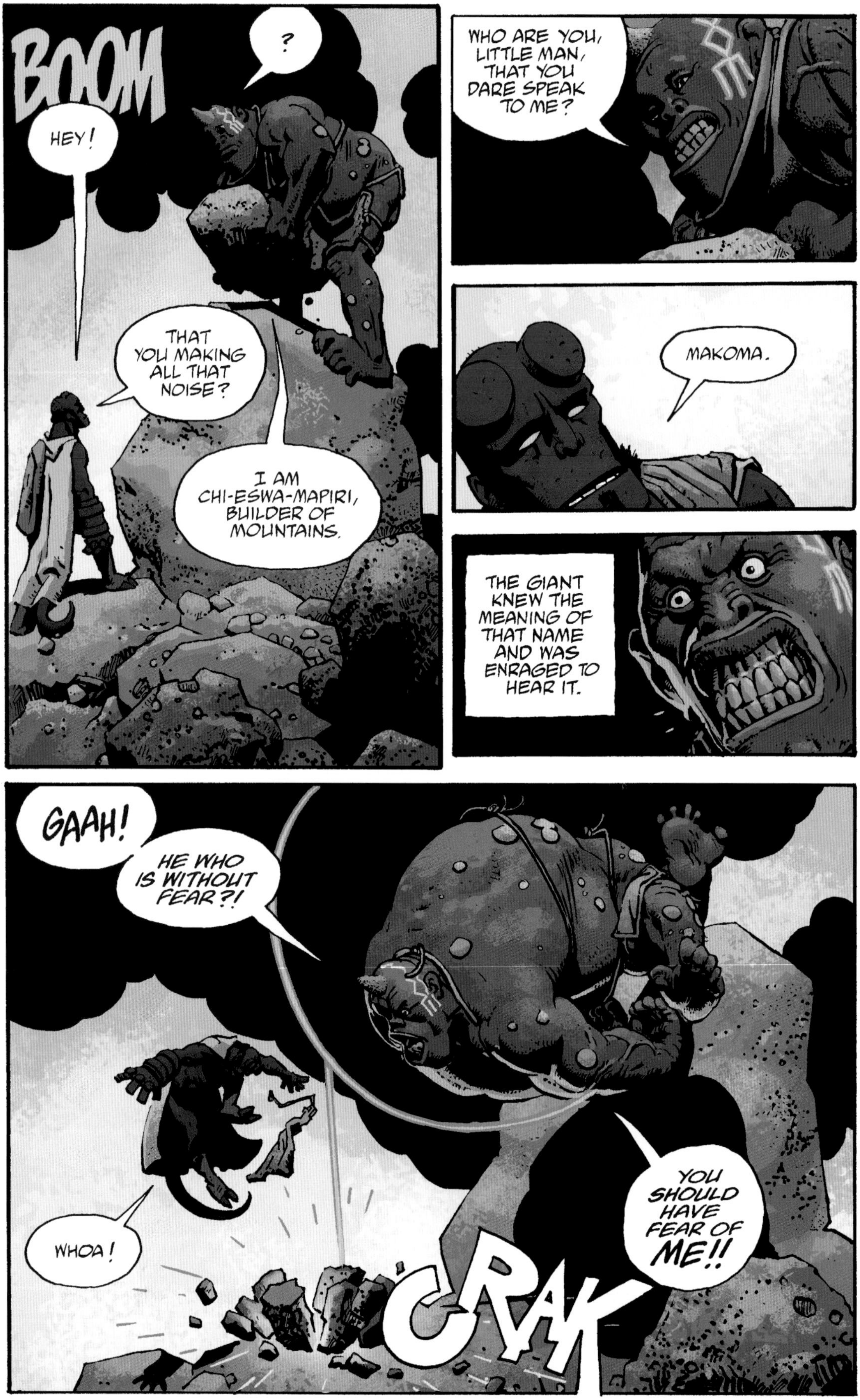
BOOM
?
HEY!
THAT YOU MAKING ALL THAT NOISE?
I AM CHI-ESWA-MAPIRI, BUILDER OF MOUNTAINS.
WHO ARE YOU, LITTLE MAN, THAT YOU DARE SPEAK TO ME?
MAKOMA.
THE GIANT KNEW THE MEANING OF THAT NAME AND WAS ENRAGED TO HEAR IT.
GAAH!
HE WHO IS WITHOUT FEAR?!
YOU SHOULD HAVE FEAR OF ME!!
WHOA!
CRAK

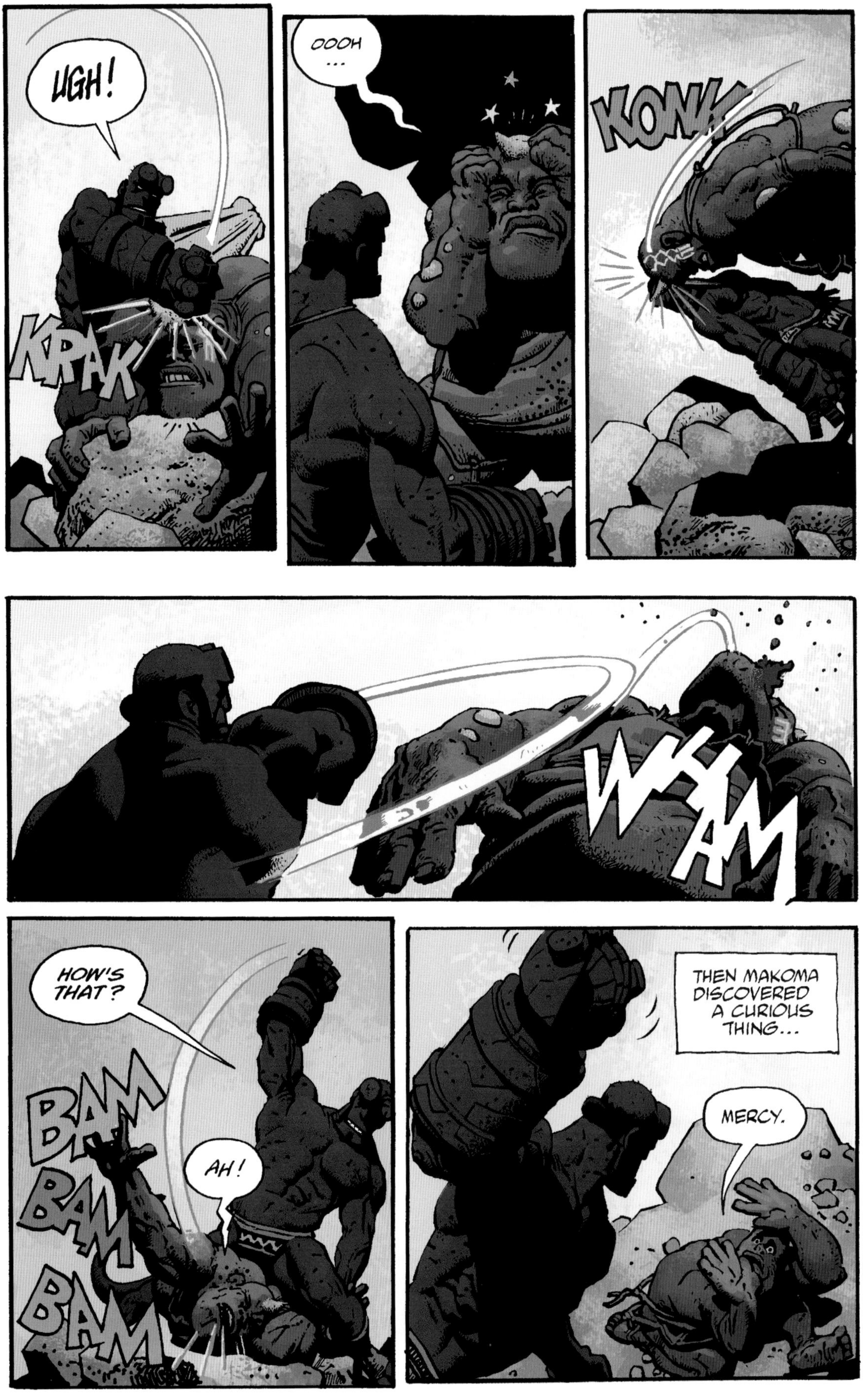
UGH!
KRAK
OOOH ...
KONK
WHAM
HOW'S THAT?
BAM BAM BAM BAM
AH!
THEN MAKOMA DISCOVERED A CURIOUS THING...
MERCY.

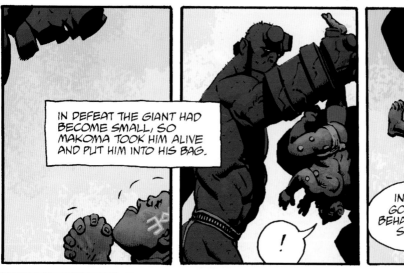

IN DEFEAT THE GIANT HAD BECOME SMALL, SO MAKOMA TOOK HIM ALIVE AND PUT HIM INTO HIS BAG.

!

IN YOU GO, AND BEHAVE YOUR-SELF.

MAKOMA THE MERCIFUL, MAKOMA THE--

QUIET BACK THERE.

HE CONTINUED ON, AND IN A SHORT TIME CAME UPON A SECOND GIANT.

CHI-DUBULA-TAKA, DIGGER OF RIVER BEDS.

WHO ARE YOU?

MAKOMA.

UPON HEARING THAT NAME THIS GIANT WAS ALSO ENRAGED. THE TWO FOUGHT, AND THE RESULTS WERE THE SAME.

MERCY.

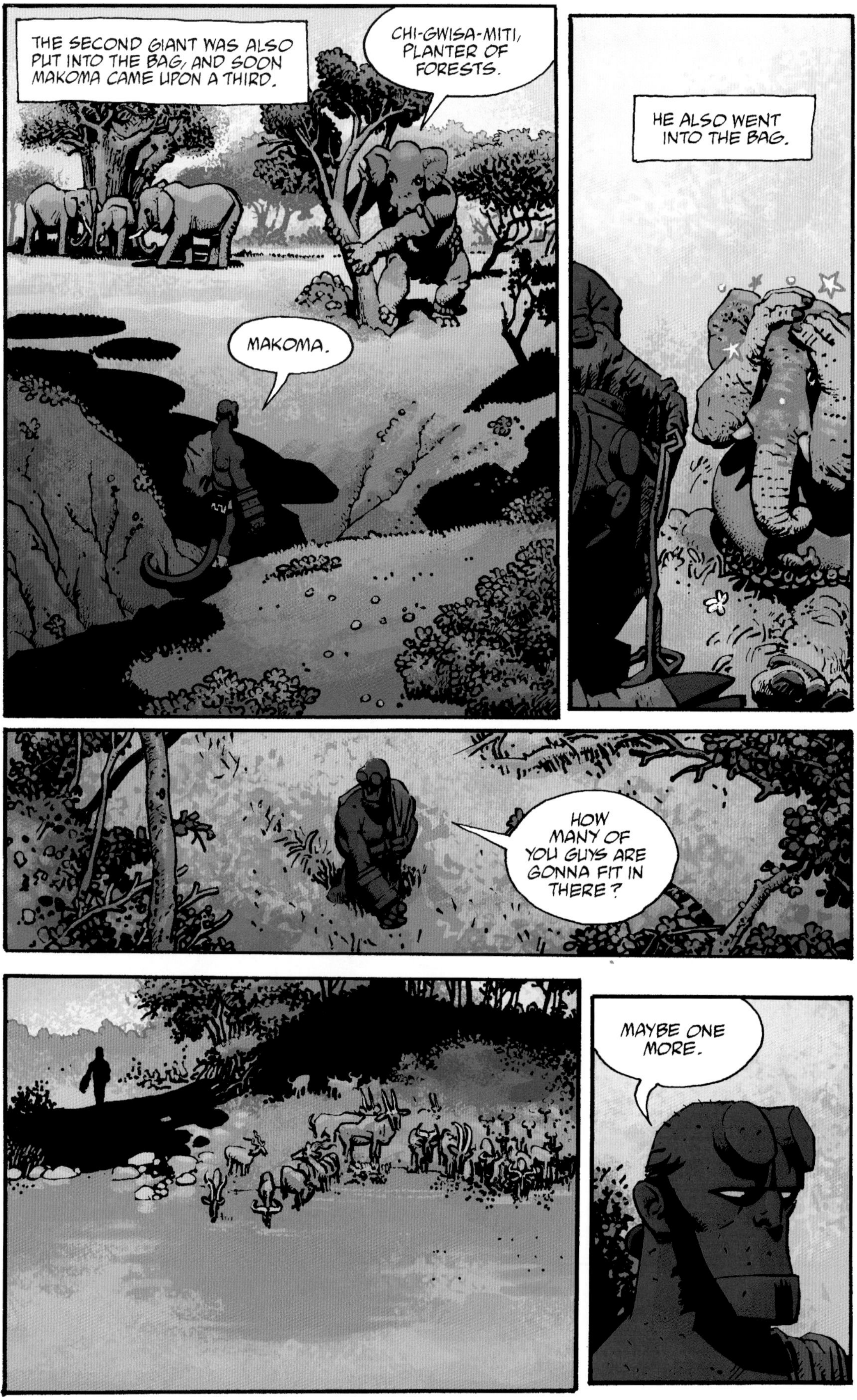
THE SECOND GIANT WAS ALSO PUT INTO THE BAG, AND SOON MAKOMA CAME UPON A THIRD.
CHI-GWISA-MITI, PLANTER OF FORESTS.
MAKOMA.
HE ALSO WENT INTO THE BAG.
HOW MANY OF YOU GUYS ARE GONNA FIT IN THERE?
MAYBE ONE MORE.

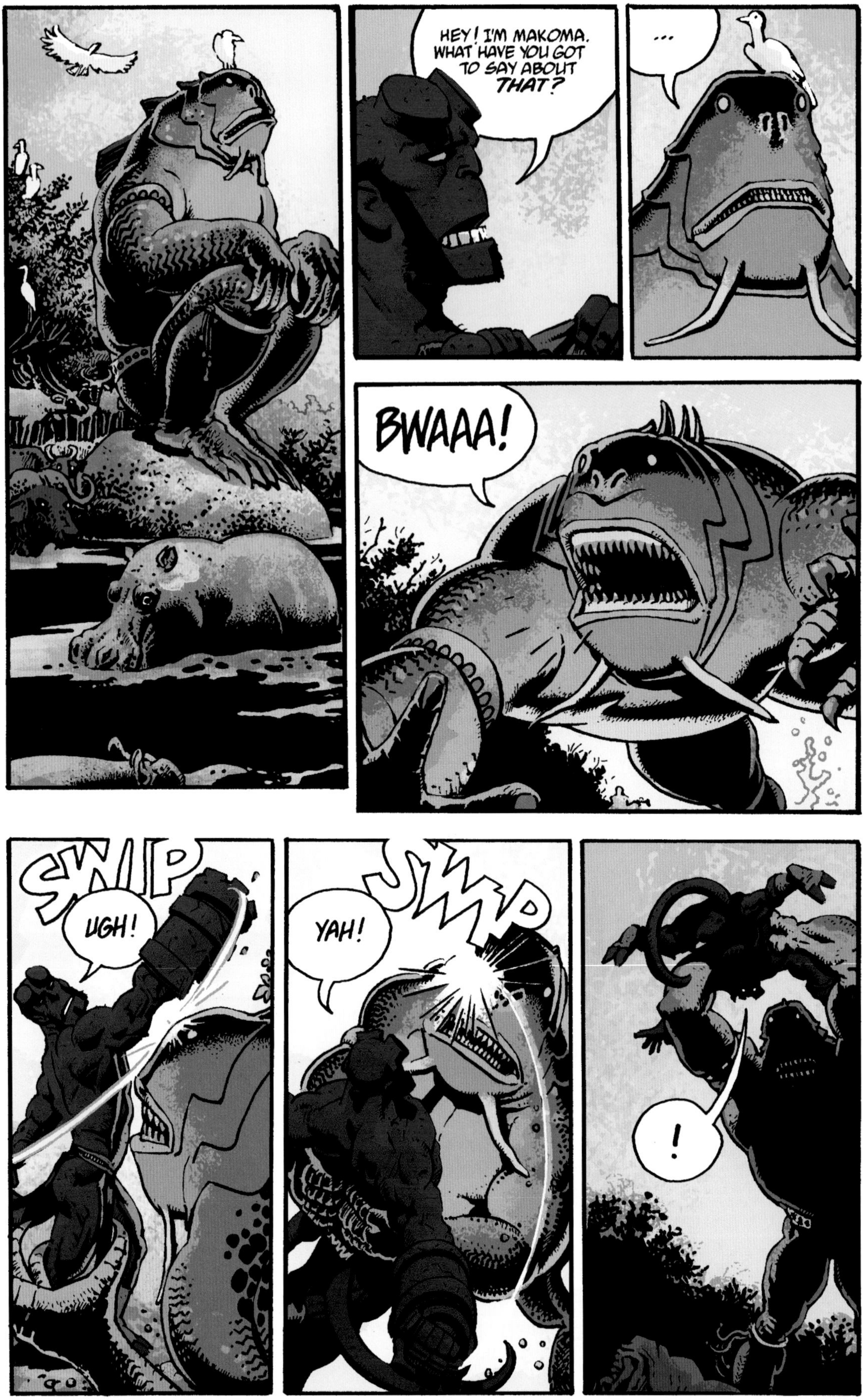
HEY! I'M MAKOMA. WHAT HAVE YOU GOT TO SAY ABOUT *THAT*?
...
BWAAA!
SWIP
UGH!
SWP
YAH!
!

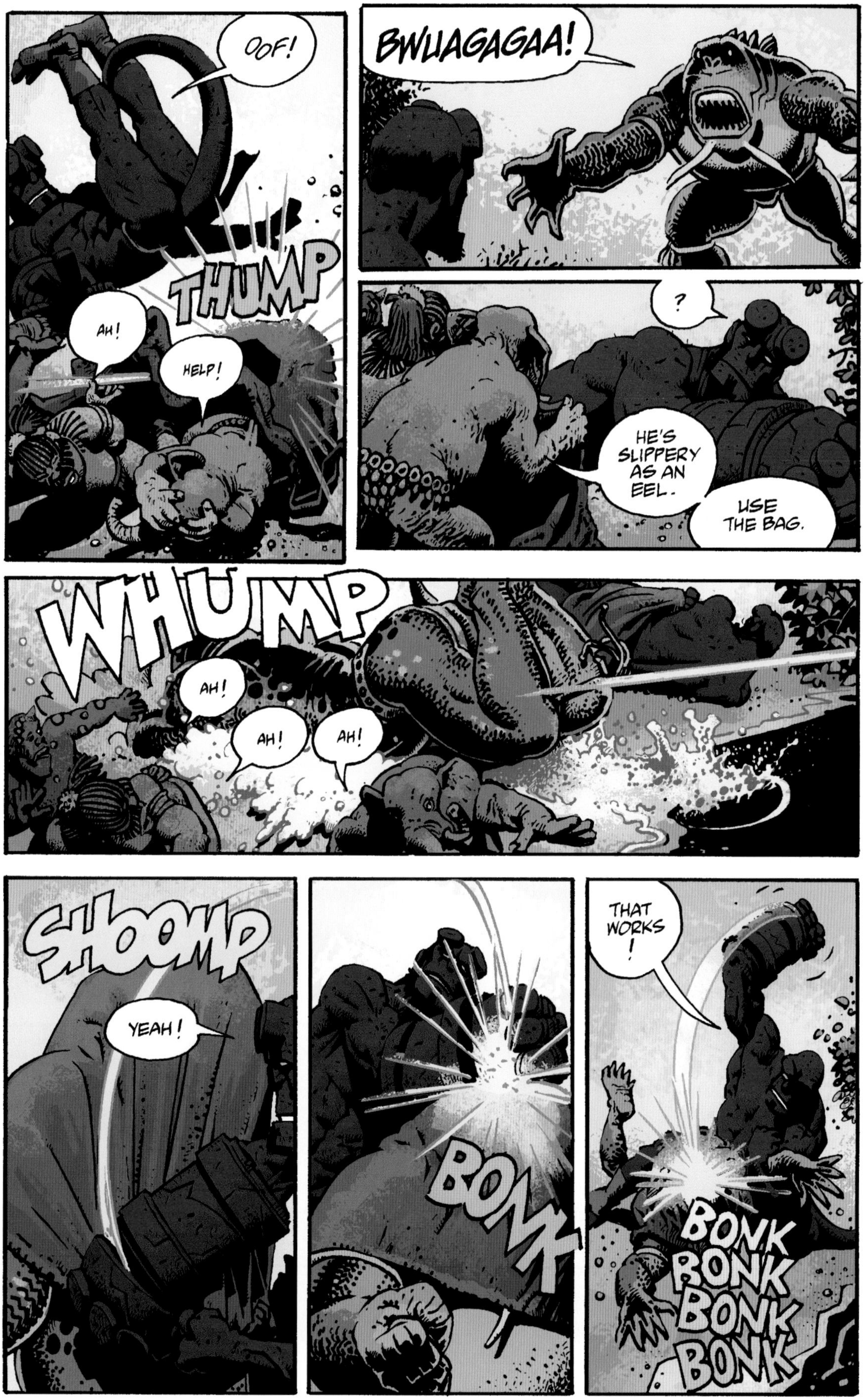
OOF!
THUMP
AH!
HELP!
BWUAGAGAA!
?
HE'S SLIPPERY AS AN EEL.
USE THE BAG.
WHUMP
AH!
AH!
AH!
SHOOMP
YEAH!
BONK
THAT WORKS!
BONK
BONK
BONK
BONK

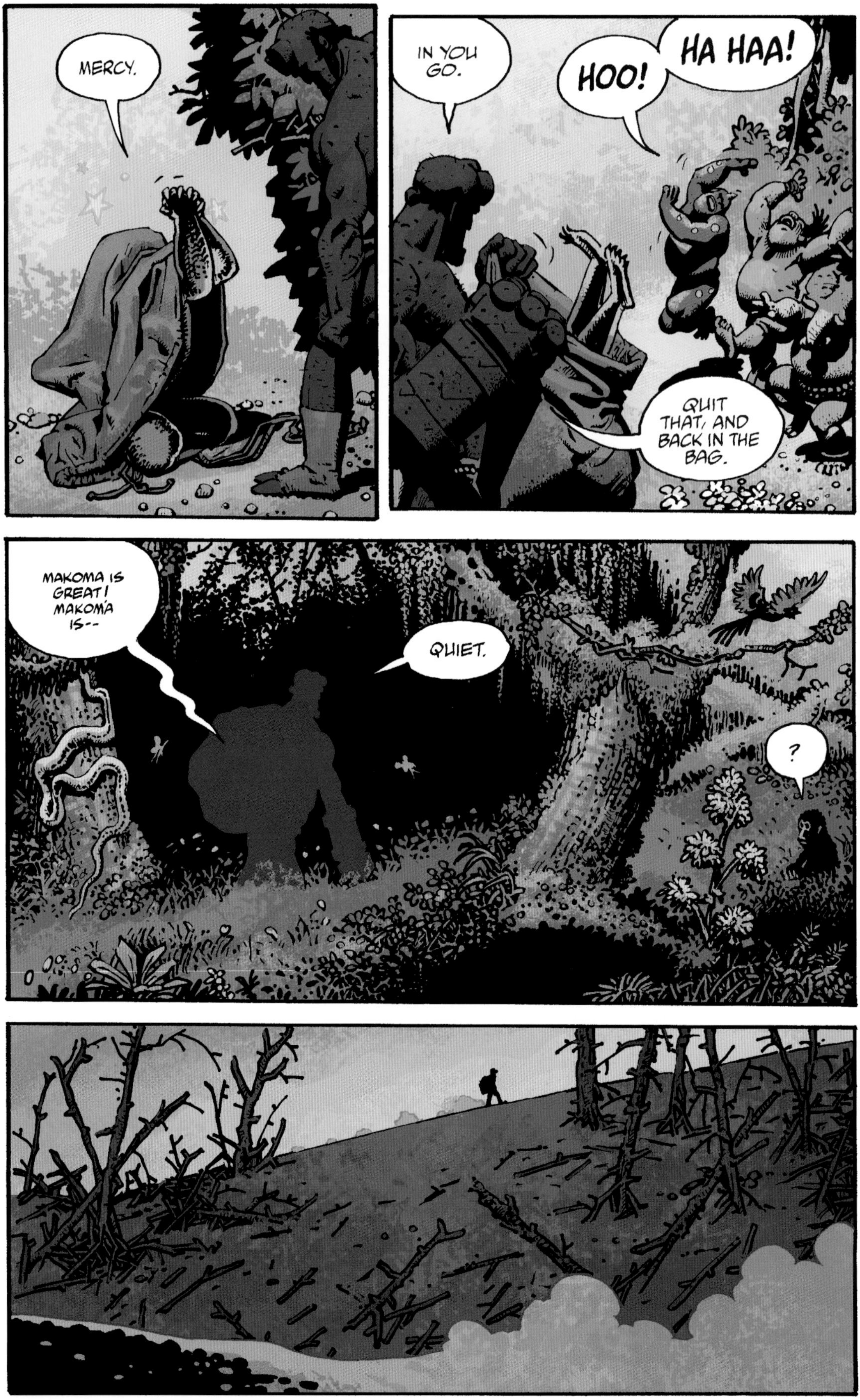
MERCY.
IN YOU GO.
HOO!
HA HAA!
QUIT THAT, AND BACK IN THE BAG.
MAKOMA IS GREAT! MAKOMA IS--
QUIET.
?

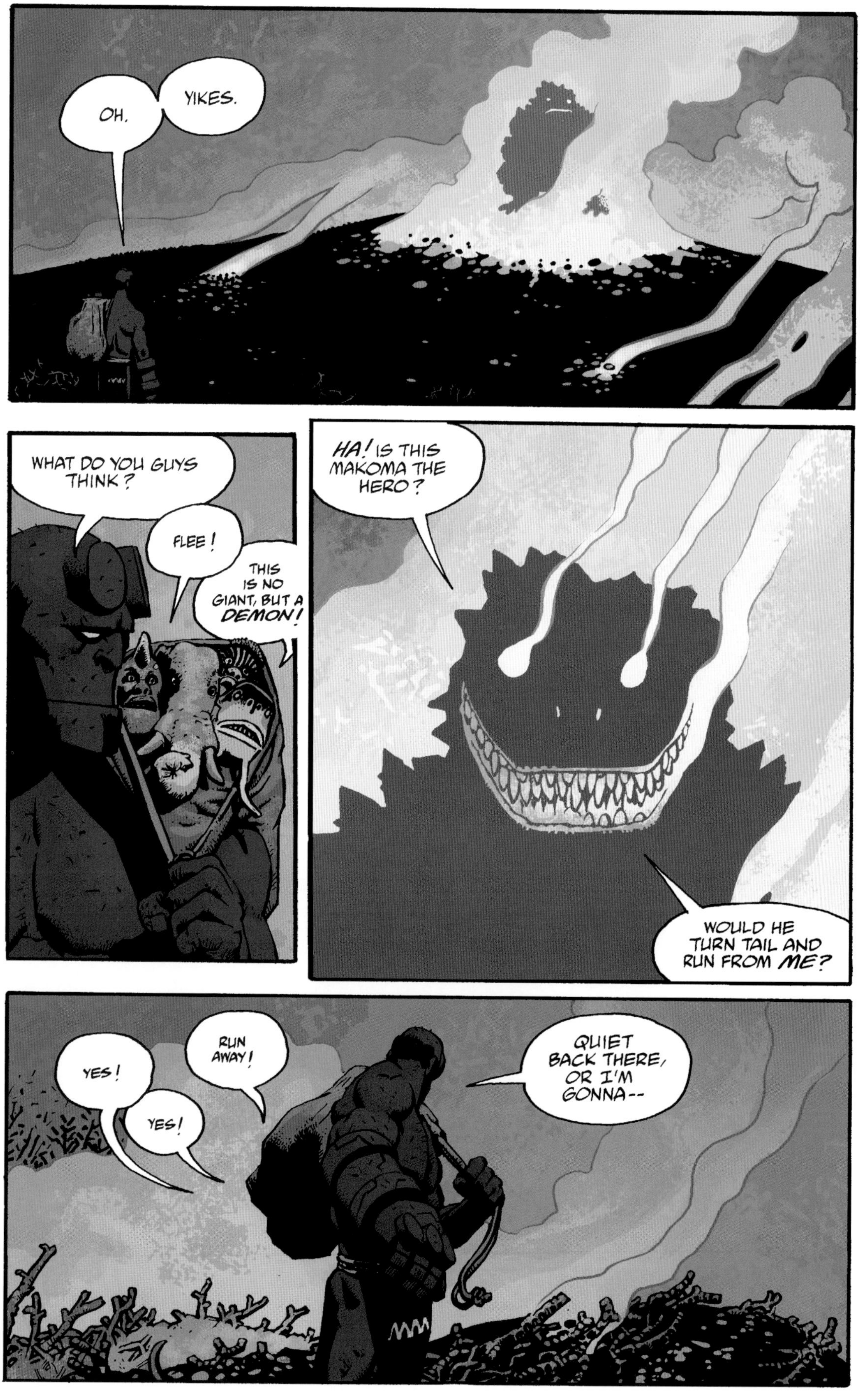
OH.
YIKES.
WHAT DO YOU GUYS THINK?
FLEE!
THIS IS NO GIANT, BUT A DEMON!
HA! IS THIS MAKOMA THE HERO?
WOULD HE TURN TAIL AND RUN FROM ME?
YES!
YES!
RUN AWAY!
QUIET BACK THERE, OR I'M GONNA--

VOOOM
OOH!
SON OF A--
HUK
HAK
COUGH
CHOKE
THUD

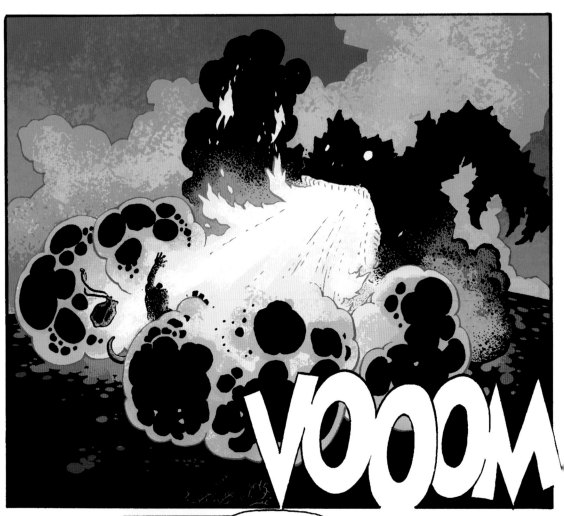

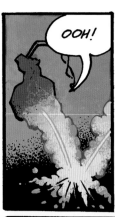

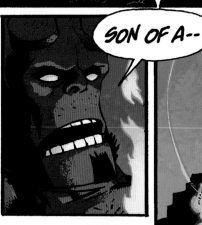

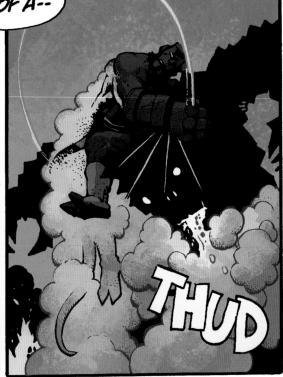

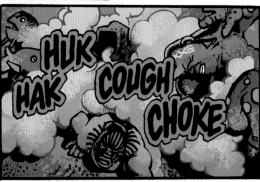

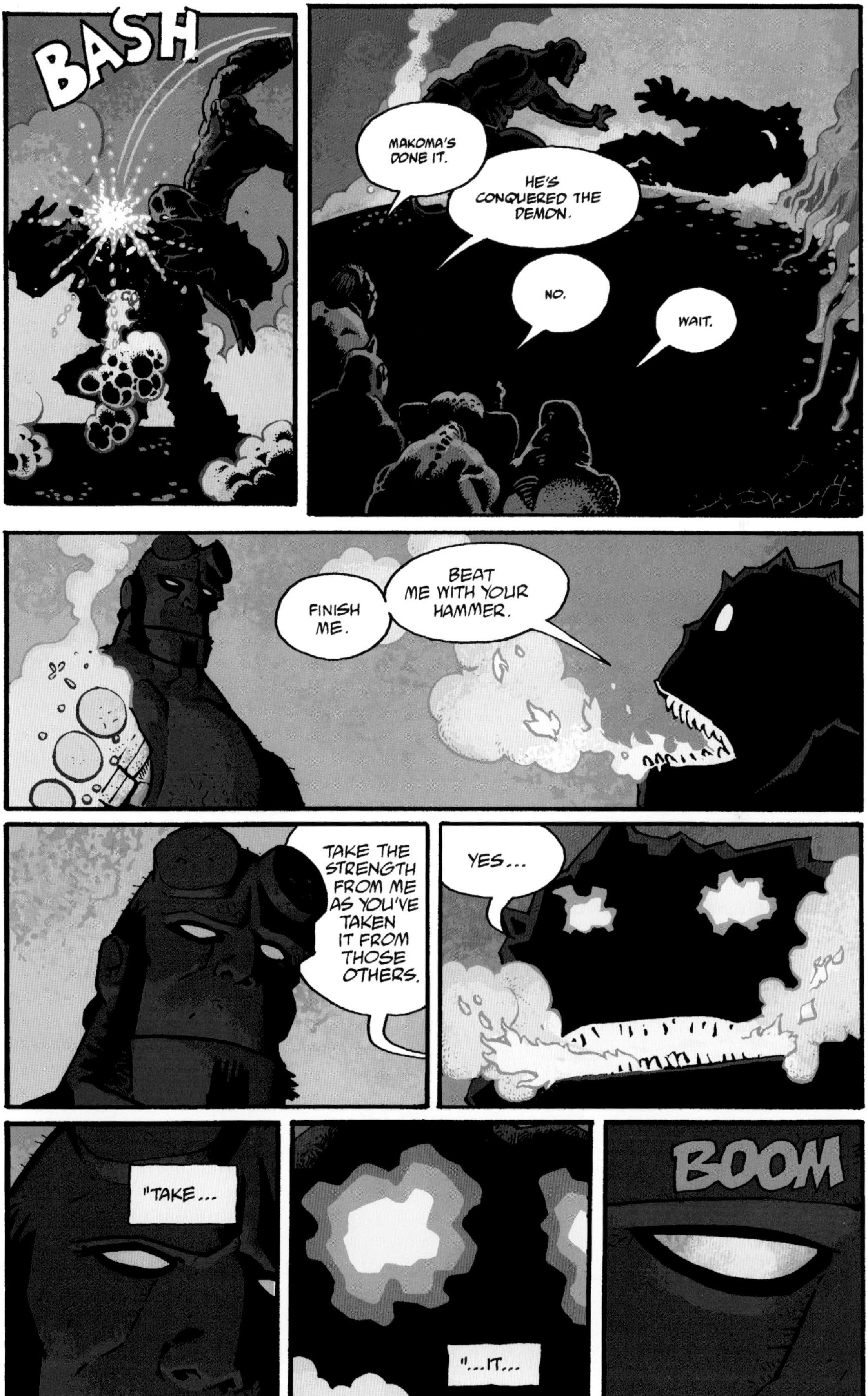
BASH
MAKOMA'S DONE IT.
HE'S CONQUERED THE DEMON.
NO.
WAIT.
FINISH ME.
BEAT ME WITH YOUR HAMMER.
TAKE THE STRENGTH FROM ME AS YOU'VE TAKEN IT FROM THOSE OTHERS.
YES...
"TAKE...
"...IT...
BOOM

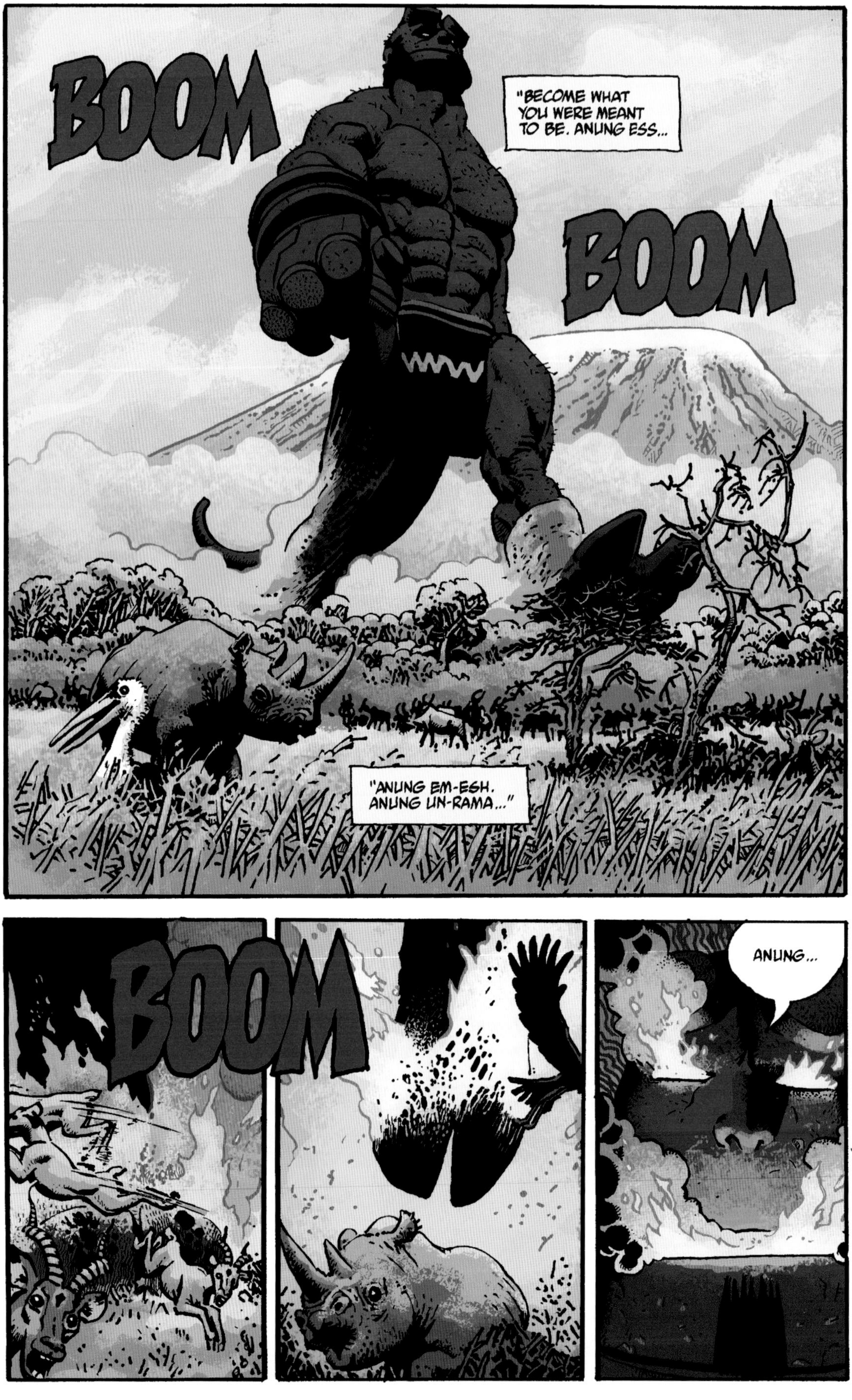
BOOM
"BECOME WHAT YOU WERE MEANT TO BE. ANUNG ESS...
BOOM
"ANUNG EM-ESH. ANUNG UN-RAMA..."
BOOM
ANUNG...

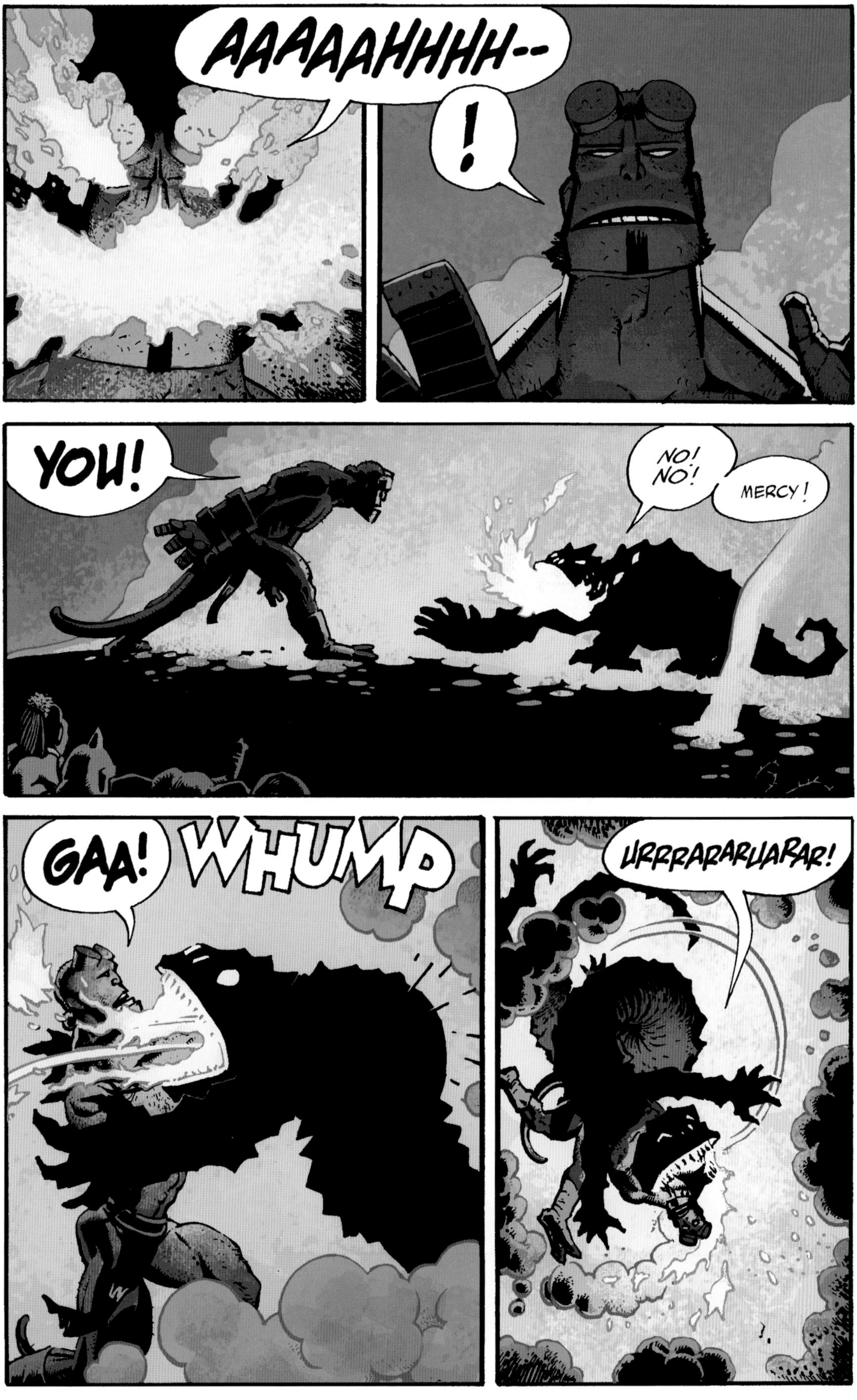
AAAAAHHHH--
!
YOU!
NO! NO!
MERCY!
GAA!
WHUMP
URRRARARUARAR!

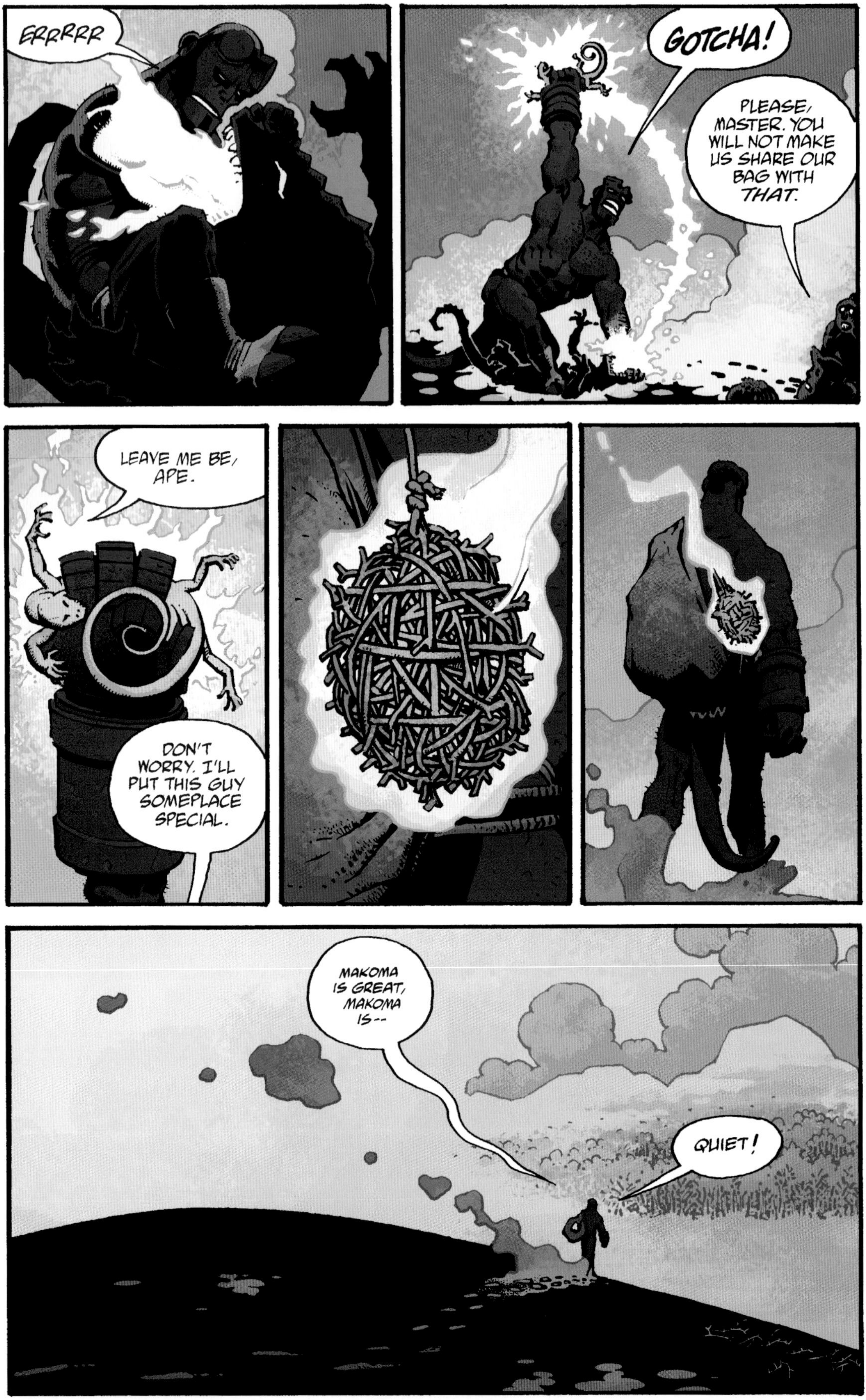
ERRRRR
GOTCHA!
PLEASE, MASTER. YOU WILL NOT MAKE US SHARE OUR BAG WITH THAT.
LEAVE ME BE, APE.
DON'T WORRY. I'LL PUT THIS GUY SOMEPLACE SPECIAL.
MAKOMA IS GREAT, MAKOMA IS--
QUIET!

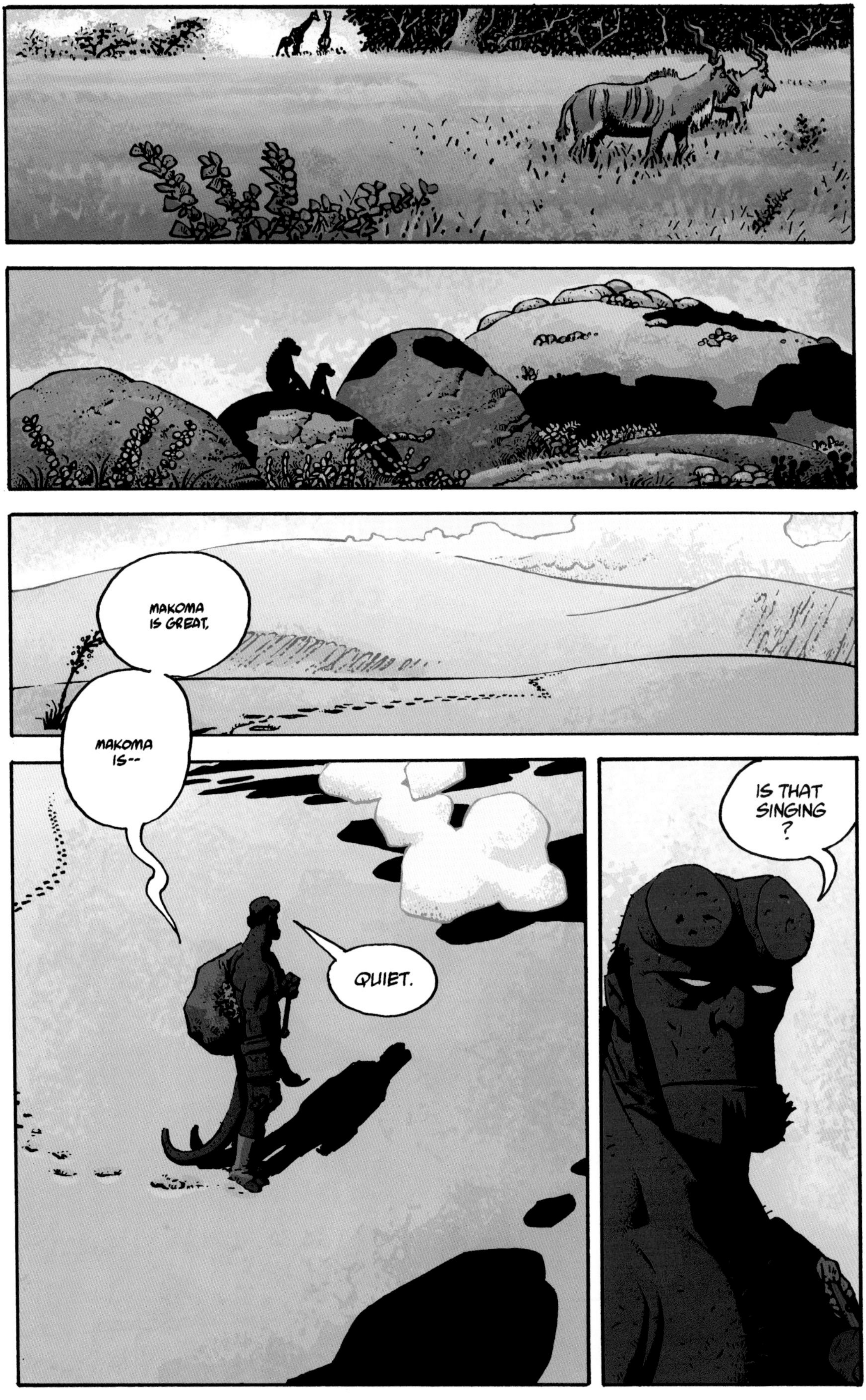
MAKOMA IS GREAT,
MAKOMA IS--
QUIET.
IS THAT SINGING?

WELCOME, HERO.

WHAT IS THIS PLACE?

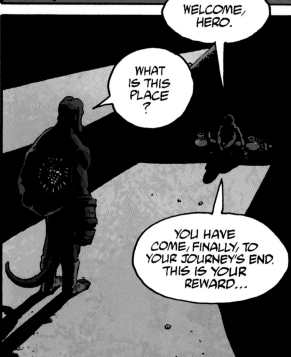

YOU HAVE COME, FINALLY, TO YOUR JOURNEY'S END. THIS IS YOUR REWARD...

PARADISE.

WHAT?

THE STRUGGLES OF YOUR LIFE ARE ENDED.

LISTEN TO THEM.

WHAT DOES THEIR SONG PROMISE?

"PEACE...

"OBLIVION.

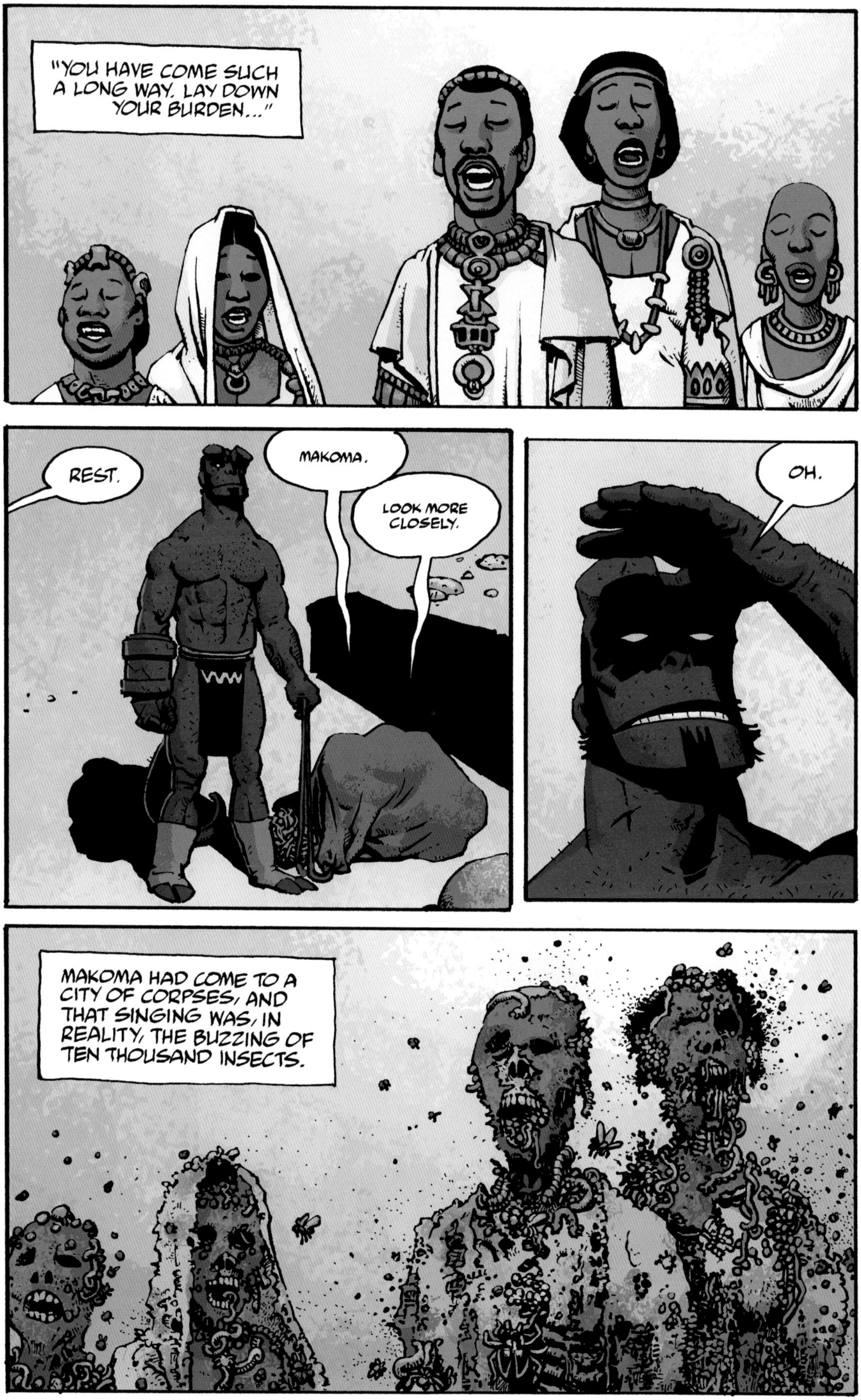
"YOU HAVE COME SUCH A LONG WAY. LAY DOWN YOUR BURDEN..."
REST.
MAKOMA.
LOOK MORE CLOSELY.
OH.
MAKOMA HAD COME TO A CITY OF CORPSES, AND THAT SINGING WAS, IN REALITY, THE BUZZING OF TEN THOUSAND INSECTS.

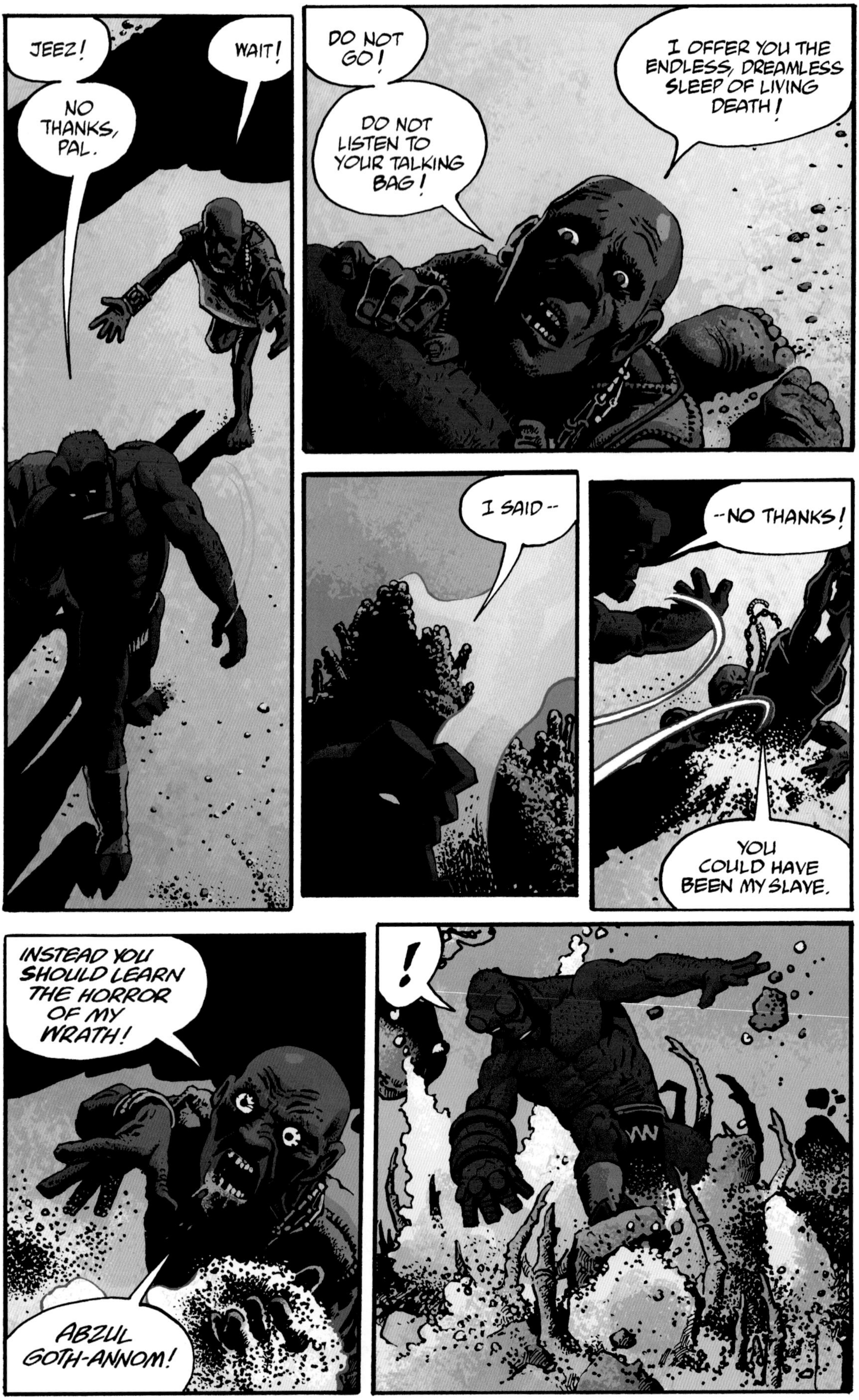
JEEZ!
WAIT!
NO THANKS, PAL.
DO NOT GO!
DO NOT LISTEN TO YOUR TALKING BAG!
I OFFER YOU THE ENDLESS, DREAMLESS SLEEP OF LIVING DEATH!
I SAID--
--NO THANKS!
YOU COULD HAVE BEEN MY SLAVE.
INSTEAD YOU SHOULD LEARN THE HORROR OF MY WRATH!
ABZUL GOTH-ANNOM!
!

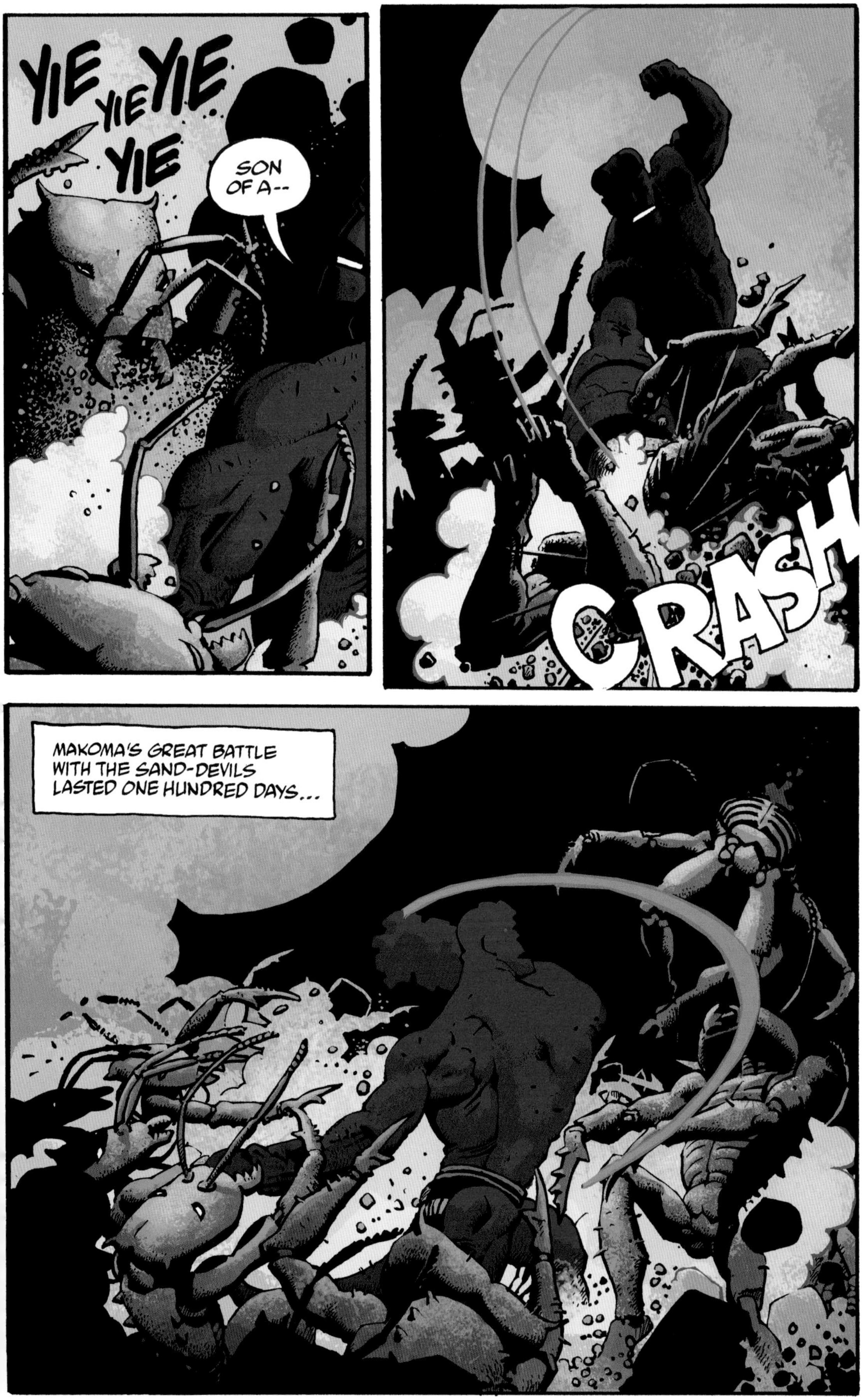
YIE YIE YIE YIE YIE
SON OF A--
CRASH
MAKOMA'S GREAT BATTLE WITH THE SAND-DEVILS LASTED ONE HUNDRED DAYS...

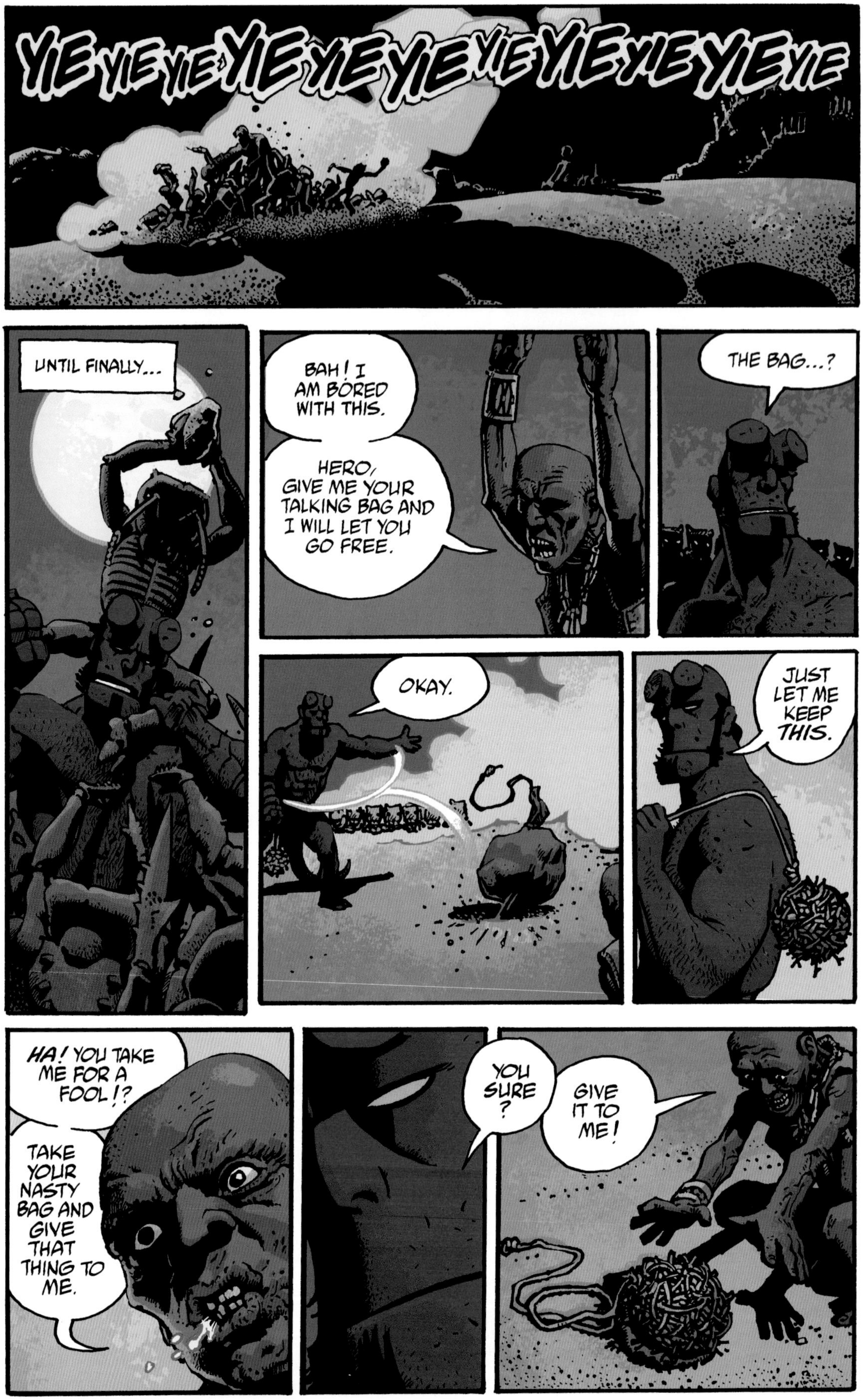
YIE YIE YIE YIE YIE YIE YIE YIE YIE YIE YIE YIE
UNTIL FINALLY...
BAH! I AM BORED WITH THIS.
HERO, GIVE ME YOUR TALKING BAG AND I WILL LET YOU GO FREE.
THE BAG...?
OKAY.
JUST LET ME KEEP THIS.
HA! YOU TAKE ME FOR A FOOL!?
TAKE YOUR NASTY BAG AND GIVE THAT THING TO ME.
YOU SURE?
GIVE IT TO ME!

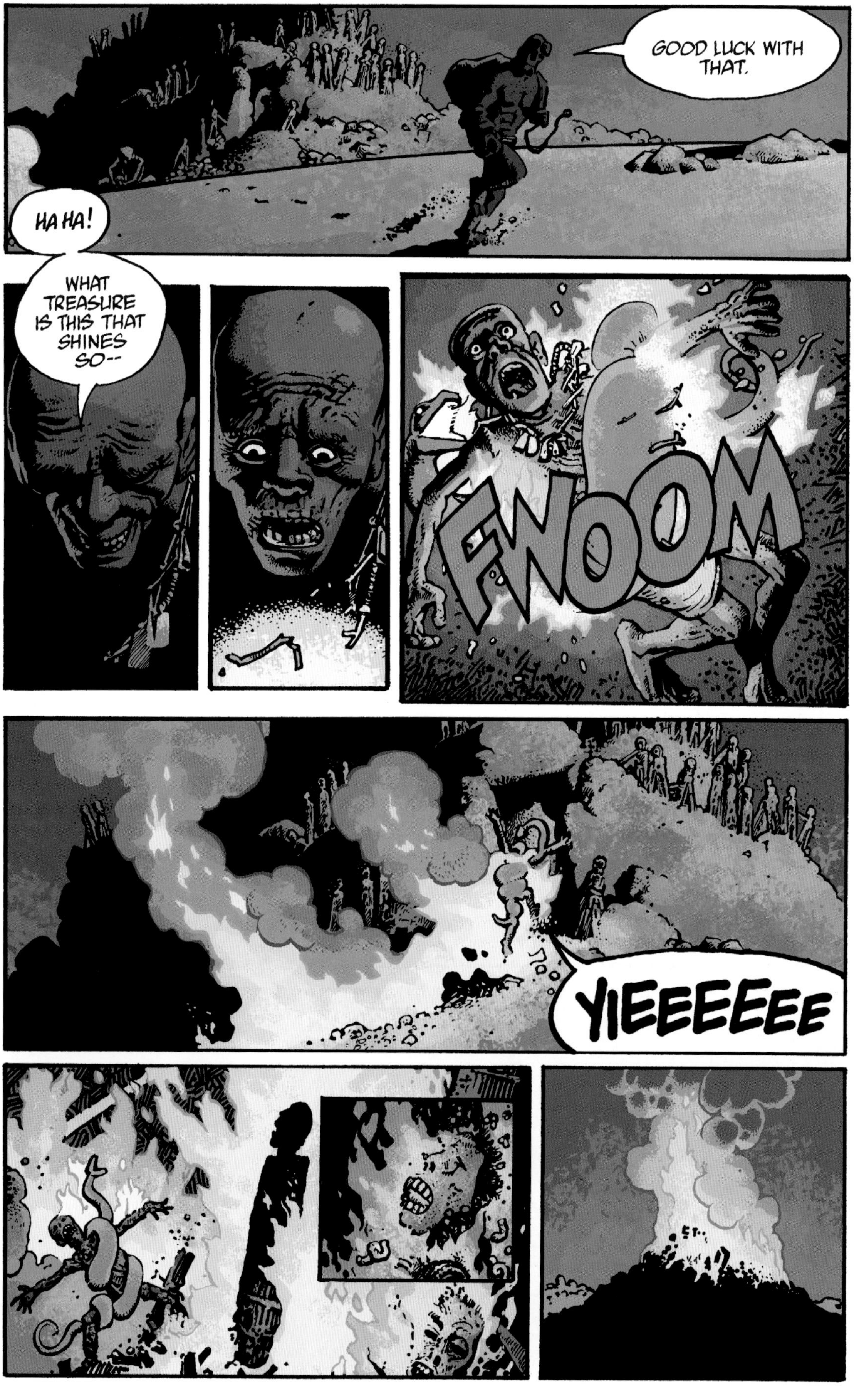
GOOD LUCK WITH THAT.
HA HA!
WHAT TREASURE IS THIS THAT SHINES SO--
FWOOM
YIEEEEEEE

SO THE EVIL MAN LOOSED THE FIRE DEMON, TO HIS OWN DESTRUCTION, AND THE RUIN OF ALL HIS EVIL WORKS.

AND MAKOMA, HAMMER AND BAG, WENT ON...

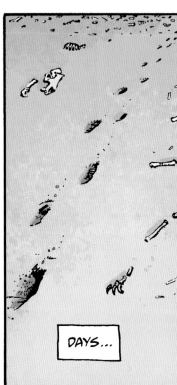

DAYS...

MONTHS...

YEARS...

UNTIL EVEN HIS GREAT STRENGTH RAN OUT.

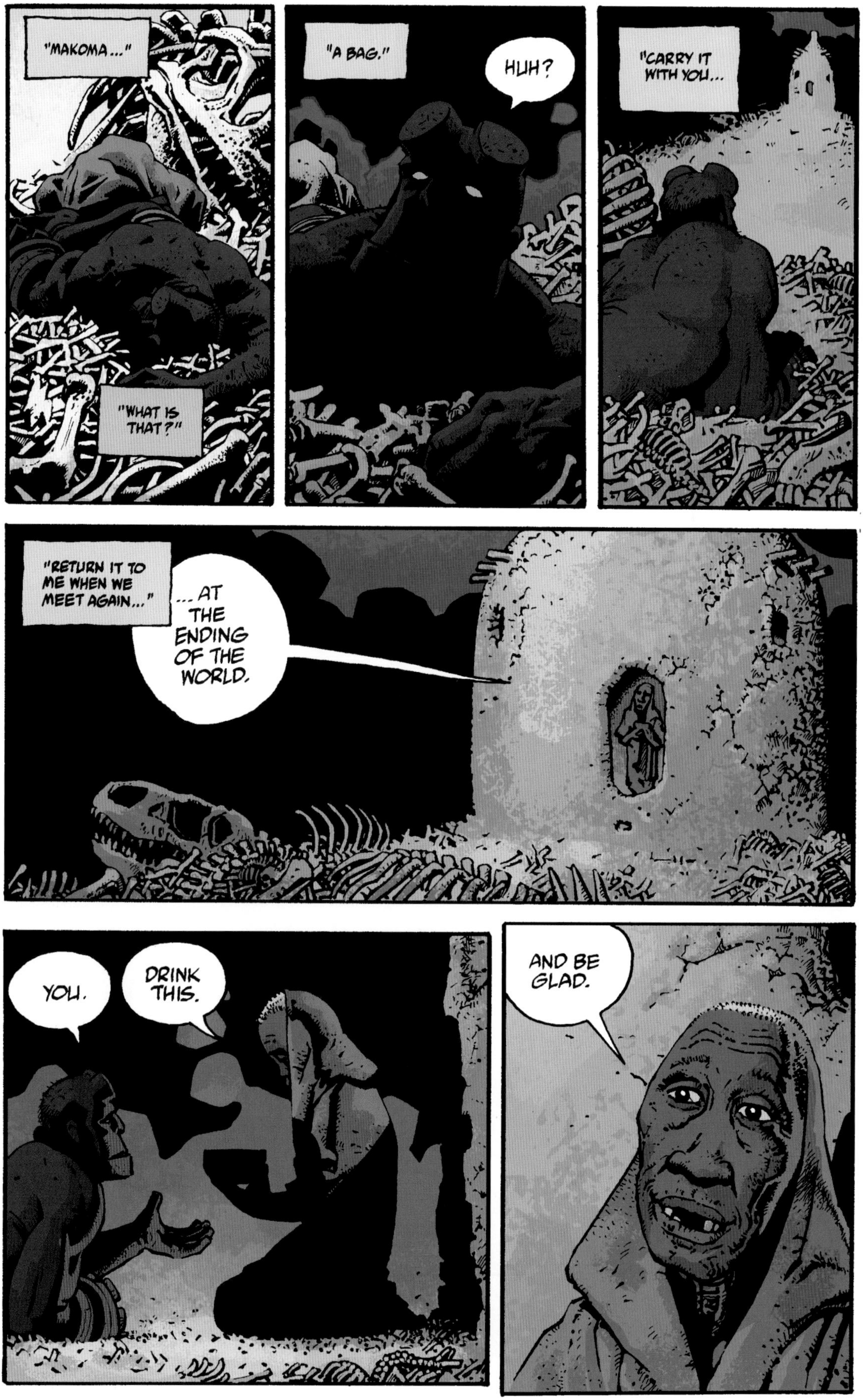
"MAKOMA..."
"WHAT IS THAT?"
"A BAG."
HUH?
"CARRY IT WITH YOU...
"RETURN IT TO ME WHEN WE MEET AGAIN..."
...AT THE ENDING OF THE WORLD.
YOU.
DRINK THIS.
AND BE GLAD.

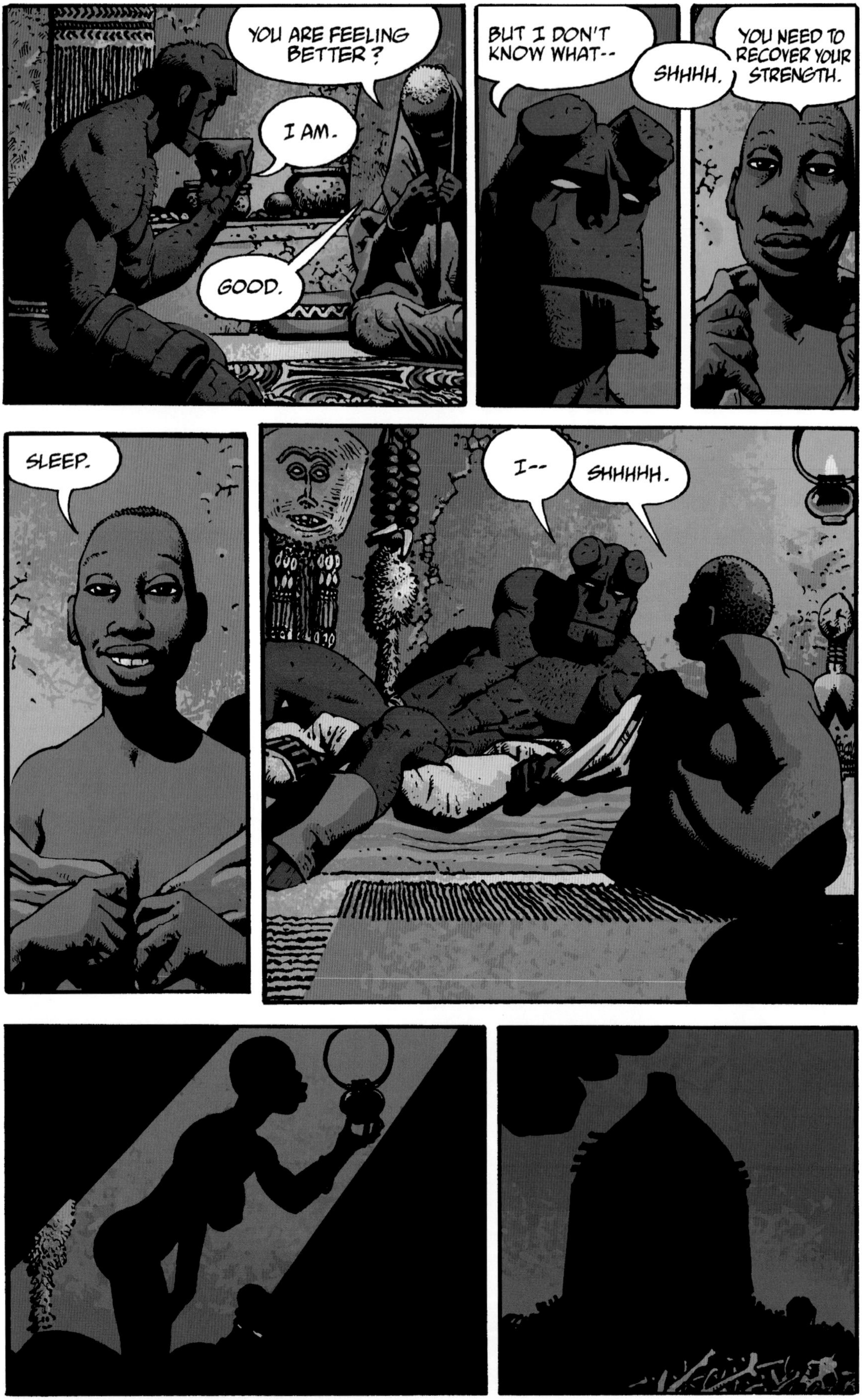
YOU ARE FEELING BETTER?
I AM.
GOOD.
BUT I DON'T KNOW WHAT--
SHHHH.
YOU NEED TO RECOVER YOUR STRENGTH.
SLEEP.
I--
SHHHHH.

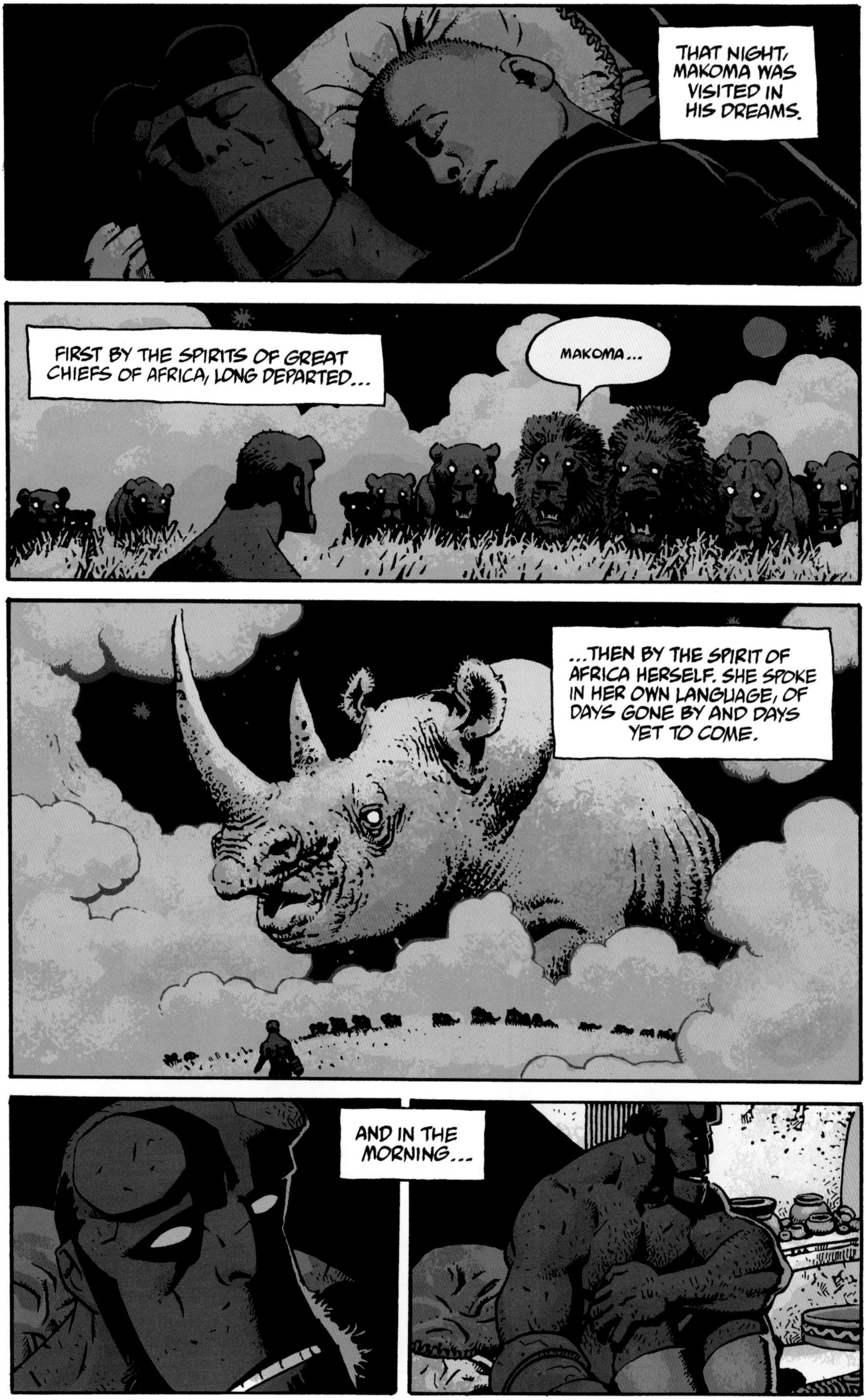
THAT NIGHT, MAKOMA WAS VISITED IN HIS DREAMS.
FIRST BY THE SPIRITS OF GREAT CHIEFS OF AFRICA, LONG DEPARTED...
MAKOMA...
...THEN BY THE SPIRIT OF AFRICA HERSELF. SHE SPOKE IN HER OWN LANGUAGE, OF DAYS GONE BY AND DAYS YET TO COME.
AND IN THE MORNING...

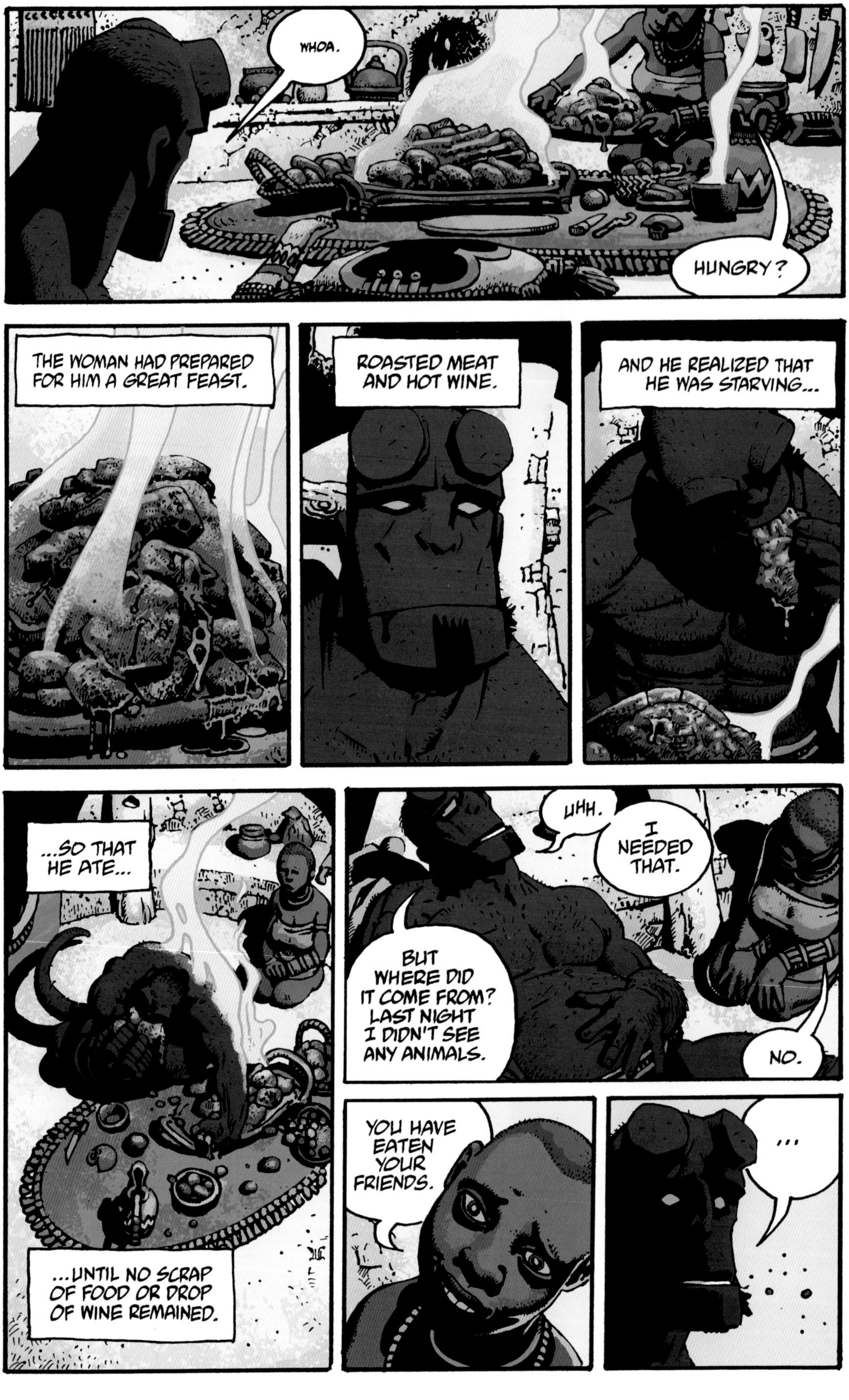
WHOA.
HUNGRY?
THE WOMAN HAD PREPARED FOR HIM A GREAT FEAST.
ROASTED MEAT AND HOT WINE.
AND HE REALIZED THAT HE WAS STARVING...
...SO THAT HE ATE...
...UNTIL NO SCRAP OF FOOD OR DROP OF WINE REMAINED.
UHH.
I NEEDED THAT.
BUT WHERE DID IT COME FROM? LAST NIGHT I DIDN'T SEE ANY ANIMALS.
NO.
YOU HAVE EATEN YOUR FRIENDS.
...

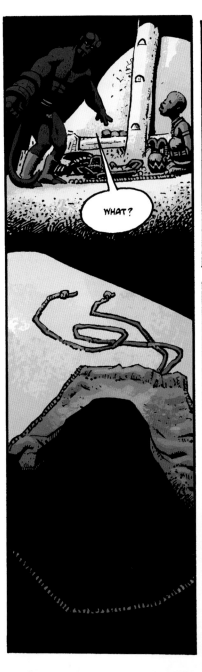

WHAT?

AH...

NO.

WHO'S THE BOY?

HE IS THE LIFE YOU GAVE BACK TO THE WORLD.

YEARS AGO, HE WAS POSSESSED BY A FIRE DEMON...

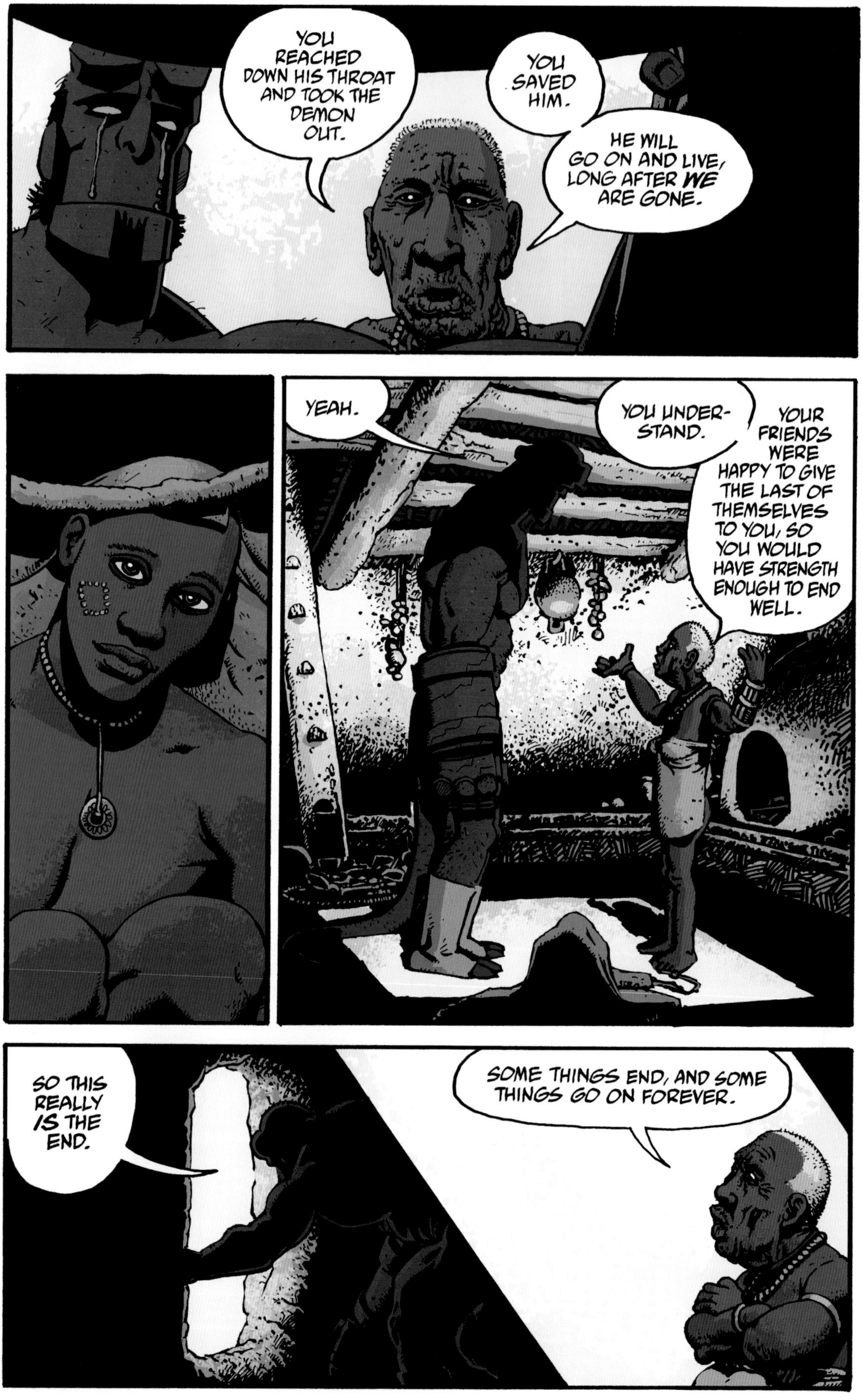
YOU REACHED DOWN HIS THROAT AND TOOK THE DEMON OUT.
YOU SAVED HIM.
HE WILL GO ON AND LIVE, LONG AFTER *WE* ARE GONE.
YEAH.
YOU UNDER-STAND.
YOUR FRIENDS WERE HAPPY TO GIVE THE LAST OF THEMSELVES TO YOU, SO YOU WOULD HAVE STRENGTH ENOUGH TO END WELL.
SO THIS REALLY *IS* THE END.
SOME THINGS END, AND SOME THINGS GO ON FOREVER.

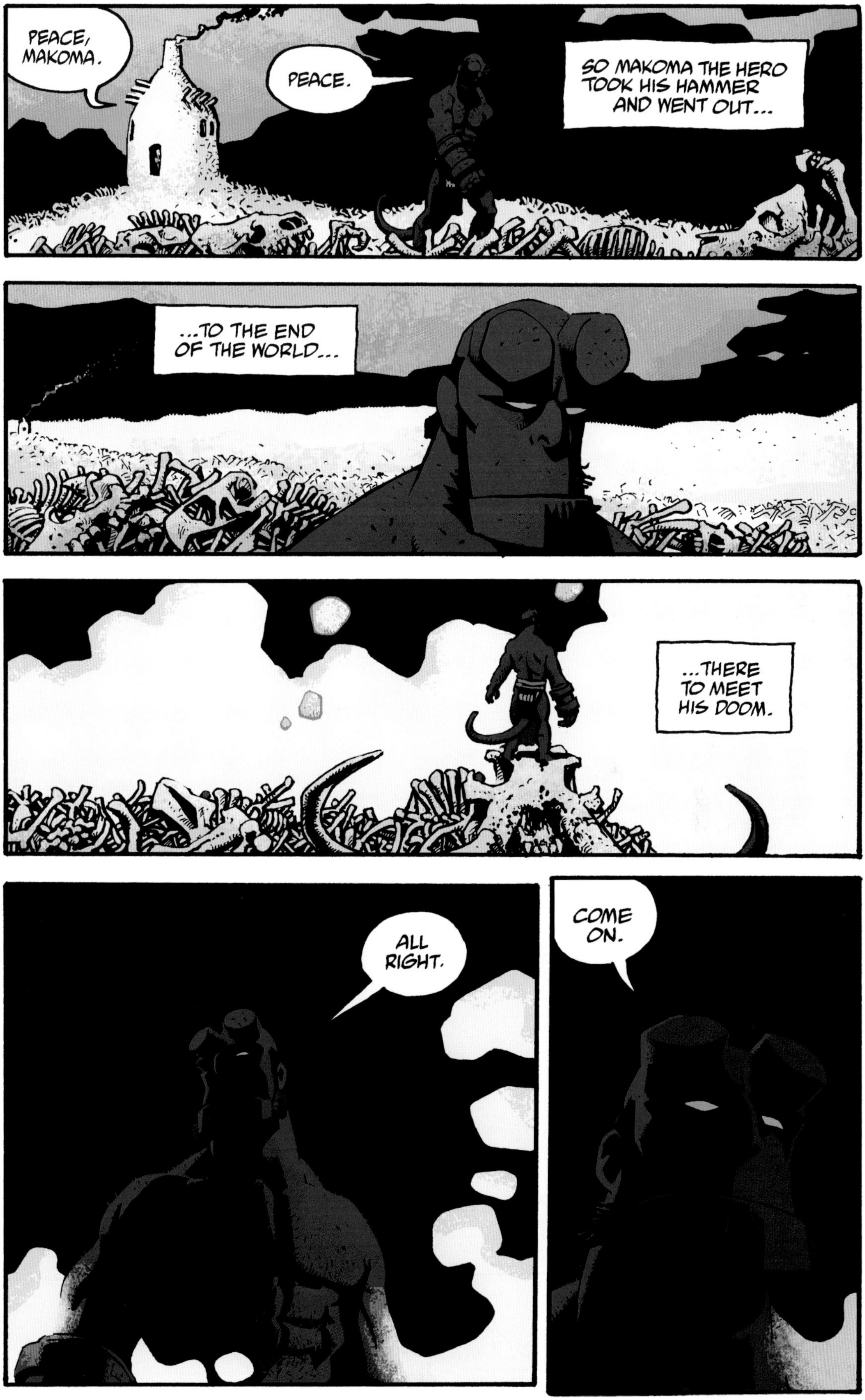
PEACE, MAKOMA.
PEACE.
SO MAKOMA THE HERO TOOK HIS HAMMER AND WENT OUT...
...TO THE END OF THE WORLD...
...THERE TO MEET HIS DOOM.
ALL RIGHT.
COME ON.

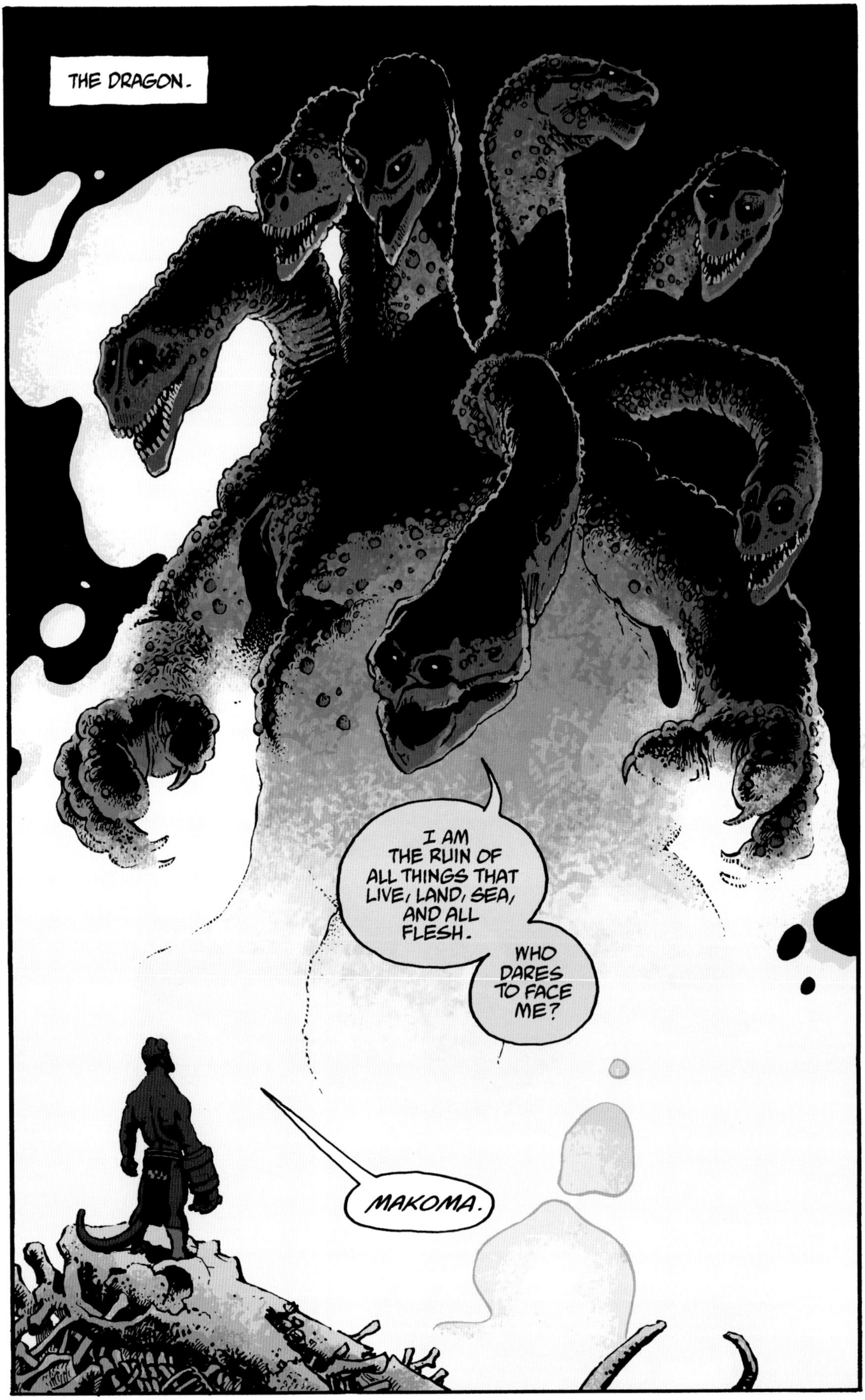
THE DRAGON.
I AM THE RUIN OF ALL THINGS THAT LIVE, LAND, SEA, AND ALL FLESH.
WHO DARES TO FACE ME?
MAKOMA.

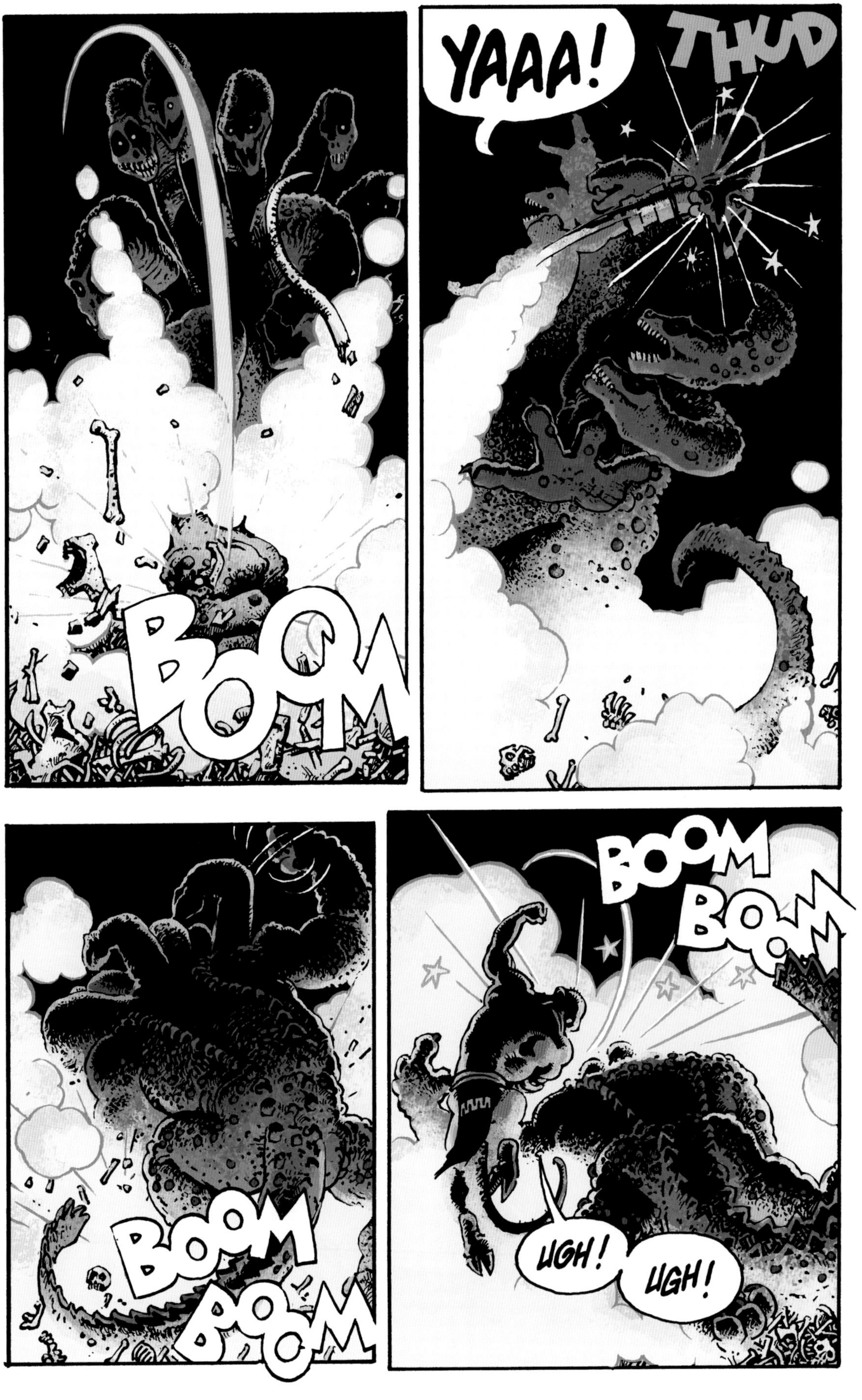
BOOM
YAAA!
THUD
BOOM
BOOM
BOOM
BOOM
UGH!
UGH!

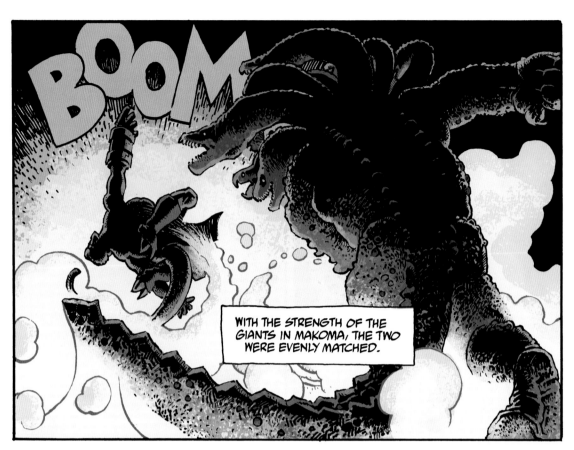

WITH THE STRENGTH OF THE GIANTS IN MAKOMA, THE TWO WERE EVENLY MATCHED.

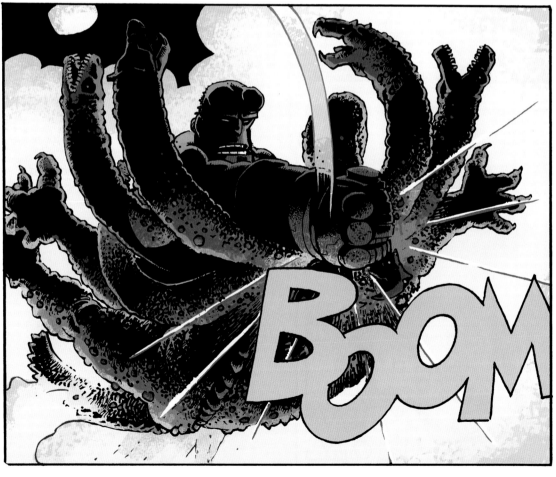

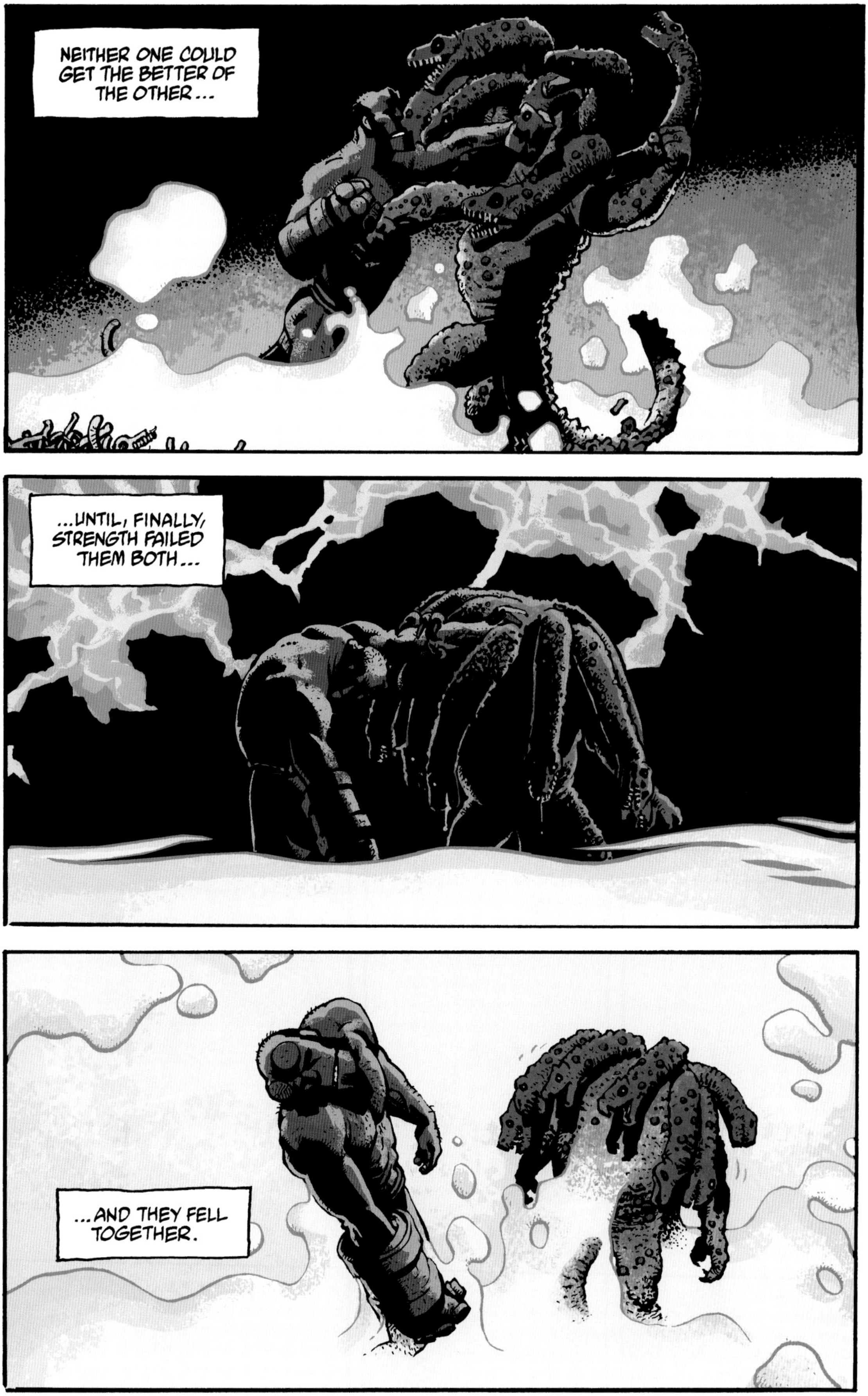
NEITHER ONE COULD GET THE BETTER OF THE OTHER...
...UNTIL, FINALLY, STRENGTH FAILED THEM BOTH...
...AND THEY FELL TOGETHER.

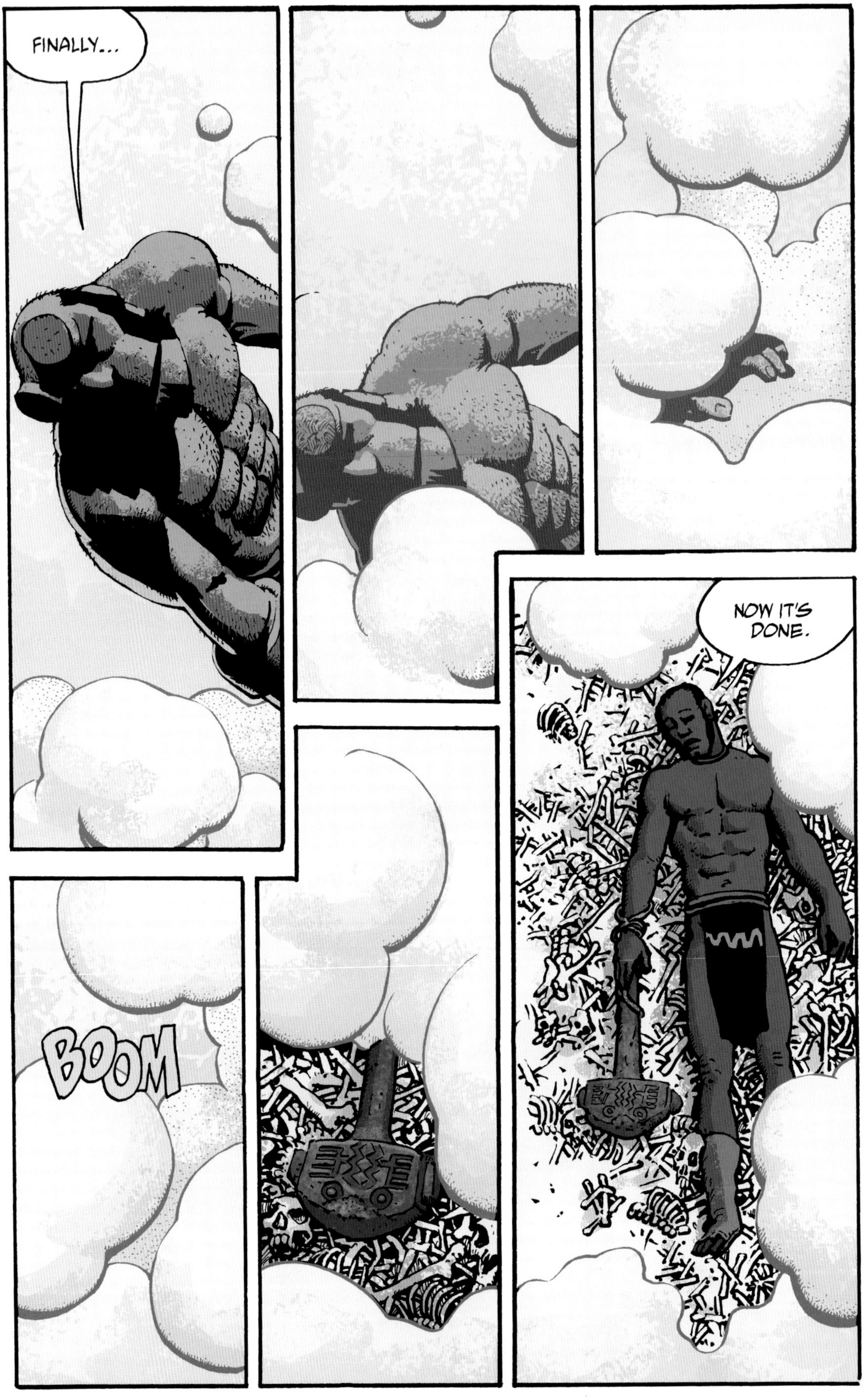
FINALLY...
NOW IT'S DONE.
BOOM

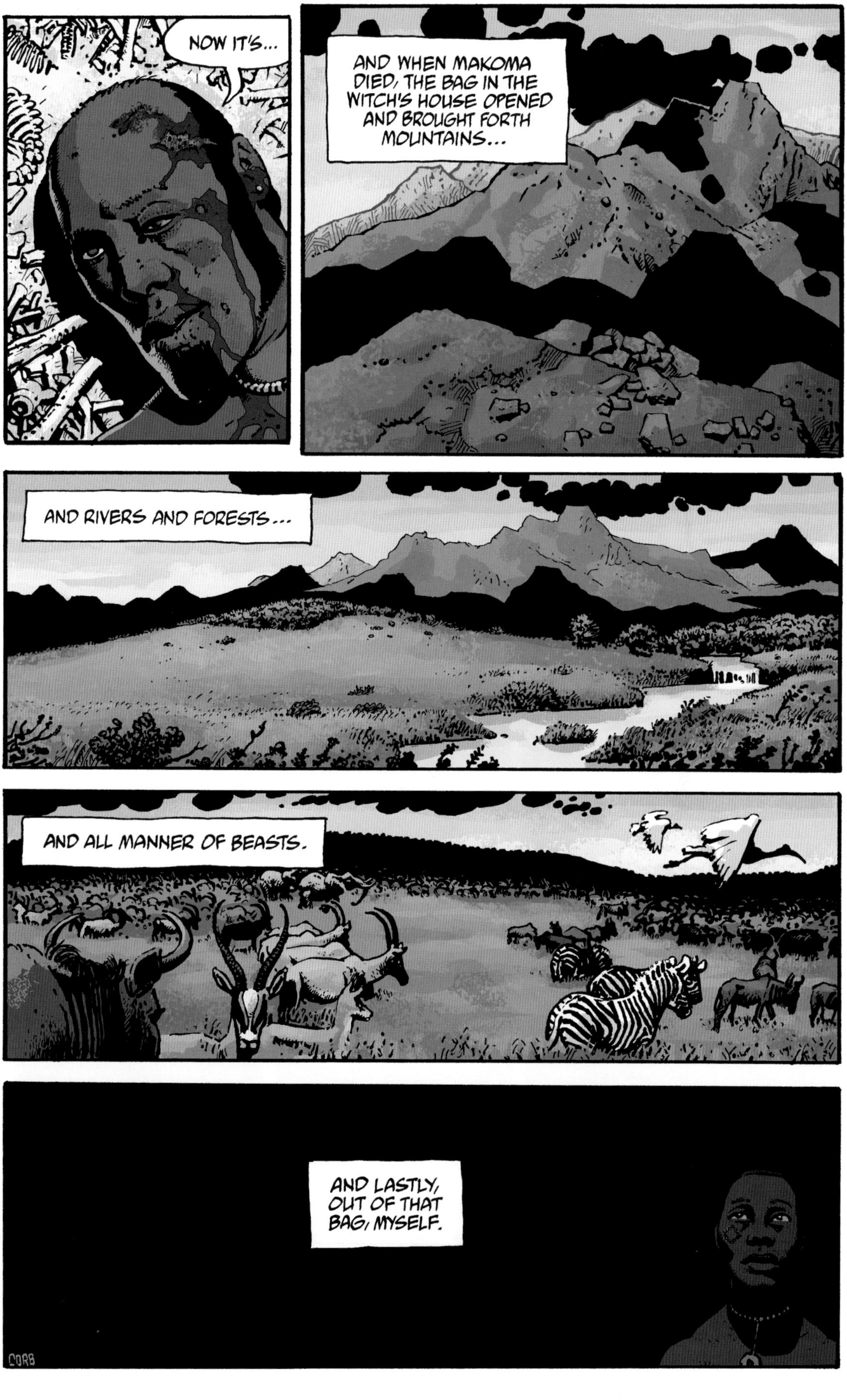
NOW IT'S...
AND WHEN MAKOMA DIED, THE BAG IN THE WITCH'S HOUSE OPENED AND BROUGHT FORTH MOUNTAINS...
AND RIVERS AND FORESTS...
AND ALL MANNER OF BEASTS.
AND LASTLY, OUT OF THAT BAG, MYSELF.
CORB

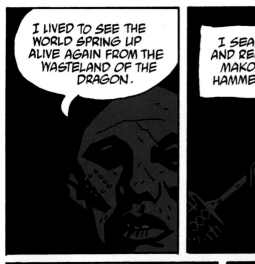

I LIVED TO SEE THE WORLD SPRING UP ALIVE AGAIN FROM THE WASTELAND OF THE DRAGON.

I SEARCHED FAR AND RECOVERED MAKOMA'S HAMMER AND BONES...

...AND BROUGHT THEM HERE.

WITH MY OWN HANDS I CARVED HIS MONUMENT AND HIS TOMB.

AND I WENT ON TO LIVE FIVE HUNDRED YEARS, TO HAVE WIVES AND CHILDREN, BUT ALWAYS IN THE SHADOW OF HIS LIFE.

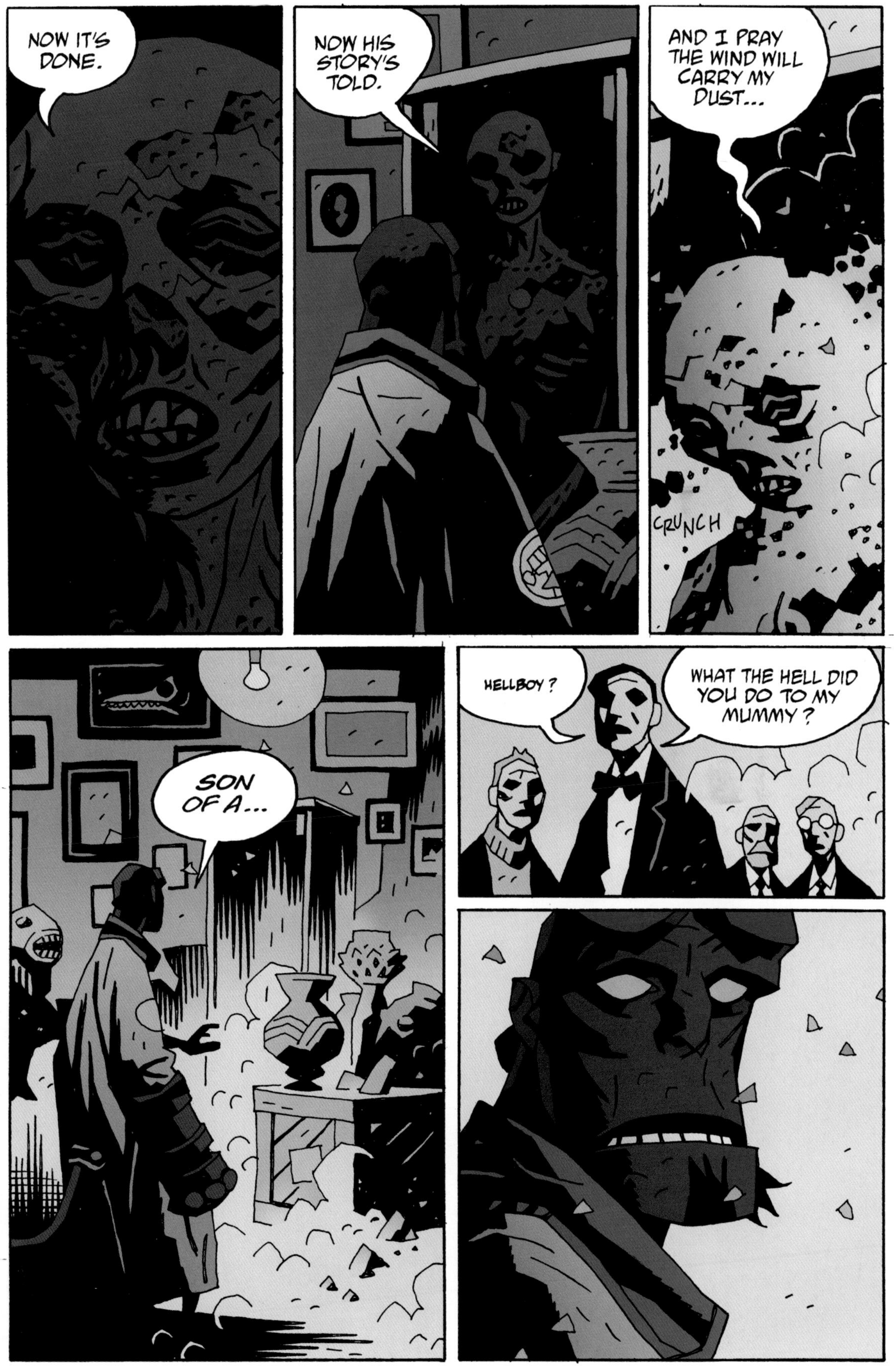
NOW IT'S DONE.
NOW HIS STORY'S TOLD.
AND I PRAY THE WIND WILL CARRY MY DUST...
CRUNCH
SON OF A...
HELLBOY ?
WHAT THE HELL DID YOU DO TO MY MUMMY ?

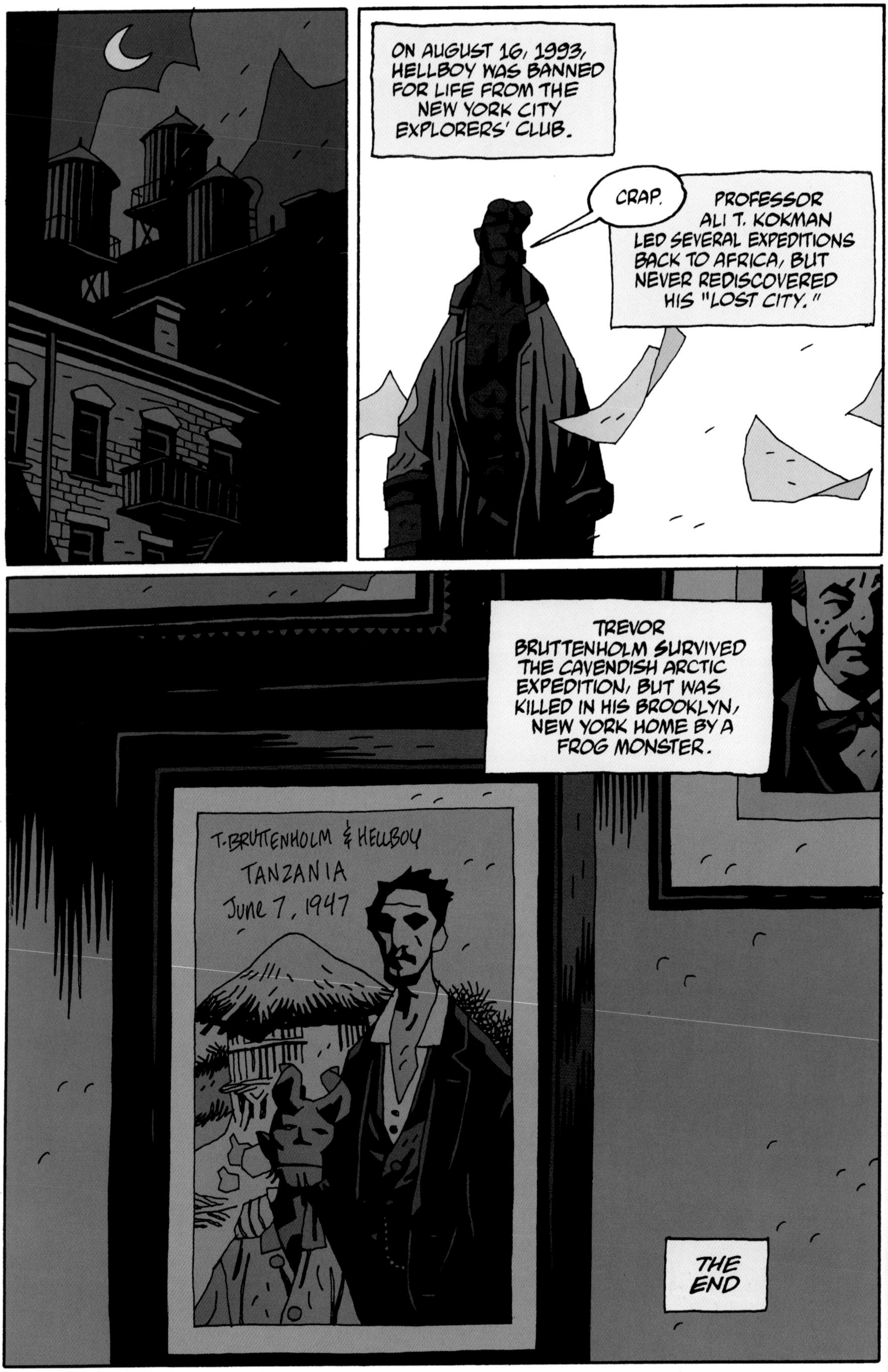
ON AUGUST 16, 1993, HELLBOY WAS BANNED FOR LIFE FROM THE NEW YORK CITY EXPLORERS' CLUB.
CRAP.
PROFESSOR ALI T. KOKMAN LED SEVERAL EXPEDITIONS BACK TO AFRICA, BUT NEVER REDISCOVERED HIS "LOST CITY."
TREVOR BRUTTENHOLM SURVIVED THE CAVENDISH ARCTIC EXPEDITION, BUT WAS KILLED IN HIS BROOKLYN, NEW YORK HOME BY A FROG MONSTER.
T. BRUTTENHOLM & HELLBOY
TANZANIA
June 7, 1947
THE END

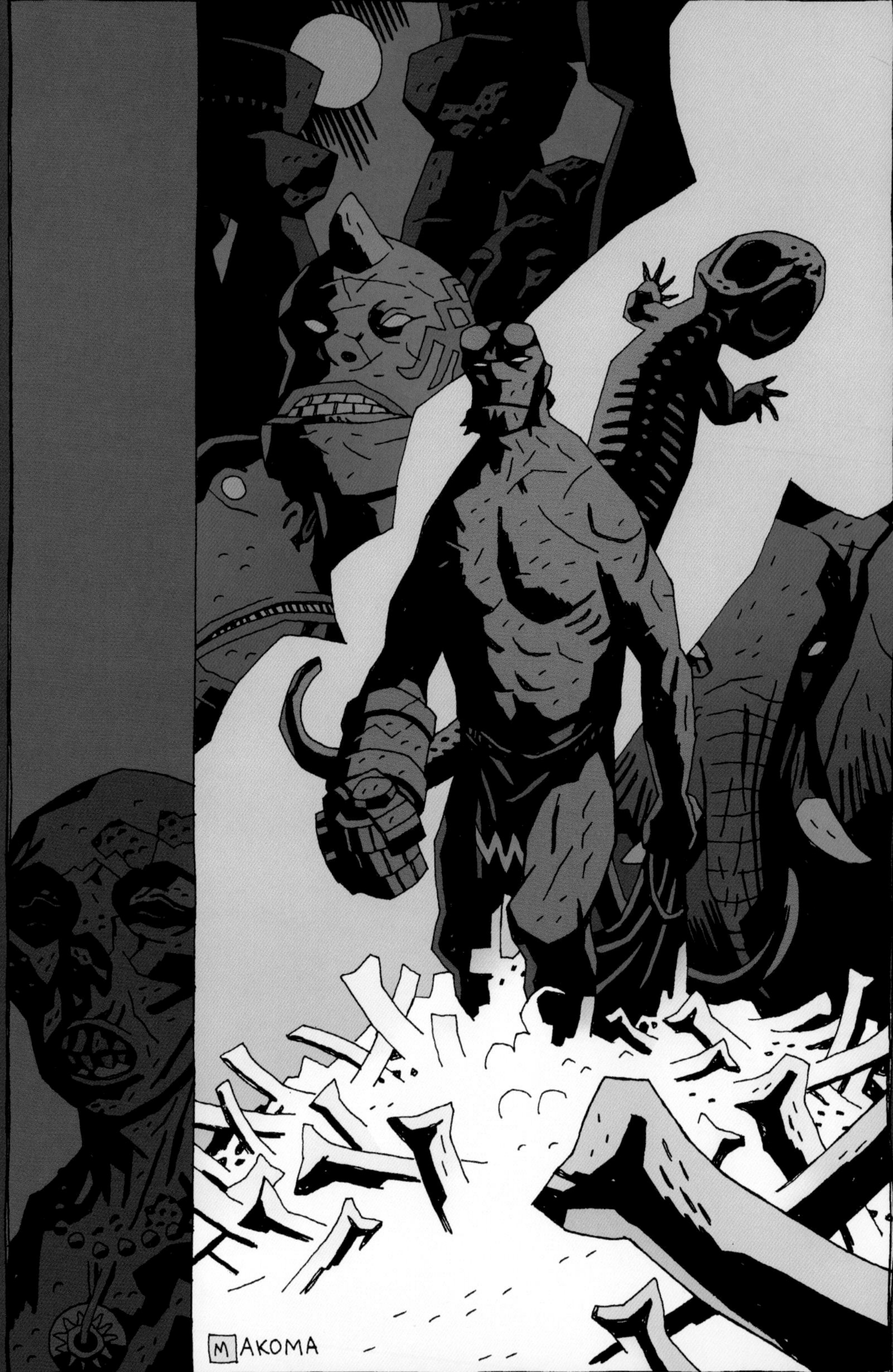

MAKOMA

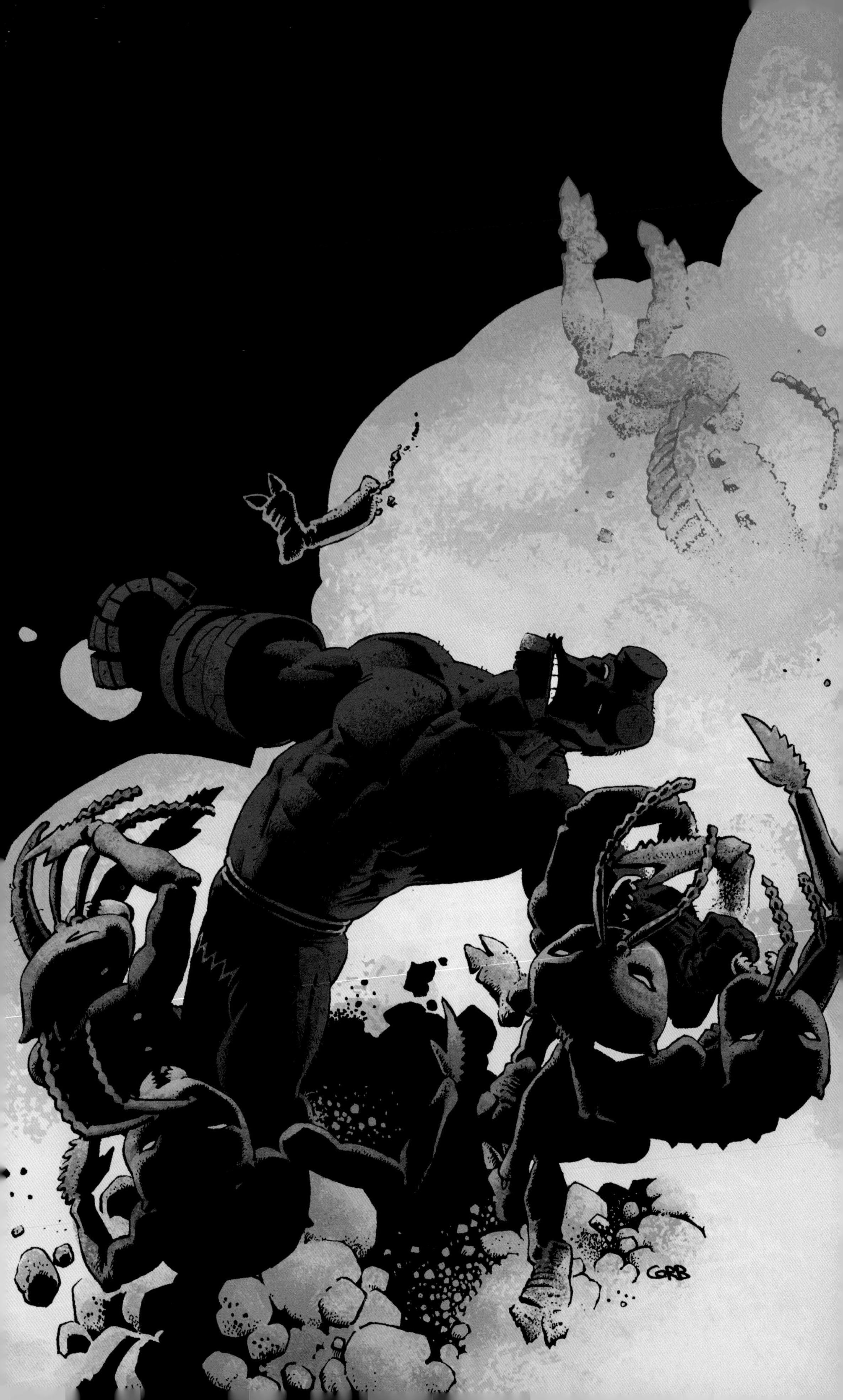

Sketchbook

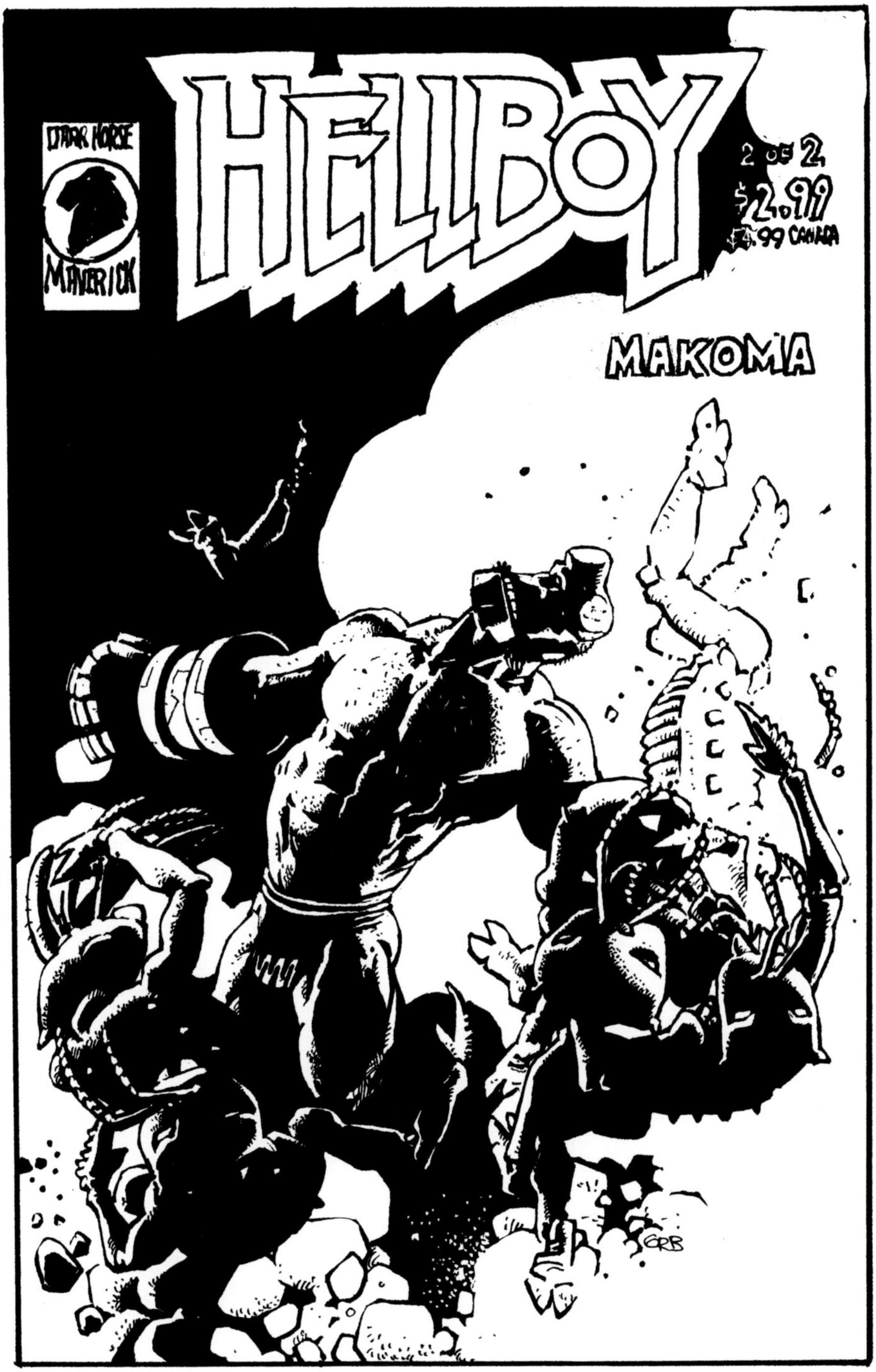
HELLBOY
DARK HORSE
MAVERICK
2 OF 2
$2.99
$4.99 CANADA
MAKOMA
CORB

Richard Corben's sketch for the *Makoma* #2 cover—This sketch is so tight that it's almost identical to the finished version on the opposite page.

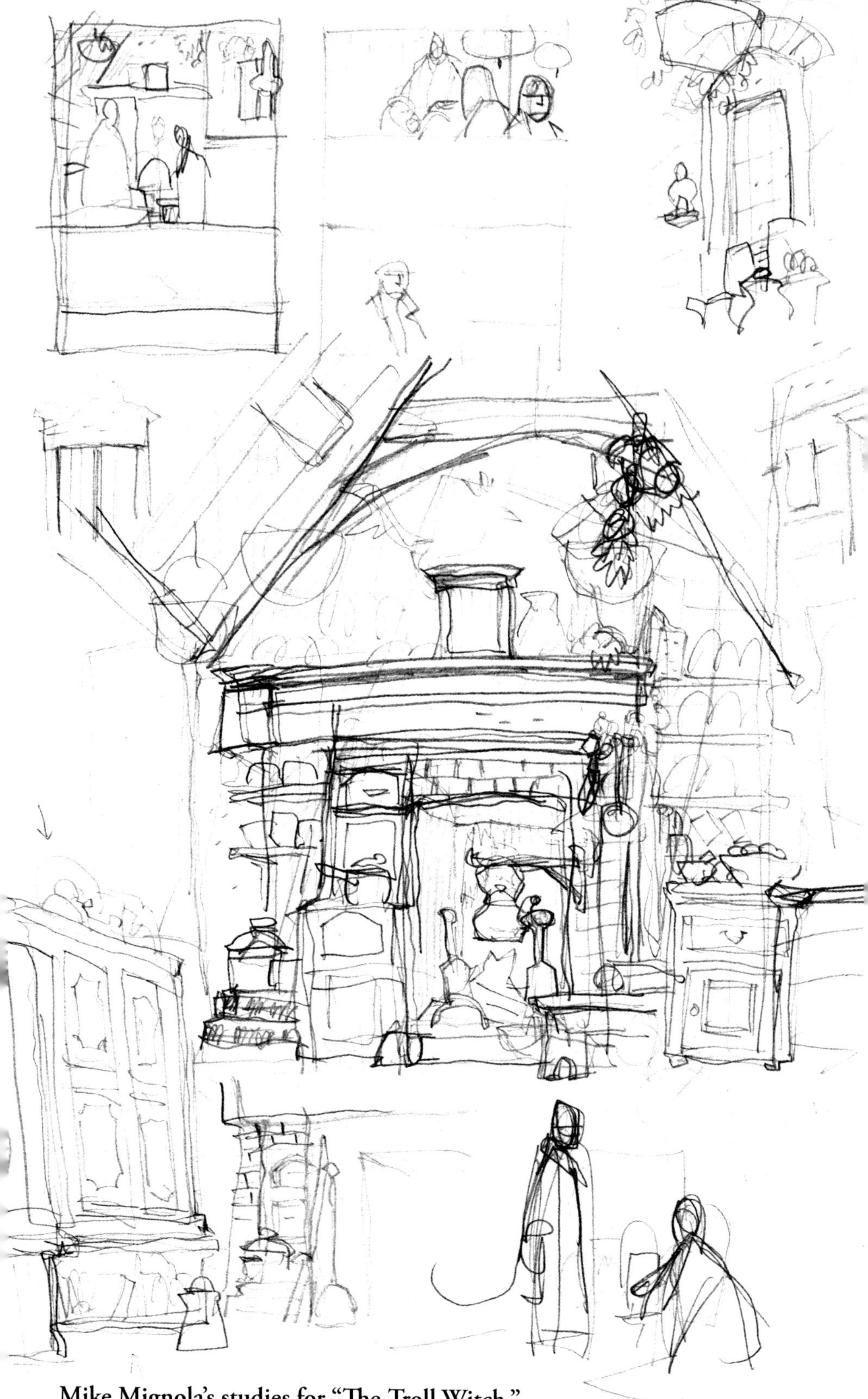

Mike Mignola's studies for "The Troll Witch," including the cover of this volume.

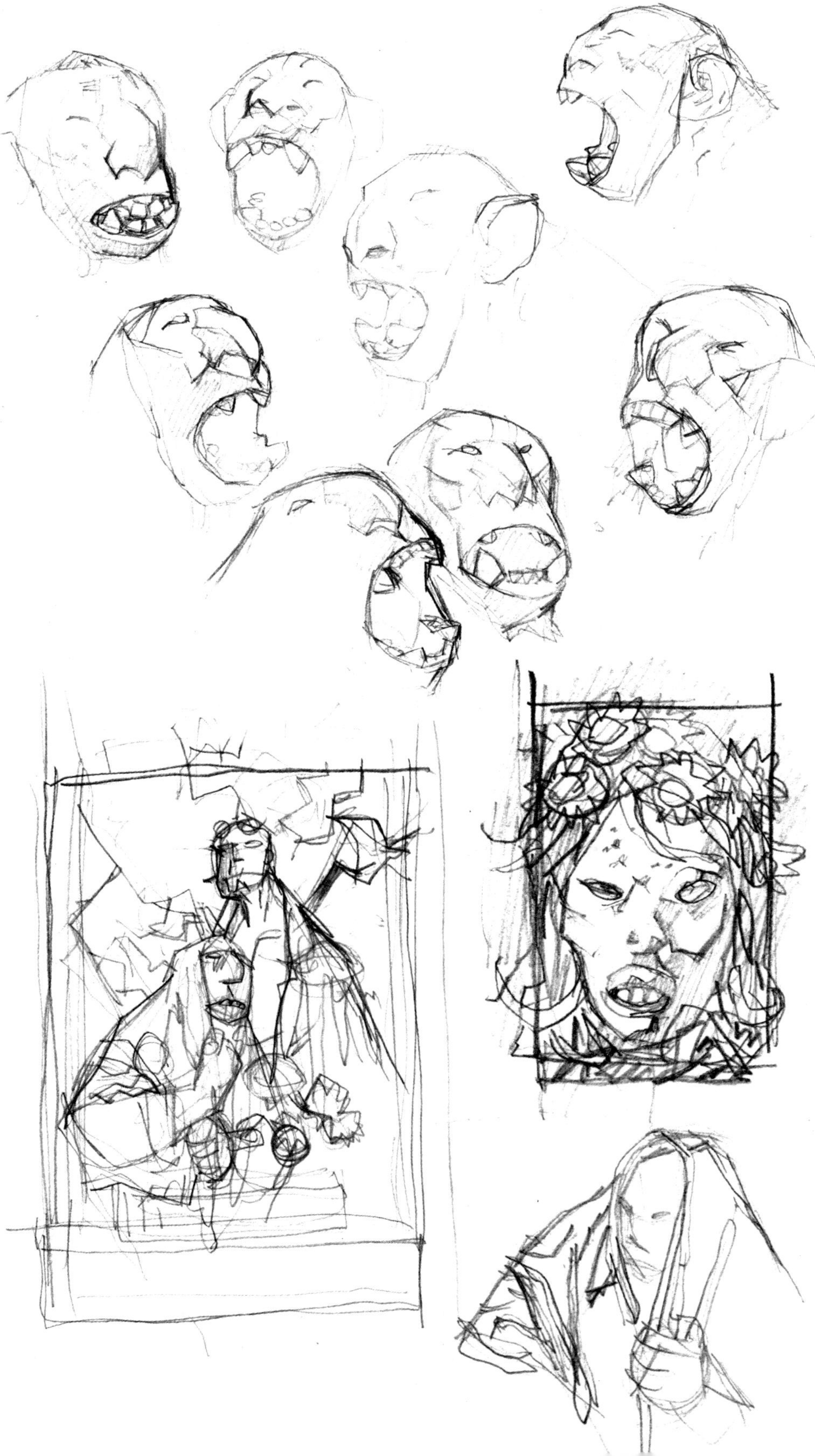

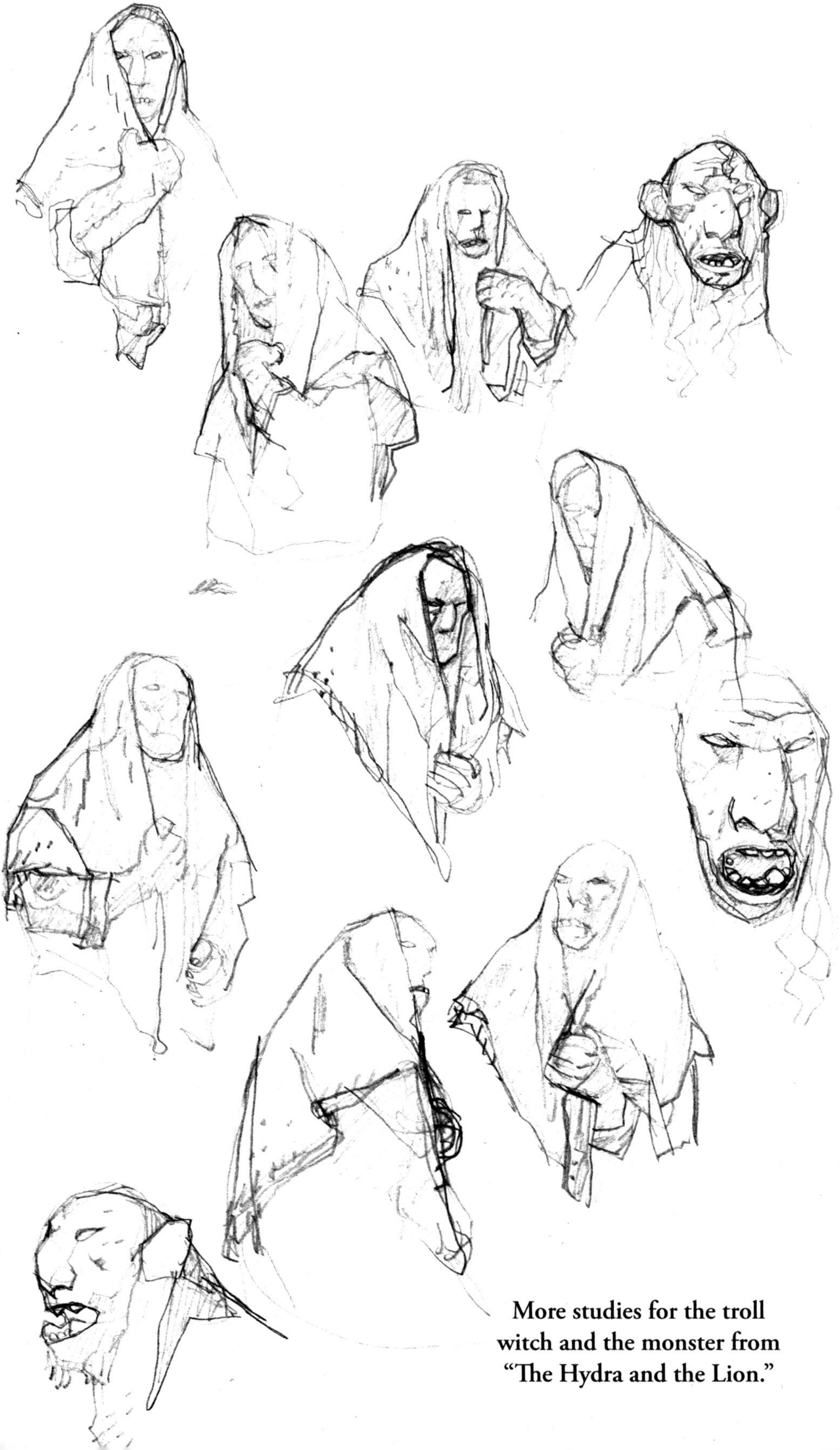

More studies for the troll witch and the monster from "The Hydra and the Lion."

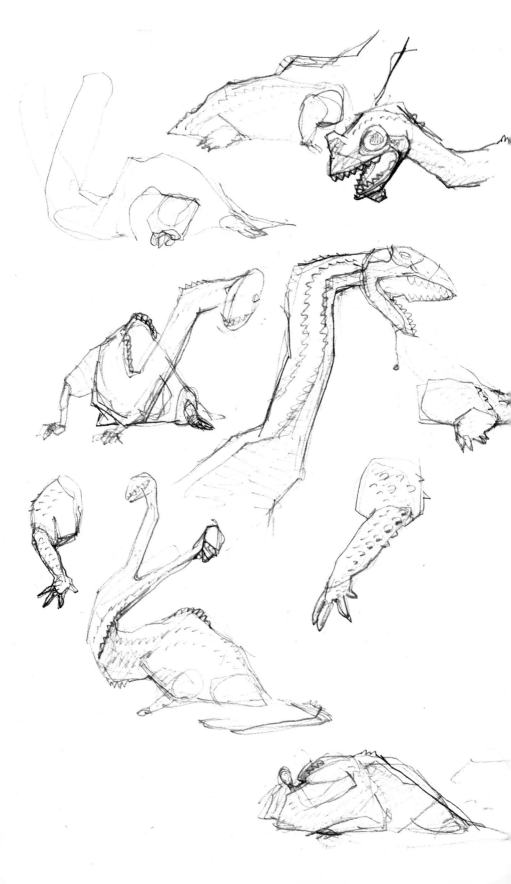

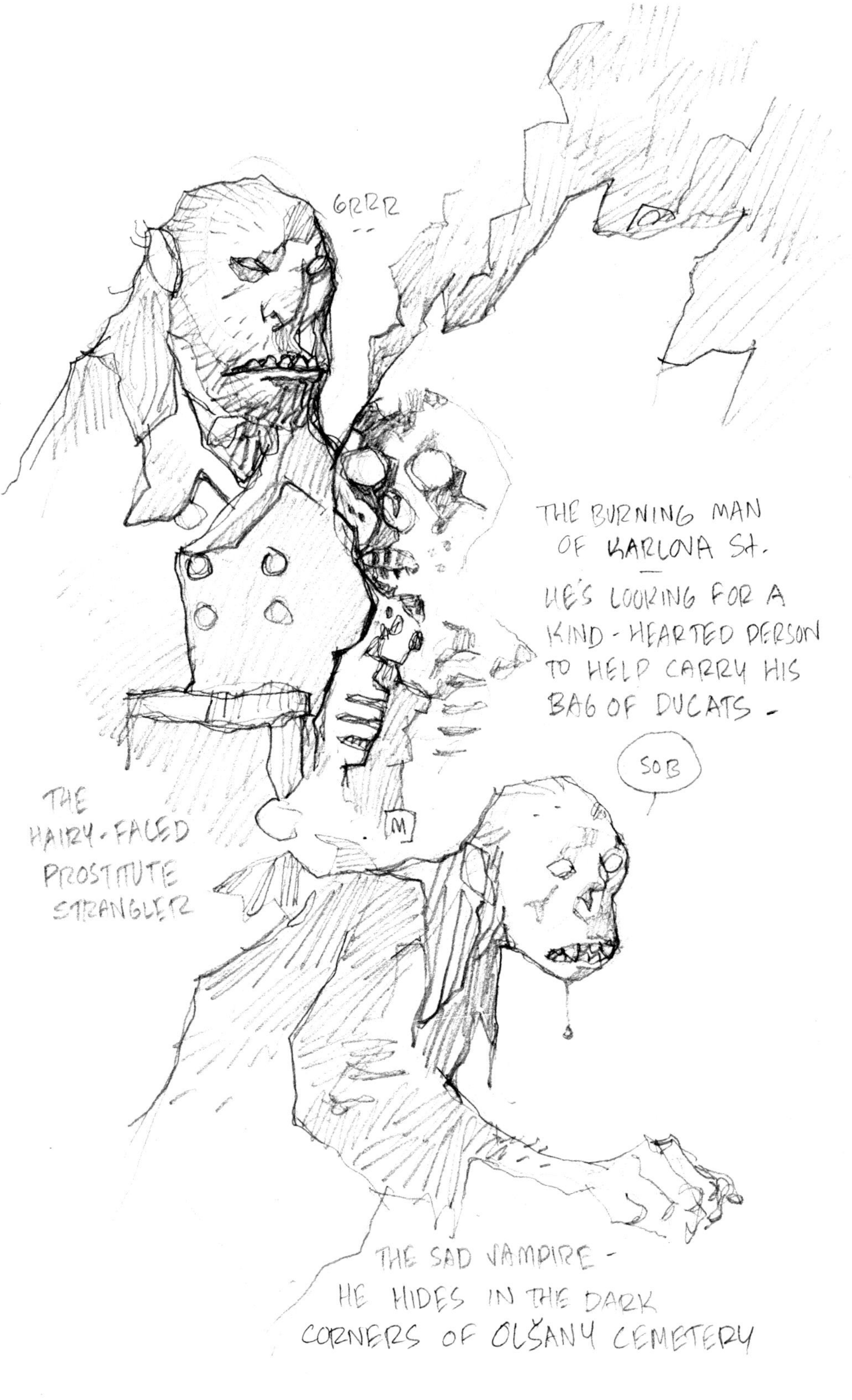
GRRR
THE BURNING MAN OF KARLOVA St.
HE'S LOOKING FOR A KIND-HEARTED PERSON TO HELP CARRY HIS BAG OF DUCATS -
SOB
THE HAIRY-FACED PROSTITUTE STRANGLER
THE SAD VAMPIRE -
HE HIDES IN THE DARK CORNERS OF OLŠANY CEMETERY

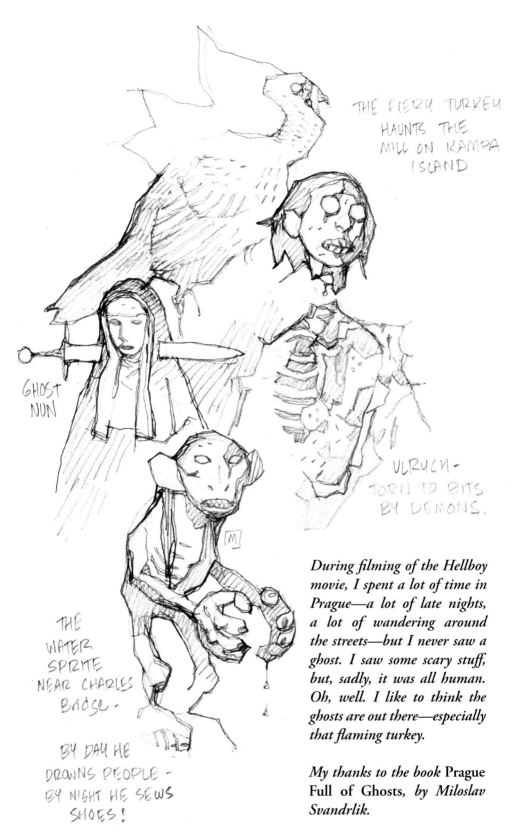

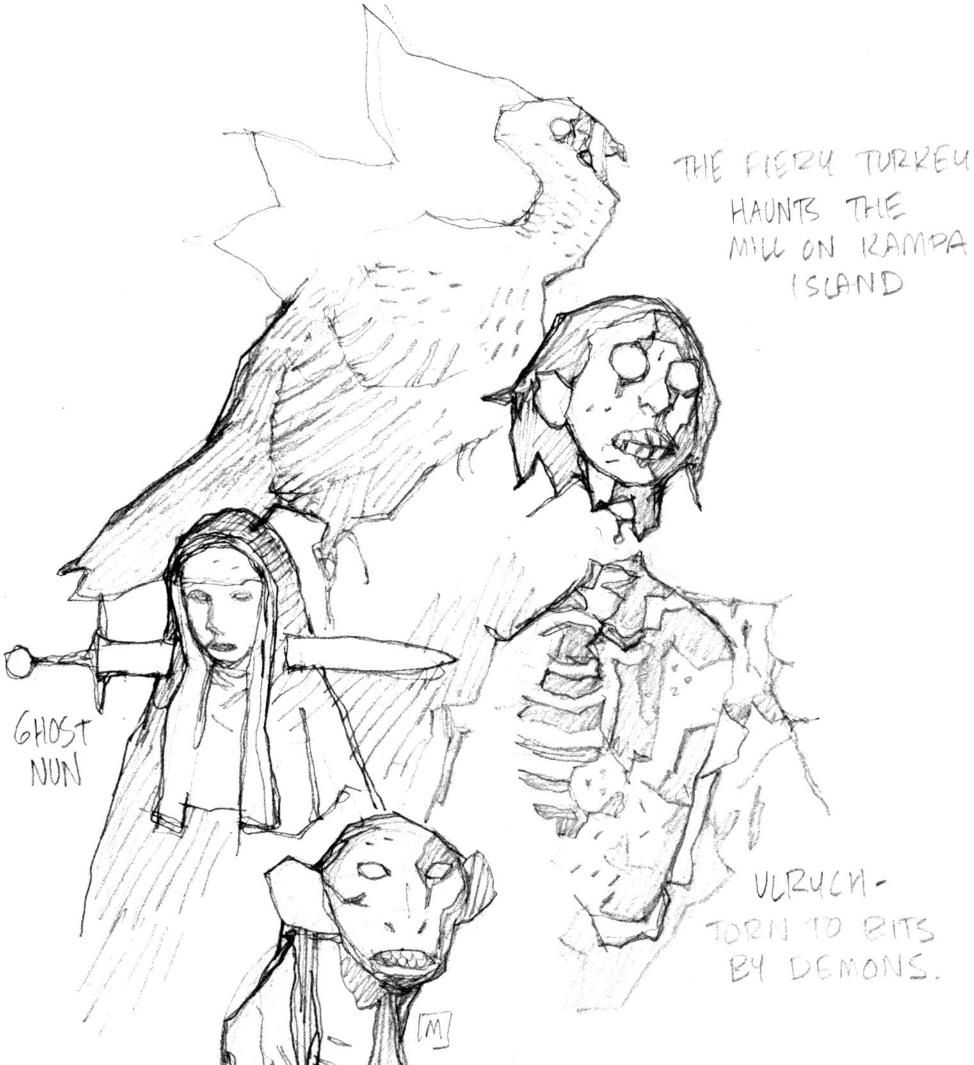
THE FIERY TURKEY
HAUNTS THE
MILL ON KAMPA
ISLAND
GHOST
NUN
ULRYCH-
TORN TO BITS
BY DEMONS.
M

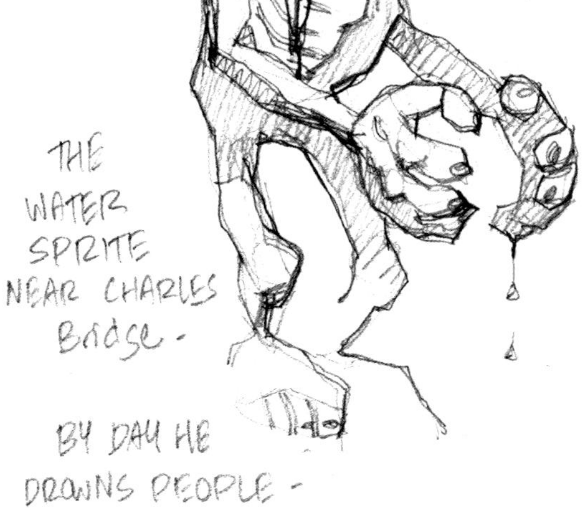
THE
WATER
SPRITE
NEAR CHARLES
BRIDGE-
BY DAY HE
DROWNS PEOPLE-
BY NIGHT HE SEWS
SHOES!

During filming of the Hellboy movie, I spent a lot of time in Prague—a lot of late nights, a lot of wandering around the streets—but I never saw a ghost. I saw some scary stuff, but, sadly, it was all human. Oh, well. I like to think the ghosts are out there—especially that flaming turkey.

My thanks to the book Prague Full of Ghosts, *by Miloslav Svandrlik.*

—Mike Mignola

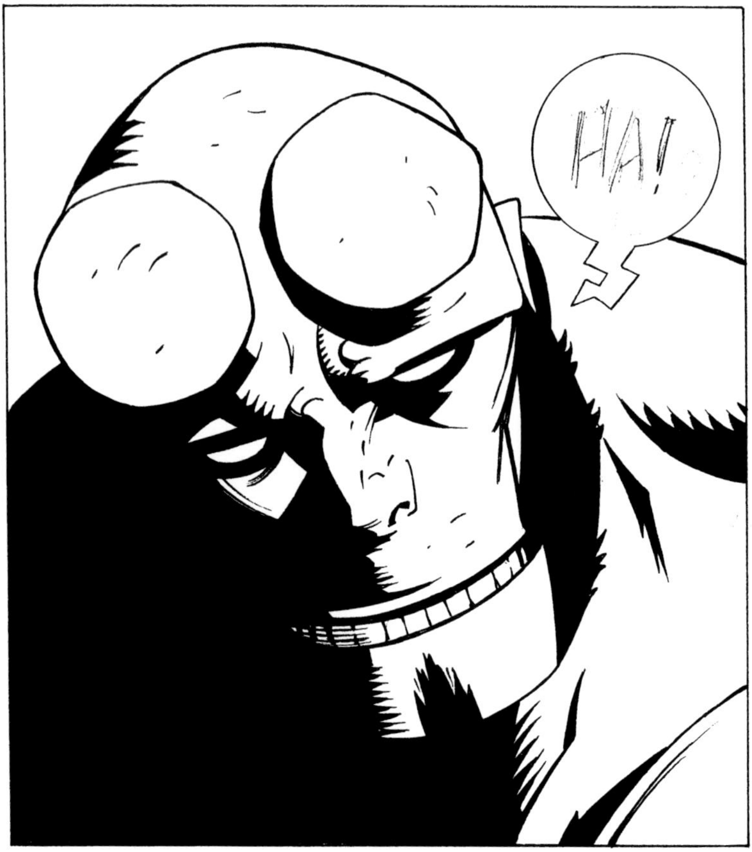
HA!

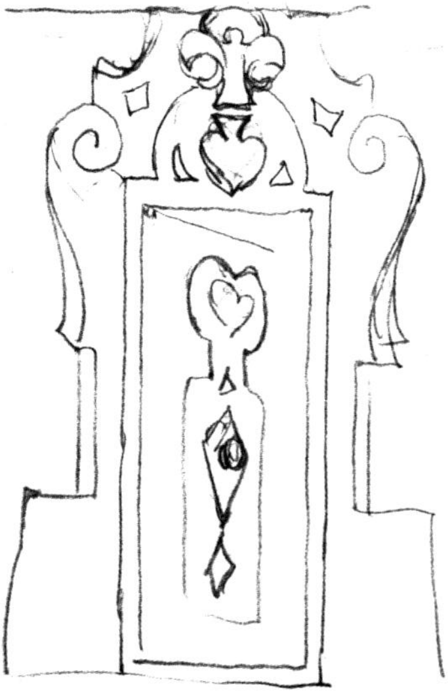

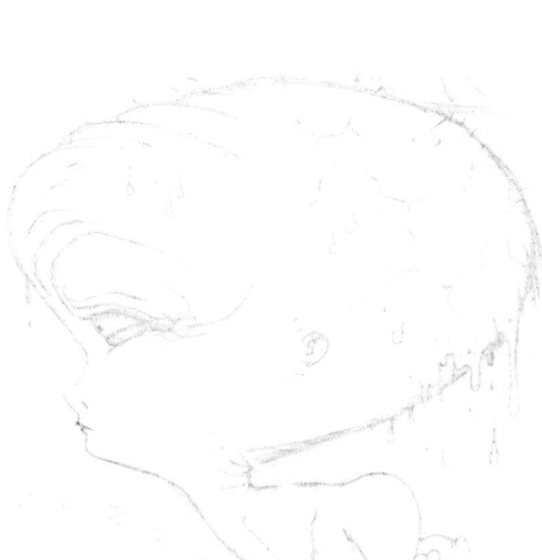

P. Craig Russell's sketches and unused designs from "The Vampire of Prague."

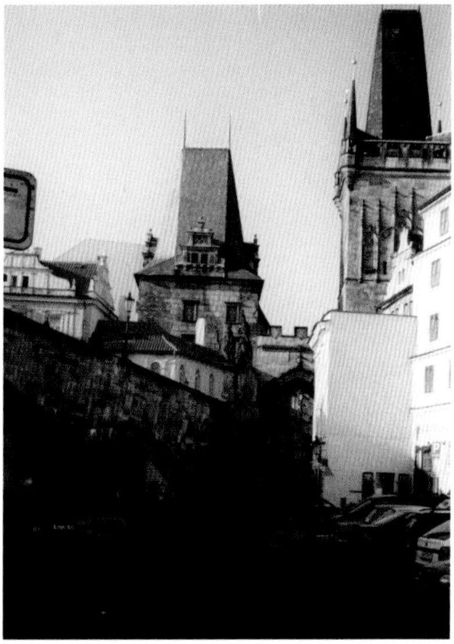

Photo by Mike Mignola,
which served as reference
for page twelve, panel one of
"The Vampire of Prague."

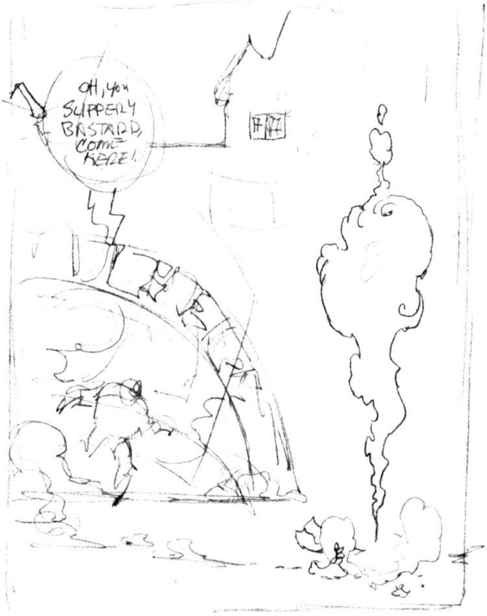
OH, YOU SLIPPERY BASTARD, COME HERE!

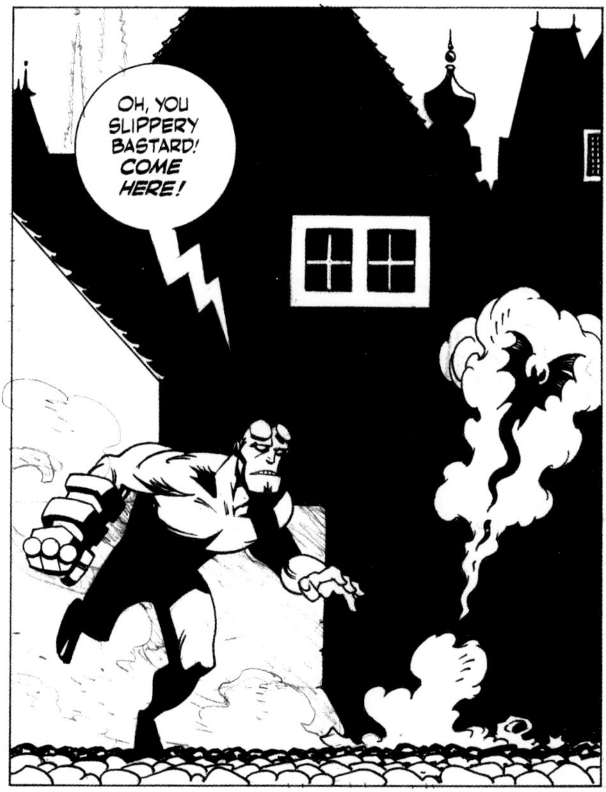
OH, YOU SLIPPERY BASTARD! COME HERE!

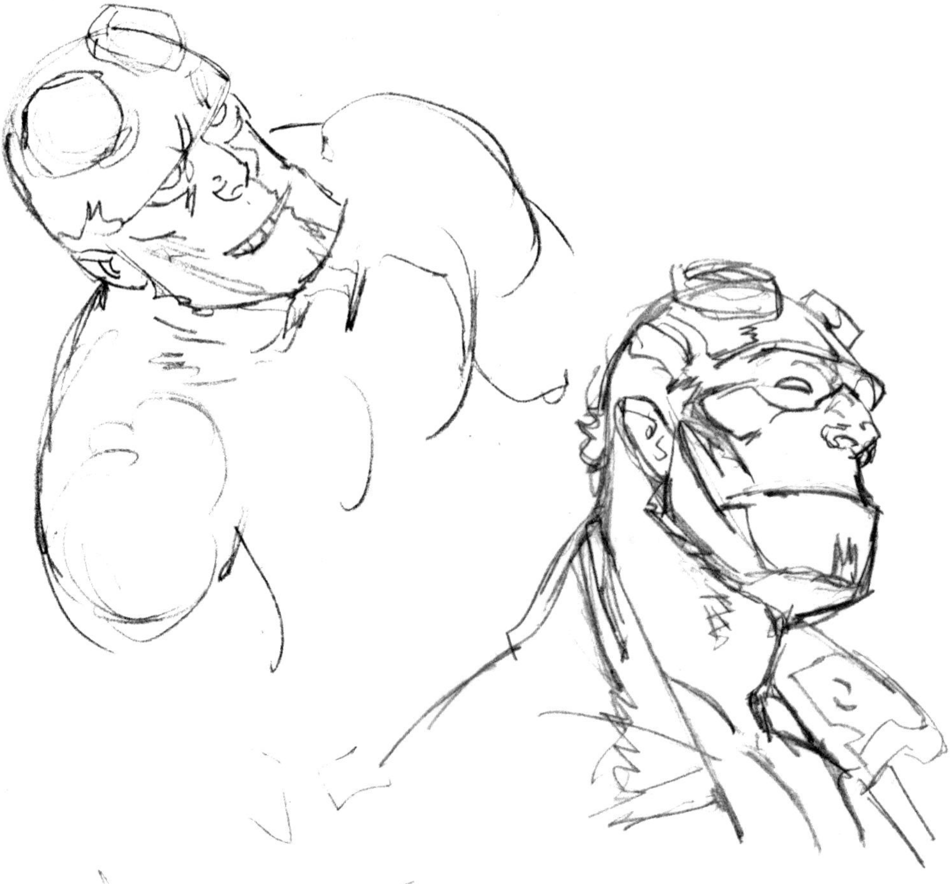

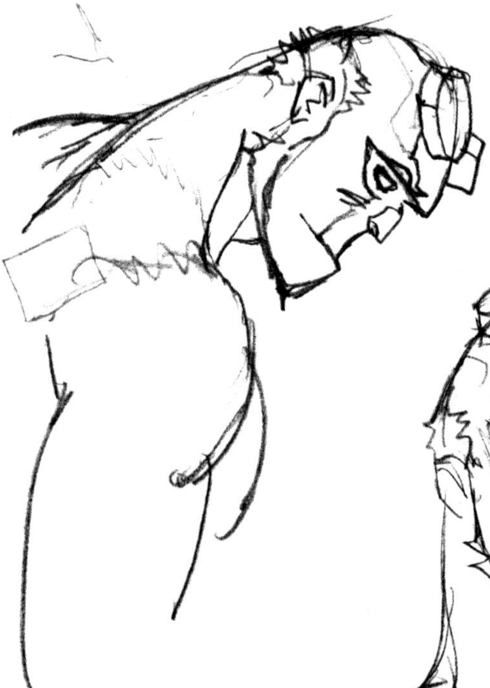

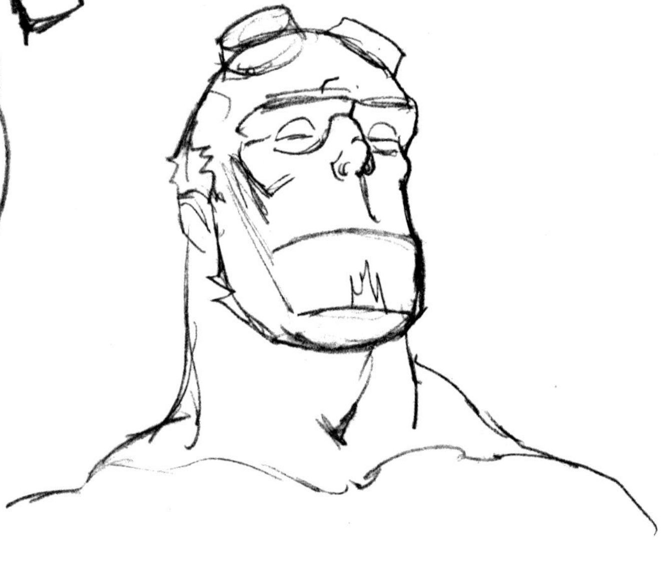

Hellboy studies
by P. Craig Russell.

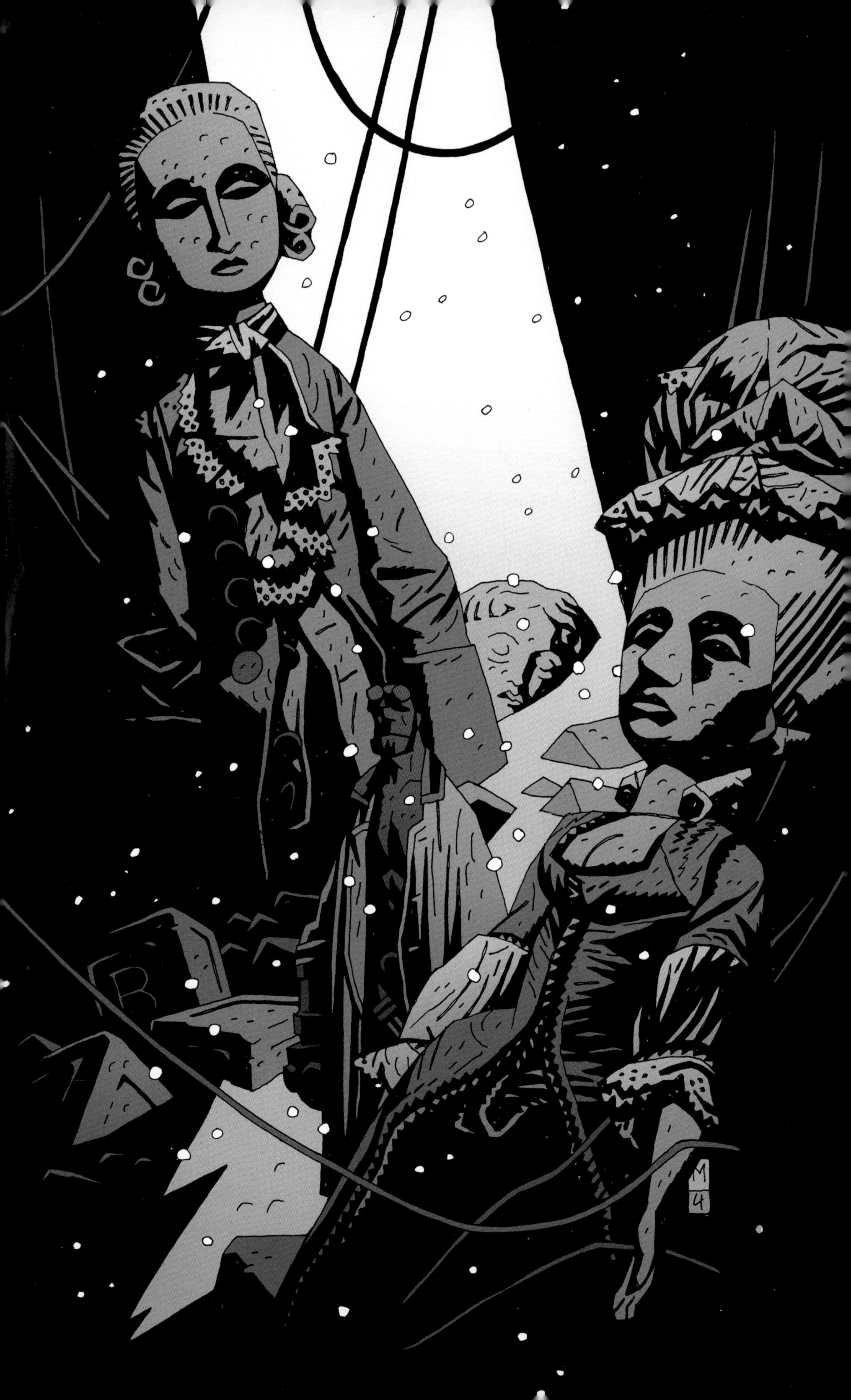

HELLBOY™

by MIKE MIGNOLA

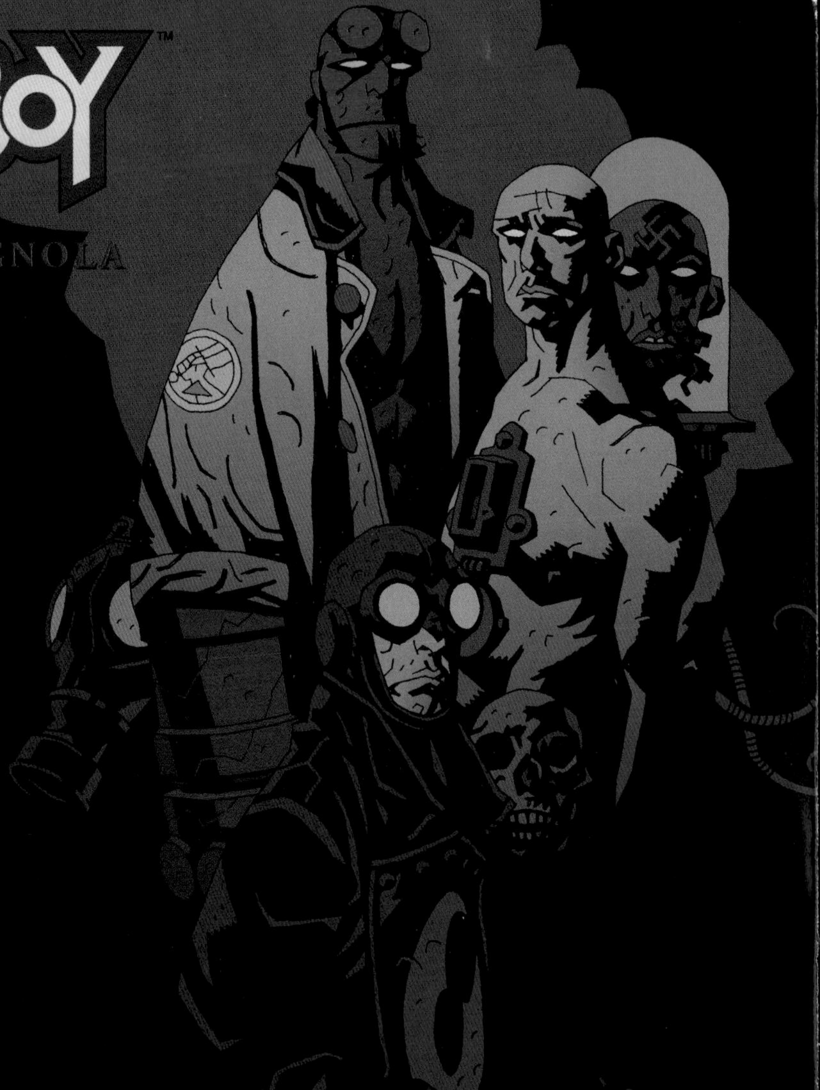

SEED OF DESTRUCTION
with John Byrne
ISBN-10: 1-59307-094-2
ISBN-13: 978-1-59307-094-6
$17.95

WAKE THE DEVIL
ISBN-10: 1-59307-095-0
ISBN-13: 978-1-59307-095-3
$17.95

THE CHAINED COFFIN AND OTHERS
ISBN-10: 1-59307-091-8
ISBN-13: 978-1-59307-091-5
$17.95

THE RIGHT HAND OF DOOM
ISBN-10: 1-59307-093-4
ISBN-13: 978-1-59307-093-9
$17.95

CONQUEROR WORM
ISBN-10: 1-59307-092-6
ISBN-13: 978-1-59307-092-2
$17.95

STRANGE PLACES
ISBN-10: 1-59307-475-1
ISBN-13: 978-1-59307-475-3
$17.95

THE ART OF HELLBOY
ISBN-10: 1-59307-089-6
ISBN-13: 978-1-59307-089-2
$29.95

HELLBOY WEIRD TALES
Volume 1
ISBN-10: 1-56971-622-6
ISBN-13: 978-1-56971-622-9
$17.95

Volume 2
ISBN-10: 1-56971-953-5
ISBN-13: 978-1-56971-953-4
$17.95

ODD JOBS
Short stories by Mignola, Poppy Z. Brite, Chris Golden and others
Illustrations by Mignola
ISBN-10: 1-56971-440-1
ISBN-13: 978-1-56971-440-9
$14.95

ODDER JOBS
Short stories by Frank Darabont, Guillermo del Toro and others
Illustrations by Mignola
ISBN-10: 1-59307-226-0
ISBN-13: 978-1-59307-226-1
$14.95

B.P.R.D.: HOLLOW EARTH
By Mignola, Chris Golden, Ryan Sook and others
ISBN-10: 1-56971-862-8
ISBN-13: 978-1-56971-862-9
$17.95

B.P.R.D.: THE SOUL OF VENICE
By Mignola, Mike Oeming, Guy Davis, Scott Kolins, Geoff Johns and others
ISBN-10: 1-59307-132-9
ISBN-13: 978-1-59307-132-5
$17.95

B.P.R.D.: PLAGUE OF FROGS
By Mignola and Guy Davis
ISBN-10: 1-59307-288-0
ISBN-13: 978-1-59307-288-9
$17.95

B.P.R.D.: THE DEAD
By Mignola, John Arcudi and Guy Davis
ISBN-10: 1-59307-380-1
ISBN-13: 978-1-59307-380-0
$17.95

B.P.R.D.: THE BLACK FLAME
By Mignola, Arcudi and Davis
ISBN-10: 1-59307-550-2
ISBN-13: 978-1-59307-550-7
$17.95

HELLBOY ZIPPO LIGHTER
#17-101 $29.95

HELLBOY TALKING BOARD
#10-248 $24.99

HELLBOY DELUXE TALKING BOARD
#10-380 $99.99

HELLBOY COASTER SET
#13-252 $9.99

HELLBOY QEE FIGURE: HELLBOY
#13-821 $7.99

HELLBOY QEE FIGURE: ABE SAPIEN
#13-822 $7.99

To find a comics shop in your area, call 1-888-266-4226
For more information or to order direct:
• On the web: darkhorse.com
• E-mail: mailorder@darkhorse.com
• Phone: 1-800-862-0052
Mon.-Fri. 9 A.M. to 5 P.M. Pacific Time

DARK HORSE COMICS™ *drawing on your nightmares*
darkhorse.com